# CONTOURS OF HINDU RASHTRA

# CONTOURS OF HINDU RASHTRA

## Hindutva, Sangh Parivar and Contemporary Politics

Ram Puniyani

Publications

KALPAZ PUBLICATIONS

DELHI-110052

Contours of Hindu Rashtra

Rs. 690

ISBN : 81-7835-473-X



Published in 2006 in India by
Kalpaz Publications
C-30, Satyawati Nagar, Delhi-110052
E-mail : Kalpaz@hotmail.com

*Laser Typesetting at* : Master Computers, Delhi
*Printed at* : Salasar Imaging System, Delhi

*This book is dedicated to my wife Smita, whose unflinching support has made it possible for me to carry on my work*

# Contents

## SECTION–III
## HINDUTVA AND MINORITIES



## SECTION–IV
## HINDUTVA'S THREAT PROJECTION—ISLAM, TERRORISM

## SECTION–V
## COMMUNALISM-VIOLENCE



## SECTION–VI
## POLITICAL CHESSBOARD

## SECTION–VII
## HINDUTVA AND DALITS



## SECTION–VIII
## WOMEN AND HINDU RIGHT

## SECTION–IX
## FAITH AND REASON

# Preface

Indian political scene has witnessed a massive change in its focus during last few decades. The decade of 80s was marred by intensification of communal violence and most the events revolved around the identity politics. It was a big affront to one's sensibility to see the heinous acts being committed in the name of religion. After the anti-Sikh pogrom of 1984, the communalism manifesting itself around Ram temple, Rath Yatras, demolition of Babri Masjid and the anti-Muslim pogrom, which took place mainly in Mumbai and also in some other cities. While during the 80s one felt that the communal events are bound to pass, after the Babri demolition it became more than clear that communalism, communal violence is here to stay.

Initially Muslims were the sole and major victims, after the BJP's first coming into power in 1996, the Christian community also came under the severe threat, especially the Christian missionaries working in the remote places. The effort to understand the underlying social and political dynamics of these so far unheard of 'problems' forced me to go into the issues which normally should be of no consequence in a democratic society. In this direction one had to look back a bit into history of India's freedom struggle, role of British colonial powers and the emergence of communalism during this period. I was struck by the understanding that different social sections responded very differently during British colonial period. While the emerging classes of new educated sections, the businessmen industrialist and deprived sections of society, veered towards democratic values, the Landlord-clergy combine, from both Hindus and Muslims felt threatened by the new sections coming to the social scene and also the coming in of the nascent values of Liberty Equality and Fraternity (community). The declining classes which opposed the formation of first the Indian National Congress and then the national movement were the repositories of communal politics, Hindu or Muslim. The trajectory of the multiple forces working in the society led to the partition and the consequent formation of Pakistan, the rise of communalization of societies which culminated in the violence over a period of time.

While grappling with the ongoing political events it started becoming clear that the real conflict is not between the Hindus and Muslims or between any religious communities. These communities are also not uniform and monolithic. The real conflict is between the two set of values, the one's deriving their legitimacy from Religion, which in turn are based on the hierarchy of caste and gender, and the other the one's based on the values of formal equality. The one's taking the garb of religion have the potent threat of creating mass hysteria and there by creative violence against the 'others'. This politics of this set of values, the one's deriving legitimacy from religion, is generally supplementary to the goals and agenda of colonialist-imperialist powers. No wonder that communalist did not participate in the struggle against British colonialists and even today are on the 'right' side of imperialist powers supplementing their global agenda.

The effort to understand communalism me to realize that minorities become the victim of this politics and rising tide of this politics puts severe social pressure on the march of the human rights movements of the oppressed sections of society. Women, dalits and workers, in Indian context, become the particular victim of the social and political processes. The responses to the themes started emerging into a coherent whole, the issues of minorities, gender equations, rational thought, way to look at history, the attitude towards the issues of Human Rights and what have you. The central link starts becoming clear with a deeper engagement with struggle to oppose communal politics. Though these essays and articles came up over a time frame the central running theme has a deeper connection, and the same thread runs all through, the issues of human rights, the question of gender, caste and labour.

While the volume was being compiled, India saw a pleasant change of the defeat of BJP led NDA coalition and the inability of BJP, the hand maiden of RSS, to hold itself together. It has realised that it cannot come to power without shedding its Hindutva agenda, its leadership wants to strive towards moderate language while retaining the communal core of Hindu National ideology. Adding to its travails is also the personality problems, the issue of generation next; who will be the supreme leader after the present ageing leadership is unable to physically lead the party. Its hypocrisy, 'party with a difference' is more than obvious, its power greed raging supreme in its calculated moves. On the top of everything else it has been yielding the opposition space to the left, it has been paralyzed to act as an opposition party of any consequence barring its regular move to stall the parliament, the highest forum for democratic debates. It is shy to debate the issues in parliament while feels confident in raising the emotional pitch in the political sphere mainly through the media. So it is today neither ruling party nor the party in opposition. It is just hanging around, trying to come to terms with the humiliating waiting defeat in 2004 elections. The defeat appeared more humiliating especially in the light of its boasts of a sure and unchallenged victory.

But the threat of communal politics is no less than it was before. Muslim community under the scanner all over the world is mired with multiple problems. Feeling insecure and threatened a section of community is getting ghettoized, a small miniscule section has taken the path of orthodoxy and the Ulemas have become more prominent at places. Some of them have resorted to terror for diverse reasons. The image of Muslim community all over the world is taking a beating, and terrorism is being linked to Islam and Muslims. The Imperialist efforts to demonize Islam and Muslims have 'succeeded' to some extent. It has become a sort of vicious circle, oppression, ghettoization further strengthening of orthodoxy, giving strong pretext to the communal politics.

In Indian context in the states where BJP Governments have been ruling, the RSS progeny is having a free run. While in Gujarat the insecurity of Muslim community has reached severe proportions, In Gujarat, MP and in some other states like Orrisa the atmosphere is becoming anti minority. At places the other minority Christians has also come under severe threat. The RSS shakhas continue unabated to spew their poison against weaker sections of society in the grab of cultural work. Vanvasi Kalyan Ashrams, Vishwa Hindu Parishad and Bajrang Dal, with a clever division of labour do the indoctrination work, supplemented by physical intimidation. The violence is projected to be a response to the anti-national work of this or that minority. Due to good deal of 'efficient management' of media and other mechanism the social common sense generally comes to stereotype the minorities, preparing a ground for their ghettoization. These pose severe obstacles to the work really needed for carrying further the struggle for the rights of exploited, poor and marginalised sections of society.

While working in the direction of understanding the ongoing political processes one has been enriched by going through the works of eminent scholars on the topic and also by interactions which the social activists who have taken up the threat of communal fascism seriously. I wish to thank to magazines and journals where some of these pieces first appeared.

August

**Ram Puniyani**
Mumbai

# Introduction

## I

The results of 2004 Parliament elections came as a big surprise. It was a big relief to some and big jolt for some others. No other election, barring perhaps the post-emergency one in 1977 had such a profound impact on the polity of the nation. The results defied the predictions of psephologists and spelt the doom for National Democratic Alliance led by Bharatiya Janata Party (BJP). The broad expectation was that the same alliance will romp back to power and the agenda unleashed during last five years will be taken at higher levels. The period preceding the elections saw many severe changes, which affected the civic society, the civic institutions, the changes, which frightened the democratic aspirations of many a people.

The preceding period was the one heavily influenced by the state sponsored anti-Muslim pogrom of Gujarat 2002. The nature and intent of the government was most obvious during this period. The blatant disregard for the rights of minority, the total insensitivity to the plight of weaker sections of society sent adverse signals to the society. These signals shook the very foundations of the democratic edifice, created during last fifty years. These riots and the aftermath saw a total disregard for post-violence rehabilitation, it showed the total erosion of civic institutions in which either the riot crimes were not registered or if registered under pressure were not pursued, and if pursued the witnesses were intimidated to withdraw their charges. Finally, it was the Supreme Court, which had to come out with scathing criticism of state Governments' handling of the legal processes.

The leaders of BJP called this period as the glory of Hindu Nation, and the presiding BJP man, Narendra Modi who was handling this pogrom on behalf of Sangh combine, was regarded as the best chief minister by the top leadership of BJP. While the Gujarat pogrom showed the basic agenda of BJP and its parent organisation, the RSS, there were many other acts of commission during the same period, which brought to fore the deeper goals of this outfit. It was during this regime that anti-Christian violence came to the fore. The peak of this was seen in the dastardly burning of Pastor Graham Stuart Stains along with his two innocent sons when they were sleeping in the jeep. The charge was that the Pastor, working amongst leprosy patients, was converting the gullible Adivasis. This period also saw the total change in the school textbooks, making them communal, the RSS version of History and understanding was dished out in these books, which apart from other things were academically substandard. Education system was further mauled by bringing in the obscurantist subjects like Jyotishi, Karmakand and Astrology in the universities, dressed up as scientific disciplines. The attempt was also made to tamper with the democratic fabric of the Constitution.

The country was watching helplessly as the alliance partners of BJP succumbed to the RSS agenda for the pelf and perks of power which they came to enjoy with forging of partnership with BJP. The mindless globalisation and the ignoring of the plight of peasants and poor sections were extreme. The social welfare schemes were dumped on regular basis leading the people to face the worsening economic scenario without anything to fall back upon. This was supposed to be just the superficial aspect of BJP programme as they claimed that they couldn't implement full Hindutva agenda as they are in alliance. Also, that the goal of Hindu Rashtra has been put on hold for the time being. The hope was that in future with the coming to power with improved strength would clear the ground for implementing the core Hindutva agenda, with ease. Hindutva forces expected that a victory in the elections will pave the way for Gujarat type Hindutva consolidation all over. The democractic streams feared that BJP's coming back to power will stifle the democratic norms further, the intimidation of libertarian streams will be stepped up and the democratic space will shrink further, taking the country a notch up in its being gripped by the Hindu Fundamentalist politics.

## II

The words Hindutva and Hindu Rashtra were new to the Indian psyche in the recent past. They started re-emerging in the early eighties. This period was a period of gross changes in the social dynamics and emergence of religiosity in the social space. The conversion of some Dalits to Islam in 1981 gave the pretext to Vishwa Hindu Parishad to step up its activities. The Shah Bano judgement and Rajiv Gandhi Government's response in reversing the judgement by an act of Parliament gave a further fillip to the Hindutva elements, which assumed their aggressive worst with the opening of the locks of Babri Masjid, on the ground that this is the precise place where our revered Lord Ram was born. BJP, which was formed on the plank of Gandhian Socialism, took up the issue of Ram Janmbhoomi, Advani took out his Rath Yatra from Somnath. This was to herald the shape of things to come. The communal polarisation started getting intensified. Rath Yatra was planned a few weeks before

V.P. Singh for his own compulsions implemented the Mandal Commission. This was perceived by Dalit OBCs as the move which they were longing for, at the same time the upper caste/affluent sections of middle class saw it as a threat to their hegemony in the jobs and other privileges associated with them for centuries. The Rath Yatra got an unprecedented response and gave rise to the plans, which in due course were to demolish the Babri Masjid and unleash one of the most ghastly violence, which India has witnessed in the post-independence era. All this led to the strengthening of BJP in the political arena; a marginal outfit now started becoming more assertive and powerful at electoral level. It was during this period that the words like Hindu Rashtra, Hindutva and cultural nationalism started coming to the fore.

As such the word Hindu Rashtra had been articulated with Vinayak Damodar Savarkar after he got himself released from the Andaman prison by giving and undertaking to the British that he abhors the methods, which he had used in the past and that he will cooperate with the British Empire, the colonial powers in implementation of Montague-Chelmsford reforms. He put forward the theory that Religion is the basis of Nation states and that this is a Hindu Rashtra, Hindu Nation. The word, Hindu was redefined and he coined word Hindutva for the politics of this Nation, it meant a politics based on Aryan race, Sanskrit language, this holy land and the Brahminic culture and social-political values. In a nutshell, it meant a politics based on the values of Brahminical Hinduism. This was the foundation of Two Nation theory, which laid the basis of partition in times to come. It identified religion to be the basis of a nation state.

It was parallel to the other similar stream, the stream that argued for Islamic Nation, Islamism. Though Islamism was not a word coined at that time, Muslim Nation was the parallel of the word Hindutva. There were basic similarities between these concepts. Both were having a social base amongst the declining sections of kings, landlords and their affiliated clergy, they both kept aloof from anti-British struggles, they both argued that religion is the basis of Nation state, they both were critical of the concept of democratic secular India, and they both were critical of the politics of Mahatma Gandhi. It was Gandhi whose politics articulated the national aspirations of composite Indian nationalism, nationalism based on the geographical notions of citizenship. The notion that all those living in a country are equal citizens and form the nation state. The concept of state derived its basis from all the people irrespective of their religion, caste and gender.

Both these streams (based on religion, the components of Two Nation theory) had a marginal support from the average people. Both of them escaped the repression by British and spewed the poison against the other community. Due to this, in due course, the communal violence kept on becoming intense and sections of middle classes started veering round to communal politics. The partition tragedy was outcome of the British policy of 'divide and rule' and the role of Muslim and Hindu communal politics. While Pakistan, which was formed due to the partition, was supposed to be the Muslim Nation, India opted for democracy and secularism. The Indian Constitution based on the values of Liberty, Equality and Fraternity (Community). This was accompanied by the policies of the Indian states towards industrialisation and popularisation of education. The economic policies also resulted in the rise of a middle class, affluent professionals, petty industrialists and rich peasants. The politics of Bharatiya Jansangh remained on the margins, till the early eighties. While many a factors boosting Hindutva politics were prevalent more in North India, and to some measure in other parts of the country. Gujarat was a state where most of the prerequisites of the rise of Hindutva were present in abundant measure.

## III

In late eighties Iran witnessed the coming to power of Ayatollah Khoemini. It was called Islamic Fundamentalism. It was also called a revolution and the call was given for the Islamic revolution all over, in Islamic countries. This regime was very strongly anti-U.S., unlike many other Islamic countries. To begin with the Socialist (state sector dominated countries) economies started showing the signs of degeneration and in due course they collapsed, leaving the world as a uni-polar Capitalist one. The domination of U.S. in the international affairs was on ascendance U.S. ambitions went on for hegemonising the whole world and for this oil zone of Middle East was the preferred target. It was also the area where the Islam was the major religion and so later the flag of Imperialism changed its symbol from anti-communism to anti-Islam. The process of demonising Islam as a backward religion, orthodox and violent was drummed up ad nauseum. The theory of Clash of Civilisation of Samuel Huntinogton became the *raison dẽtre* of U.S. imperialism's lust for oil wealth around the globe. It provided the much-needed general pretext for the forthcoming invasions on Islamic states.

The U.S. intervention in the Middle East led to the training of Al Qaida, the increase in the terrorism and the rise of Osama bin Laden. The events of 9/11 came as a big shock to the world. U.S. on the pretext of punishing Osama bin Laden attacked Afghanistan and installed the puppet government there. This new regime, a puppet of U.S. was compliant enough to let them lay the oil pipeline from Caspian Sea to the Arabic Sea. Nothing could have been a better pretext than 9/11 to achieve the aims of U.S. administration. Who did it, was immaterial so far as Osama could be implicated and Afghanistan attacked.

Attacking Iraq was a different ball game. It had been weakened immensely due to the 1991 attack on Iraq and the subsequent sanctions. Various pretexts were thought of, weapons of mass destruction, Iraq's links with Al Qaida, Saddam's atrocities on the Iraqi people and all that. In opposition to the world opinion and sidetracking the U.N. totally, U.S. launched its attack on the ground of liberating Iraqi people. The U.S. army was presented as the liberation army, while in due course the local population was targeting this occupation army. Many a body bags started arriving in U.S. Many of the soldiers employed to trample Iraq were mercenaries. So far the response to body bags is not a strong enough reason for U.S. occupation armies to be pulled out from Iraq. The hanging of four American soldiers in Faluja was the gory act committed by local frustrated people. The acts of U.S. army in Abu Ghraib prison, the perversion and torture of Iraqi soldiers, was too horrific for words and it created abominable reaction all over the world.

All this led to the thinking as to what is primary: imperialism or terrorism. The debate continues on streets and in the torture chambers of U.S. army. But all the same the denomination of Islam and Muslims continues serving the goals of U.S. imperialism abroad and the Hindutva politics at home. The global demonisation of Islam by imperialists coincided with the same process at home by the Sangh combine. The coincidence has more to it than meets the eye.

## IV

The core agenda of Hindutva is not anti-Islam so to say. Similarly the core agenda of imperialism is not anti-Islam in that sense. Hindutva is essentially an attempt to foster the feudal hierarchical social relationships on society. Imperialism is an attempt to control the raw materials and markets in the world. But the language of both gets merged in the anti-Islam for that matter.

Savarkar, Golwalkar and Deendayal Upadhaya articulated Hindu Rashtra's ideological underpinnings in the years past. Last two decades these ideologies have been widely percolated through the popular mechanisms of media and rise of cults. The two hierarchies which Hindutva aims to impose, perpetuate in the society, are the one's of caste and gender. Media's presentations, popular films, *Hum Apke Hain Kaun*, and serials like *Saas Bhi Kabhi Bahu* Thi present these in a very popular format. The gender hierarchies come out very well in these. The struggling women of seventies, coming into her own self, has been replaced by the subservient Tulsi, who takes up and becomes the aggressive vehicle of patriarchal values, the real embodiment of gender equations. It is no coincidence that anti-women atrocities have also gone up during this period.

The new middle class has the need for a soothing balm. One recalls the clergy blessing the kings and feudal lords. The middle class in addition requires those who can calm its tense nerves, preserve its status, those who can also present the feudal hierarchies in a modern language. The rise of cults in last two decades is a fascinating study. At one level, to assuage the anxiety of existence and at another to talk of *Manusmriti* in a modern language is what has been done by the tribe of Asaram Bapu, Sudhanshu Maharaj, Sri Sri Ravi Shanker etc. These five star sants are the ideological bases of the Hindutva politics. Pandurang Shastri Athwale's outpourings are a proactive defense of *Manusmriti* values deriving legitimacy from some odd scientist here and there.

That Hindutva is a phenomenon of caste and gender hierarchy also becomes clear if one looks at the statements of RSS ideologues. They are the one's explicitly uncomfortable with Indian Constitution and want to bring in something based on Hindu Holy Scriptures, basically *Manusmriti*.

Hindutva like all other religion-based nationalisms is against the democratic values of liberty, equality and justice.

It is the ideology and its percolation, which makes the phenomenon complicated on the first appearance. This applies to cultural nationalism in particular. This is again a very impressive word at the first sight. But in its structure it ignores the multiple cultures, which are present in the country. It upholds the Brahminic culture in the modern language. It is a ploy to oppose the diversity and pluralism. In a way it is a way to impose the homogenisation sought in by the elite. In a way it is exclusionist, more so for the non-brahminical religions and tendencies. One part of analysis, which is not very commonly articulated, is the one related to social hierarchies. Also that in pre-independence times the Hindutva had base amongst landlords, Brahmins and Banias (traders) and post-eighties the major supporters, its core base, of this ideology come from the affluent middle classes like rich professionals, petty industrialists and rich peasants. The commonality between these two groups needs to be drawn out. In pre-independence times the groups supporting this ideology were the one's who can broadly be called as declining classes, declining in the face of industrialisation and introduction of modern education. Again the two phenomena were crucial in the eroding the hierarchical structures. It is nobody's argument that these hierarchies got abolished. The point is the attempt was on to go against the prevalent social relationships, in the direction of abolishing them.

The present supporters of Hindutva type ideologies are those privileged in their social situation, those fearing that the lower strata may usurp their privileges. It is this existential anxiety of privileged middle class, which draws them to the ideologies of status quo, or better still the ideologies, which can talk sweat but hide the inbuilt social inequalities in their structure and thereby promote the values of inbuilt hierarchical differences.

It is precisely for this that faith based knowledge derives a lot of respectability with these groups. The use of reason will challenge the social inequality and so the emphasis on the blind upholding of traditional systems of knowledge, rituals, astrology and the like.

## V

The persistence of Hindutva type onslaughts has a lot to do with the incomplete process of land reforms and democratisation of society. This symptom complex persists in many post-colonial societies in different degrees. In India the earlier phase of industrialisation kept such political streams on the margins. Post-eighties combination of global changes, economic and political, have a great influence on the rise of this phenomenon. The coincidence of Islam being at the centre of both the global and local offensive needs to be understood as more than a mere coincidence. The problem with such Hindutva type of formations is that they cannot come to power on their own in the parliamentary structures as they cater to a small section of society. The large sections not only remain aloof but unconcerned about this agenda. To incorporate those sections into their electoral support base the emotive issues are brought to the fore, and these emotive issues consolidate a section of the population around this politics.

The campaigns for Hindu Rashtra were built mainly around the Ram temple, Uniform Civil Code, abolition of Article 370 in Kashmir. The coming to power for the party of Hindutva was a major event, as it could woo the opportunist middle of the road parties. In order to increase its electoral base, it also went in for social engineering in which the large section of Adivasis was won over. It was for this reason that Vanavasi Kalyan Ashram launched a strong campaign against Christian missionaries. The same Adivasis came in handy to act as foot soldiers for Hindutva during the Gujarat violence. The same Adivasis contributed to the massive electoral success of BJP in cow belt states, MP, Rajasthan,

Chhattisgarh and of course Gujarat. It seems that lately they are getting disenchanted from the politics of Hindutva, but time alone will tell how far social engineering wins over the worldly needs of this deprived section.

The period, 1996-2004 was the period of major transition for the strategies of Hindu Rashtra politics. Its electoral child the BJP learnt the art of coalition politics, came to power and led a coalition. During this regime the assertion of its politics went up by the day and it sounded as if it will return to power to really take the country towards the so-called Hindu Rashtra. Gujarat had already shown the way as to where minorities will be placed in the scheme of things being hatched by the Hindutva politics. The return to power of BJP would definitely have been the doom for democracy and those yearning for secular society. Now the furtherance of agenda towards Hindu Rashtra would have meant, change of Constitution, and all other tactics of intimidation, whereby the concept of human rights, affirmative action and democratic space would have been laid to rest for a long time. It's just fortunate that combination of various forces saw that BJP does not come back to power. It is a big respite for the democratic movements, for those struggling to ensure that democracy, the values of Liberty, Equality and Fraternity (Community) survive.

## VI

The idea that one will have to be working for the preservation of community amity, against the communal venom was alien to the progressive movements till the early eighties. It was presumed that the Indian freedom and secular constitution has buried these irritants for good. The communal violence in Jabalpur in 1961 came as a grim warning that communalism is lurking in the sides. In response Pandit Nehru that time went on to lay the foundation of National Integration Council, which was put in suspended animation with BJP coming to power 1998 onwards. Barring that no other response in this direction came from the state or the social action groups. Till practically the late seventies not many efforts were put in this direction barring of course few exceptions, like Dr. Asghar Ali Engineer. To work especially against communal poison was not made into a social campaign by most of the progressive groups till late nineties.

With communal violence taking ghastly shape in the decades of 80s many an eyebrows were raised in sheer amazement. During this period the attack on secular values went on getting worse by the day. The progressive groups used to respond as a knee jerk in the aftermath of riots and then went back to their own previously defined agendas, which were/are relevant any way and are of paramount importance, leaving this issue unattended. The demolition of Babri Masjid saw many a secular action groups coming up for the time and then keeping quiet barring the few, which took it upon themselves to struggle for this on ongoing basis. This state of affairs prevailed till the Gujarat genocide. This anti-Muslim pogrom woke the social groups' conscience in a deep manner. Now the progressive groups have realised that ignoring this issue would be most suicidal for the survival of our democratic ethos. And many serious groups all over the country have taken up the issue of communalism in a significant way.

The hope, optimism and the wish that the poisonous propaganda done by the politics of Hindu Rashtra is combated at all the levels needs to be actualised. The task is to see that the communal divide brought in by this divisive politics is opposed tooth and nail. The goal is to ensure that different religious communities form the national community as a part of emerging global community. The aspiration is that the politics and ideology of exclusionism is replaced by inclusive spirit of Indian Constitution. And this is the prerequisite for the struggles for just and humane society. This is the bedrock on which the values of justice, social; gender and economic can stand.

## VII

The march of the movement for Hindu nation was all pervasive and affected different aspects of our lives. The most papable part of this movement was the myths and sterotypes which came to the fore in an overt manner. History of Muslim kings as presented by the motivated British historiography became the base of many a myths which picked up (Temple destructions, forcible conversions, atrocities on Hindus in general and Hindu women in particular). Similarly the norms of family, large families due to poverty and lack of education, the traits emerging due to ghettoisation, and the international situation resulting in the prominence of Al Qaeda, terrorisim started being attributed to Islam and Muslims. Christians also came under the fire as the Christian missionaries were working amongst Adivasis whom Hindutva politics wants to recruit for political purpose and whose empowerment due to education being spread by Christian missions is a big threat to the status quo, the aim of Hindutva movement.

At slightly different level one sees the state apparatus being communalised more and more. The role of large sections of Police and bureaucracy in Gujarat carnage was too shocking for words. Harsh Mander merely had to blow the lid, which was loosely covering the phenomenon widely perceived by the social workers. About its impact on sections of judiciary and police, the lesser said the better. The arena of culture, totally left unattended by the progressive movement has been swiftly occupied by the conservative values of Hindu right. The communisation of media which began long ago and was boosted during Lal Krishna Advani's tenure as information and broadcasting minister in the

Janata Party's rule, became much more visible lately and of course Gujarat carnage saw the role of a section of the media in its worst light. Here again language press, the media of regional languages, seems to be worst hit by this phenomenon.

As the processes were worsening during the BJP-led NDA rule, its electoral debacle did come as a respite for those who thought that all stones need to be turned to protect the democratic and secular values. All these components are the ingredients of the larger agenda of Hindu Nation, they constitute the contours of the agenda of Hindu Rashtra so to say.

# Section–I

# Religion and Society

Religion had a very complex relationship with society, power and traditions. Nation state has been a late phenomenon, starting from 17th century. The very notion of Hindu Rashtra, Hindu Nation, is based on Brahminical Hinduism. It does use the identity of Hindu religion and is based on particular set of elite versions of Hinduism. It has nothing whatsoever to do with the moral values of saint tradition of Hindu religion for example. It does raise the question as to what has been the role of religion and politics. In the era of kingdoms, which preceded modern nation states the most visible part of the religion, the clergy was closely allied with power structure of the society, the feudal lords and kings. On the other pole were saints of those religions and saints were close to the downtrodden, weak, poor sections of society. The clergy sanctified the social hierarchy and gave legitimacy to the power of the kings and feudal lords, their power was divine and above being challenged by the ordinary mortals.

Clergy had vested interests and all around and in different religions it created and perpetuated the hierarchy between ordinary mortals and the divinely ordained kings. It also presented the caste/class and gender hierarchy in the language of religion. The medieval times saw the unbridled powers of the duo king-clergy in different forms, but the core of this remained the same.

Religion was the major language of expression of the battles of kings. While power and wealth were the central motives of this battle, they were presented as Crusades, Jihad and Dharmayudha, when kings happened to belong to different religions. When belonging to same broad religion, the sects of religions provided the pretexts for wars. The present politics, whenever stalking in the name of religion, does hide the vested interests of the powerful sections of society.

While the Mullahs have been on the prowl in the countries where Islamic fundamentalism has come up, in India, the Godmen have mushroomed in dozens. Apart from being the most lucrative business, it has the support and sanctions of the layers of society, which are either opposed, to the transformation of caste and gender equations or want to preserve the status quo.

This section looks at the role of religion as an institution, the role of clergy, the process of secularisation in West and here in India. This complex process essentially means the abolishing of hierarchies at all the levels, paving the way for Liberty, Equality and Fraternity (Community). The types of politics, which derive their legitimacy from religion, are against the erosion of this hierarchy under the banner of religion. This section also looks at the trajectory of religion in its changing role over a period of time. The simple fact that religion has been abused by kings, cutting across religions, for their expansionist goals, is so apparent but so hidden. The wars launched by kings are looked at with reverence while these were essentially power games. The clergy whose social power declined with modern values is being supplanted by new associates, the modern elite saints, the Godmen with air-conditioned cars, mansions and mobiles and enormous wealth, have been on a rise more so after the Hindutva politics has been on ascendance.

# 1

# Religion, Secularism and the State

Secularism has been the topic of discussion and controversy in this society for the past two decades or so. In a way this issue is linked with the issue of the separation or non-separation of religion from politics. With Indian Independence, came the formation of the Constituent Assembly, which after long deliberations formulated the Constitution in a way, which had all the basic ingredients of a secular state. We are using the term secularism here to mean *Dharma Nirpekshta* (i.e., religious authorities should have no say in matters of the State). There is another interpretation also which is being imputed to secularism, *Sarva Dharma Samabhava* (equal respect for all religions).

In the years immediately after Independence, the State was criticised for not being 'secular enough' and for compromising with religion. This is a far cry from the present attacks on secularism. The present attacks and misinterpretation of secularism are on the ground that : (a) secularism is a western concept and it has been brought into the Indian Constitution as a result of our mental slavery to the West, (b) secularism is anti-religion and is unsuitable in a religious country like India, and that if at all secularism is to be practiced in India it should mean equal respect for all religions.

**Religion and Human Society**

Religion has multiple subsets like institutional, ritualistic, doctrinal, mythical and ethical components. Religious experience has a definite reference to the transcendental which is expressed in various religious goals like 'Kingdom of Heaven', 'Nirvana or Moksha'. Religious beliefs are social compilation of pre-modern human wisdom related to the entire world-view. 'Ritualistic dimension' of religion provides an occasion for community sharing of religion and creating social bonds. 'Ethical and moral dimensions' of religion set the norms of behaviour for human beings. The most predominant aspect of religion, however, is the clergy *(dharmaguru)*, which is supposed to mediate between 'man' and 'God'. This clergy has different levels of organisation, varying from the most well organised clergy in Christianity to the most fragmented priestly class in Hinduism. Religion has played diverse social roles in history. For example the clergy has mostly served to provide legitimation to the existing social systems. On the other hand, some religions have also provided the vehicle for expression of social dissent. The major change in the role of religion takes place with the advent of industrialisation, and this process is known as secularisation. Secularisation is the broad term referring to the changes in the social relationships between different social groups and also the change in power equations at social level. In Feudal societies (Kingdoms) clergy is the legitimizer of the prevalent social hierarchies of class, caste and gender and holds a powerful place in the society.

From 17th Century discoveries of science began challenging the deeply held beliefs and faith which were integral part of broad canvass of religion. This phenomenon was first observed in Europe, where medieval period was characterised by supremacy of church over all aspects of life. There were not a few, who had through life long dedication discovered the secrets of nature, but were seen as heretics, blasphemous or otherwise. For example, in 1553 Servatus was burnt at stake for publishing his work in the field of medicine, which was labeled by church as against the idea of trinity. Similarly Palissy who was a great natural scientist with several contributions in the field of minerals, geology and chemistry had to die in prison in 1590 for converting to Protestantism. Copernicus had to present his discovery that Earth went around the Sun, merely as a mathematical formulation rather than as a real life phenomenon for the fear of persecution.

**Secularisation**

European secularisation movement took root during the period of Renaissance and French enlightenment. The vast mass of peasantry crushed under feudal exploitation, could see the libratory potential of "Liberty, Equality and Fraternity', the call given by the rising French bourgeoisies to break the hold of feudal-church nexus on the society. The struggle against feudal absolutism also involved struggle against the hold of Church/Religion on the society. Here on the one hand the requirements of the newly emerging industries required the peasants to be released from the social grip of feudal lord and the concomitant religious grip of the church. It is in this backdrop that one can begin to understand the meaning of social norms developing around modern rationality.

Similar to French experience industrial revolution in England projected the ideal of democratic form of government and rights of individuals as citizens proved a turning point. Thus, secularisation of civil society and polity was actually the culmination of numerous factors as new scientific discoveries and technological advancement which revolutionised the mode of production both in agriculture and industry, unleashing a novel socio-religious processes, renaissance and reformation. Navigation and new markets, emergence and rise of new class of bourgeoisie and consequent contractual relationship brought in free labour and capital accumulation.

Thus, modernity and secularisation do not just emerge from ideological constructs of the philosophers and ideologues. Primarily these twin processes are the outcome of the struggles of the emerging bourgeoisie (industrialists and their paraphernalia) and the expression of the struggles of peasants under the clutches of feudal lords. These processes get social roots in these sectors of society who emerge pari passu with development of science and technology which form the infrastructure of the newer production processes.

Modernity/secularisation occur at a particular juncture in history when the newer production processes are trying to integrate the achievements of science and technology into its gambit. The newer requirements want a labour force which till that time is not 'free floating' as it is, gripped by the traditional hierarchies, is at the service of feudal lords and its legitimiser the clergy. The prevalent system is a mix of pre-scientific social wisdom, and gender related hierarchies which are sustained by the preachings of clergy, pandits and mullahs. The secularisation movement is heralded by two parallel but opposite groups, whose interests are common at this point of time. The rising industrialist needs more social powers, and a labour force which can be hired at contractual terms. The victims of prevalent hierarchies, poor peasantry, looks forward to the work in industries as a 'relative' liberation from the prevalent oppressive hierarchies. And along with it goes the struggle for social consent, ideas in social space where the scientific reason battles it out with the pre-scientific social ideas. Thus the complex of modernity/ secularisation cannot be located in any one single arena, it is a comprehensive arrival of newer social relationships (Industrialist-labour: on social contractual terms), newer rationality (around science and reason) on one hand arrayed against the feudal-church nexus (based on birth based hierarchies) and pre-scientific social ideas.

**Secularisation in India**

The secularisation process in India has been an extremely complex and painful one. The European powers were out to colonise the rest of the world to enrich their industrial development and for creating markets for their industrial products. India came mainly under the sway of the British who colonised the country, and keeping their needs in mind, initiated a ruthless plunder of India's wealth and raw materials. They increased the taxation on land, forced the shift to cash crops, and simultaneously ensured intense plunder by laying down the railways and telegraphs as the efficient means of communication. To supplement their needs for trained-educated manpower, they introduced English education in the country. To support their efforts many an Indian came up as their 'assistant', who themselves started laying down the foundations of modern industries and eventually graduated as 'modern' business-professionals. At this time these modern ideas also found their way through the newer education system and through a class of intelligentsia which started going to England for their education.

This process again required the release of peasants from their 'ties', to the lands, and subjugation to the feudal lords and Brahmins. Simultaneously we see the twin movements, which contributed to the secularisation process. The first of these was the independence movement, aimed against the control of colonial masters, and the second was a series of regional movements against the social hierarchy, caste system and gender oppression, aimed to gain self-respect and breaking the social stranglehold of landlords, Brahmins and the caste system.

This exposure to new learning also laid the foundation of Indian Renaissance. The positive and negative factors of alien rule, e.g., Western liberalism, free press, modern system of communications, along with racial arrogance, economic exploitation of India and assertion of cultural superiority by the English, filled the Indian mind with a new spirit of national consciousness. The British policies put into motion a number of contradictory processes. The development of modernity was not just against the religious clergy and landlords but had to take on the British rulers also.

The process of breaking of the hegemony of the priest and the Zamindar was painfully slow and remained incomplete for decades to come, leaving its remnants in different pockets even today. This process was initiated by Mahatma Jotirao Phule who founded the Satyashodhak Samaj in Maharashtra with its alliance of middle and low castes, shudra and ati-shudra.

In Tamil Nadu, Periyar E.V. Ramaswamy Naicker began the 'Self-Respect Movement' in 1926. This developed into a political party Dravida Kazhgam in 1944, which centred around the struggle for secularisation of the hitherto inarticulate sections of Tamil society. Another major attempt, the one which had the deepest impact in secularising the society, was initiated by Dr. Bhimrao Ambedkar (Babasaheb) who attempted at organising a broad based caste-class front of dalits and non-Brahmins. He was able to arouse the self-respect in large sections of dalits though workers under the influence of communist parties, which had a different perception of struggle of the oppressed, remained aloof from Babasaheb's movement. He initially struggled to gain a place for the dalits within the fold of Hinduism, but failure of all his attempts forced him to convert to Buddhism with all his followers.

Workers movements began with Narayan Meghaji Lokhande and later on Communist Party picked up the thread. Workers movement had deep ramifications in the social dynamics and it broke the long slumber of passivity in social relations. It sent the villages into a turmoil and new value systems began making their inroads into the Zamindar-poor peasant relationship. Thus, the existing social relationships came under attack from multiple quarters : (a) Independent struggle, anti-British movement led by Gandhi and Nehru, (b) the anti-caste movements of Periyar and Ambedkar, and (c) Workers movement.

The secularisation/industrialisation process was slow in its trajectory because of colonial powers who permitted/initiated only as much modernisation as was needed for their 'plunder' project. The secular democratic movement led by Congress was also predominantly representing the emerging bourgeoisie, which was not very strong, and partly the aspirations of the broad layers of society. It did want to take along the anti-caste and workers movements but with lot of limitations and compromises. It is for this reason that anti-caste, anti-upper class movements never totally subjugated to the Congress, preferring to keep their separate identity as they were clear that their interests are secondary as far as the priorities of the Congress-led freedom movement are concerned. The land-reforms, land to the tiller may sound a purely economic demand but it is the social core of secularisation process, as it is this measure which frees the tiller from the clutches of the landlord. One of the reasons, as to why Nehru rejected the offer of coalition government from the Muslim League was his realisation that Muslim League, like its counterpart Hindu Mahasabha, was dominated by the landlords and they will prevent the measures for land reforms in the states wherever the coalition governments will be formed.

The movement for secularisation of society had enemies within the society itself. The weak secularisation movement, represented by Indian National Congress, as pointed out earlier was voicing, projecting the socio-economic needs of the rising, nascent industrialists, a section of professionals, and the modern businessman, who came up in the wake of newer industrial scenario. The opposition to their social aspirations came from the entrenched social powers, assuming a communal manifestation. The newer developments were breaking the back of established social hierarchy of landlords, moneylenders and the priests. Realising the dangers to their social and political interests these sectors of society hit back and threw up the political formations like Muslim League (Muslim elite, initially business groups later joined by landlords and Nawabs) and Hindu Mahasabha, RSS (Hindu Zamindars), Rajas of Riyasats (small states within Indian territory: paying tribute to British masters but not controlled by them directly), Brahmins and Banias (traditional tradesmen).

The complex development of this political triangle: British colonial aspirations, freedom struggles led by Gandhi and Nehru, and the communal forces represented by Muslim League and Hindu Mahasabha, RSS, led to the partition of the country and also retarded the growth of secularisation process to a great extent. With Muslim communal elements going to Pakistan and Hindu communal elements being a small force, the Indian Constitution which was drawn up came to represent mainly the aspirations and political agendas of the industrialists, workers and dalits. Constituent Assembly adopted a secular constitution as a response to the needs of rising industrialist class, and the pressure of social movements of the oppressed sections of society. Nehru was an overarching figure in bringing in the secular principles at the level of state policy, he had the support of modern industrialists and radical intelligentsia in this endeavour. This initiative of his was strongly supported and prompted by the social impact of aspirations of industrialists and struggles of exploited sectors of society desiring to break free from Brahmin-Bania, (priest-trader) landlord-priest nexus.

The pressure of social movements of workers and dalits gave strength and ensured a place for secular ethos in state policies. During this time the main opponent to modernity/ secularisation, the RSS remained a marginal force, and secularism as a state policy continued to enjoy respectability and admiration from different social scientists. One cannot deny that there was a strain between the secular Constitution and semi-secularised society. And if at all, state was criticised for inadequate implementation of secular policies and not the other way around.

## Indian State and Secularism

Secularism was the guiding principle of anti-British struggle. It was recognised as an ideological platform for the multi-religious, multi-caste, multi-ethnic population of the subcontinent. It was the collective expression of the aspirations of the rising classes against the power of its colonial masters and the entrenched feudal interests in the country. The resultant constitution, made different provisions to ensure that secularism has a place in the society, i.e.

(i) the state by itself shall not espouse or establish or practice any religion

(ii) public revenues will not be used to promote any religion

(iii) the state shall have the power to regulate any economic, financial or other secular activity associated with religious practice (Article 25 (2)(9) of Constitution)

(iv) every individual will have, in that order, an equal right to freedom of conscience and religion.

In the words of Jawaharlal Nehru "What it means is that it is a state which honours all faiths equally and gives them equal opportunities; that as a state, it does not allow itself to be attached to one faith or religion.... In a country like India, real nationalism is a relic of the past and no longer relevant today" (Forward in Raghunath Singh, *Dharma Nirpeksha Raj*).

In a similar vein Mahatma Gandhi said, "I swear by my religion, I will die for it. But it is my personal affair. The state has nothing to do with it. The state will look after your secular welfare, health, communications, foreign relations, currency and so on, but not your and my religion. That is everybody's personal concern". (Gandhi, quoted in T.N. Madan, TSI Vol. 3, Jan. 1997).

Secularism is not just an ideological issue. It basically stands for relegation of the clergy to the private realms of one's life. Secularism is not anti-religion but only stands for diminution of political powers of the clergy, it has no antagonism to other components of religion as such.

## References

Quoted in Uday Mehta, "Problem of 'Crisis of Indian 'Secularism'", *Indian Journal of Secularism*, April '97, Mumbai, pp. 82-85.

T.N. Madan, 'The Crisis of Indian Secularism', *Towards Secular India*, Vol. 3, No. 1, Jan. 1997, p. 2, Mumbai.

Ashish Nandy, 'The Politics of Secularism and the recovery of religious tolerance', Rajiv Gandhi Institute for Contemporary Studies, New Delhi, 1995, p. 37.

*Ibid.*, p. 49.

Wallace, Anthony, F.C., *Religion an Anthropological View*, Random House, New York, 1966, p. 62.

Rohini, P.H., 'Struggle Against Communalism', *EPW*, Oct. 23, 1993, p. 2339.

Irfan Engineer, 'Religion, State and Secularism', *EPW*, Oct. 28, 1995, p. 2726.

Colin A. Ronan, *Science—Its History and Development Among the World's Culture*, 1982.

Larry Shiner, "Conceptualisation in empirical research: Sociological perspectives", Pelican 1971, (Eds. Thompson and Tunstall).

Madhavi Yasin, *Emergence of Nationalism, Congress, Separatism*, Raj Publications, Delhi, 1996.

*Ibid.*

O'Hanlon 1985, Quoted in Heredia and Mathais (Eds.), 'Secularism and Liberation', Indian Social Institute, New Delhi, 1995, p. 29.

Omvedt Gail, 'Hinduism and Politics', *EPW*, Vol. 25, No. 14, pp. 723-29.

Anandhi S., "Collective Identity and Secularism", *Social Action*, Vol. 44, No. 1, pp. 54-68.

Jawaharlal Nehru, "Foreward in Raghunath Singh", *Dharm Nirpeksh Raj*, New Delhi, 1961.

Upendra Baxi, 'The struggle for redefinition of secularism in India, Dr. Iqbal Narain (Ed.), *Secularism in India*.

T.N. Madan, 'Quoted in Anandhi S., "Contending Identities", Indian Social Institute, New Delhi, 1995, p. 4.

T.N. Madan, 'Quoted in Anandhi S., "Contending Identities", Indian Social Institute, New Delhi, 1995.

*Ibid.*

*Ibid.*

M. Gandhi quoted in T.N. Madan, 'The Crisis of Indian Secularism', *TSI*, Vol. 3, No. 1, p. 4.

# 2

# Religion, Power and Violence

The world scene has seen immense and horrific violence in recent times. Two planes ram into the World Trade Center, nearly three thousand people perish into oblivion, an "Islamic terrorist" Osama bin Laden thanks Allah for this act. U.S. President George W. Bush launches an attack on Afghanistan to catch hold of Osama bin Laden and calls this attack as crusade.

Separated by thousands of kilometres, in another part of the world, Gujarat, India, a train coach is burned. Instant investigation by the chief minister of that state gives him the insight that this was an act of Islamic terrorists in collaboration with local Muslims. His associates give the call that Hindus are in danger and he signals that revenge process will not be disturbed. He instructs his staff to sit back. His administration goes a step further and assists the rampaging marauders out to kill Muslims. Two thousand people loose their life. The plight of women and children is beyond description. What these victims share in common is the identity of a religion called Islam. Just a few years ago people in Bosnia and Rwanda died in thousands for belonging to the 'wrong' religion.

Last three decades have seen the violence world over under the flag of religions. Is this violence done to save some religion or its followers? Is it done to protect the moral values, *din*, ethics, and *dharma* of the particular religions? Is this violence done to save the traditions and communitarian ethos of the followers of those religions? How are religions related to the massive violence, which goes on in their name?

One recalls that even in medieval times the phenomenon of crusades, *jihads* and *dharmayudhs*, which, kings undertook on the pretext of religion. Were these meant to expand religion or were they meant to expand their empires. One recalls that the identity of religions is associated more with the clergy and less with the moral values of the religions. It does not require too much of knowledge to realize that in pre-industrial society the clergy, the most visible part of religions was associated with the landlords and the kings in different forms, somewhere in direct collaboration from top to bottom, somewhere in fragmented form. Also there was another set of people associated with religions, the saints, who were away from the power centres. These were the saints, the *bhakti* saints in Hindu tradition, the sufi saints in Islamic tradition and mystiques and later liberation theologian in Christian tradition, were away from the centres of power and were close to the poor, exploited and oppressed sections of society.

The rulers did not tolerate the saints. The clergy, the official upholders of the religion, were hostile to *bhakti* saints, who were killed in various ways. The two facets of religion were always counter-posed to each other. Since the traditions close to power are more dominant, the Church, Olema and Brahmins are presented as the vehicles of religion. The parallel traditions of saint's remains on the margins, snubbed by the social and political powers.

A sufi saint Nizamuddin Auliya refused to receive the emperor in his dargah, Tukaram was done to death, Chokhamela reprimands God himself for the plight of the poor. These traditions emphasize on the message of love and amity in contrast to the clergy, which gives importance to rituals and the written word. In India the saints, mostly came from low caste and did proclaim that they have no capacity to learn the heavy tomes of their religion written in Devbhasha (language of Gods, upper caste) Sanskrit, which was denied to them anyway, because of their low caste status.

During the process of secularisation the role of clergy declined from the social and political space. The structural hierarchies of caste and gender, which this clergy legitimised in the name of religion started getting challenged, got abolished in countries where industrialisation took place in the early period. These societies strove for the values of Liberty, Equality and Fraternity (community). In colonies the nexus between colonial powers and the landlords, kings blocked the secularisation process. And in country like India these declining classes, landlord-clergy, threw up the politics in the name of religion, known as communal politics. For example, in India it came up as Muslim League and Hindu Mahasabha-RSS, but these were marginal streams. At world level the politics was dominated by the colonial powers. Later U.S. emerged as the major world power and national liberation struggles in the colonies took the inspiration from Russian and Chinese revolutions, at many places under the flag of socialism. During this era the global violence was presented as the struggle between the 'free world' and communism.

After the cold war era, the decline of socialist economies, the hegemony of U.S. started becoming indisputable. Its machinations in the oil zone where Islam was the dominant religion, the new offensive of imperialism took the garb of religious language and the 'backward Islam' started being targeted by the U.S. and its cohorts. It is to support this imperialist ambition that the theory of Clash of Civilisations (Samuel Huntington) came up as a cover for U.S. policies.

This theory very cleverly counter-poses the advanced Western Civilisation against backward Islamic civilisation. Here the Western civilisation is not Christian, and the Middle East Muslims and others are clubbed to be having the backward Islamic civilisation. The wars launched by U.S. against the people of Afghanistan and Iraq is presented as a logical extension of this thesis, to set right the wrongs of backward Muslims.

Around this time in India the rise of Hindutva politics has goals similar to the ones of the U.S. as far as targeting Muslims and Islam are concerned. This Hindutva ideology is a politics based on Brahminical stream of Hinduism and had base earlier in the declining classes of landlords and clergy (Zamindar, Brahmin, Bania) and now it flourishes amongst the new middle class thrown up by the so-called development process. This middle class, affluent and the core of 'Shining India' has gained immensely from the process of industrialisation and also from the mindless globalisation from eighties onwards. It is this middle class, which sustains a new breed of religious people, in saffron or any other color. This new set of Gurus and Acharyas, Sri Sri Ravishankar, Asaram Bapu, Pandurang Shastri Athwale, Sudhanshu Maharaj, Aniruddh Bapu and the like, are the nerve soothers for the existential tensions of the middle class. These Gurus are pushing the *Manusmriti* and the feudal values of caste and gender hierarchies in a new language, the language laced with modernity, so to say. Similarly, one notices the presence of Muslim Olamas, Mullahs and the likes of Shahi Imam who have been promoting obscurantism in the Muslim community. Starting from their role in putting pressure to reverse the Shah Bano judgment to their opposition to abolition of triple *talaq* and polygamy amongst Muslims, their retrograde role is a bane of Muslim community in India.

Globally and locally various phenomenon are overlapping. Now as the offensive of power seekers at world level is masked in the language of religion, particularly anti-Islam, those aspiring for control on social and political power at home are also using this Hindutva, religion based politics.

The language of religion is deceptive. It gives it a type of moral sanctity, it creates a sort of mass hysteria, and it offers a sort of platform for the retrograde ideology. The goals of power are creating violence, condoned by those who should have different types of social power. Violence is the superficial layer of this politics of power in the name of religion. It is more than a coincidence that while, religion targeted by U.S. at the level of the world and the one targeted in India by Hindutva are the same. The camaraderie of those using religion for their political goals cannot be missed.

Religion has diverse functions in society. The way it is being used (! abused) by Hindutva and U.S. and its cohorts, is its most dominant face. The clergy at many times plays diverse roles as well. At times it has played the role of projecting the religion, which is the opiate of the masses, it has also been the sigh of the oppressed in this heartless world. The sufis and saints had particularly played the latter role. While the opiate role has been played by the section of clergy tied to the apron strings of those in political and social power, acting as legitimizers of their exploitative and oppressive role. One sees the Church of old times associating with kings, and the one currently, which is opposing the U.S. offensives as the same institution playing diverse role with change of time. One can see in Indian context the fleet of gurus with immense wealth under their control serving as the base for creating the opinion and opium for Hindutva politics. One also sees the saffron clad sadhus of Vishwa Hindu Parishad asking for revenge against Muslims and the Shahi Imams using their sermons to rouse the passions in the name of religion.

Religion, if one regards moral values as its core, should not be associated with power. Different types of people associated with religion have at times played as handmaiden to the power centres, legitimising their violence in turn. The triad of religion power and violence gets connected once we see the ambitions of those using religion for their narrow goals. If the people of religion cannot be associated with the plight of poor and oppressed they are handmaidens of the powerful. And in turn then they are legitimizers of violence. The examples of these abound.

It is time that the people associated with religion realize the abuse to which religion has been put. Some streams of religion are for this goal in a blatant fashion. Than there are other streams of religion which play a soothing role for the exploited sections of society. This section of religious people, true to the moral values of religions, can live their religion only by associating themselves with the plight of the poor, oppressed and the underdogs. Association of religion with power is the crux of its negative role in society. A severance of this will surely put religion more as the vehicle of sigh of the oppressed and this can only be achieved by firm advocacy of the causes of this section, this can be achieved by associating with their struggles for the justice, gender, economic, social and political.

# 3

# Profane Goals: Sacred Garb

## Religion, Godmen and Contemporary Society

Shankarcharya's arrest in Shankarraman murder case (Nov. 2004) created few ripples in the civil society and some commotion in the political outfits. While BJP went on hammer and tongs to criticize the government for arresting a divine authority in a shabby manner, which according to it tantamounted to insult of Hindu religion, the Prime Minister Manmohan Singh had to state that the person of such a high religious position should be treated with the respect. With the courts granting him bail the BJP has declared it as its victory as if the decision of the courts has been on the political grounds and not on the grounds of law! It is noteworthy that while the Hindu right wing outfits were beating their breasts at the incident, the average Hindus preferred to ignore the issue and they did not join in the protests organised by these outfits. It raised a question whether there can be two sets of laws in dealing with the people, one for those with divine authority and the other for the laity, the ordinary people, not privileged, not having 'divine' authority.

Just as an aside, few happenings during and around the arrest are quite significant. It is reported that the holy seer cooked for himself, and at one occasion he refused being injected medicine by a non-Brahmin doctor. The happenings in the Shringeri Mutt of the pontiff were probably as mundane as at many other places not blessed with divinity. Sex, pornography, links with the high and mighty, money and what have you were the core ingredients of the things which appeared to be going on in the Mutt. How does one acquire divinity? Is it bestowed by some superpower unknown to the lay people or is it by the internal succession of these 'Holy' *mutts* that the divine power passes on to next generation? In places where the Godmen are having 'normal' families and children the problem is like the one witnessed in Muktanand Ashram, the struggle between brother and sister for the high throne, not much unlike the inheritance of the business enterprises, as one being currently witnessed in the wealthy, mighty Ambani family. But in places where the pontiffs are unmarried, which is the case most of the time, the succession of divinity and the accompanying moolah is through the nomination or manipulation of sorts.

The world of Godmen is fascinating and mysterious at the same time. There are types and types of Godmen. They abound in most of the traditional religious institutions, some of them have come up through their own efforts and have formed institutions. Unfortunately they are the most visible symbol of that religion or the sect of a religion or those who come up on their own form a new sect or following. Many a times they are regarded as the representative of that religious community as well. Various facets of religion do exist, various religious values do exist but the impression is that religion is synonymous with the Godmen and rituals. It is not easy to classify them and categorize or characterize them with ease. But surely some broad generalisations and their role in society can be discerned.

Most of the prophet based religions, Jainism; Buddhism; Christianity; Islam and Sikhism, began as a response and to oppose the existing injustices and to address some of the issues prevailing in the society. Soon with co option of religions by the social powers their character started changing and what started becoming dominant was the authority of clergy and symbolism of rituals. The moral values of the religion were put aside, as a marginal phenomenon. The powers that be of society associated with the religious authority to ensure that the weaker sections of society are deprived of their dues and are made to work as slaves and serfs, as dalits. The women were deprived of their equality and treated as property of men, and all this in the name of religion. The set of Godmen, Mullahs, Priests, Acharyas, Gurus became part of the established social hierarchy and gave the 'religious sanction' to the suppression of the oppressed. This section of clergy, was all through with the political authority of kings, feudal lords. Many a religions did not accept the role of clergy in the basic sense. But this was sidetracked and the social groups did come up with this role of a mediator irrespective of its non-existence in the canons of those religions.

Interpretations were conveniently changed and feudal authority derived its legitimacy from the lord almighty through the agency of clergy. The king rules on the authority of the lord almighty and so the possibility of opposition to his power by the people does not exist as it is the divine sanction due to which he is ruling. When kings, if they are from the same religion, fight with each other, the 'other' is labeled as the one from the deviant sect, a heretic and so needs to be decimated. If the fight is between the kings of different religions the convenient labels of Jihad, Crusade or Dharmayudh are marshalled to enthuse the soldiers to lay down their lives for the power of their king. As this type of laying down of life is a religious sacrifice entitling one for the much longed for Jannat, Heaven or Swarg as the case may be.

While this clergy, the Godmen are merrily dishing out the dictates for all and sundry, as to how people have to live (or die) they claim to be sole repository of the knowledge and this knowledge, it is claimed to be divine and any opposition to the prevalent divine knowledge was dealt with firmly by excommunicating, burning or condemning the dissenting voice, to Hell, *Jahannum* or *Nark* as the case may be. While one can easily understand the needs of power to make the issues of world opaque to make the rule of vested interests easy, what remains more impressive and encaptivating is the role of saints, sufis and liberation theology type of holy people.

It is through them that the downtrodden express themselves, their pain, anguish and exploitation. It is through the literature of these sufi's and saints and mystiques that one sees the germs of humanism thriving, the values of oneness of humanity finds its language through them. No wonder these saints are paupers, and identify with the paupers. The divide between these two groups of people one with power and one with the exploited is as clear as it is distinct. Most of the time the saints are not tolerated by the clergy.

Secularisation in various countries changed the scenario and the powerful duo of landlord-clergy lost their prime position. In semi-secularised societies the situation is much different. The clergy changed its character from the one of medieval times. Somewhere, more so from early seventies, we do see the emergence of a new category of Godmen, affluent, with connections with the power centres of the society, patronised by upper class and the affluent section of middle class and having a mesmerising sway over broad sections of society. Major part of their wealth and property also comes from elite sections of society. Today in India we do not see many a saints in the medieval mould who can express the anguish of the people in the language of religion or the like.

While the traditional priestly class has managed to retain their place in a slightly modified form, the new cults and Godmen have an overarching presence. To begin with the traditional *mutts* have a following, which is increasing by the day. One observed the increase in the number of visitors to Vaishno Devi, Tirupati Balaji, Sidhhi Vinayak and the like. At many of these places one observes a shameless phenomenon of different queues depending on the capacity of the person to pay to have a *darshan* of the Lord. These temple trusts are controlling millions of rupees. The *mutts* have the dynamics and logic of their own and the politics and vested interests in these places are quite akin to one's prevalent in the business houses.

To add to the variety, one has witnessed the mushrooming of new godmen and sects a la Mahesh Yogi, Rajneesh, Muktanand, ISCON, Ma Amritnand Mayi, Prajapita Brahmkumari, Anirruddha Bapu, Aasaram Bapu, Pandurang Shashtri Athawale and Sri Sri Ravishankar. They specialize in different areas of spirituality and have ever increasing clientèle. Their divinity is also of different variety. Most of these are very hot favourites of Hindu Right. In Gujarat where the laboratory of Hindu Rashtra is making a transition towards Hindu Rashtra in one state, their number has been very significant. Many of them like Asaram Bapu and Pandurang Shashtri are talking sanitised version of *Manusmriti* in the garb of spirituality. The social phenomenon as to why these are coming up and thriving during last few decades has a lot to do with the type of socio-economic processes which are unfolding in the society. Many of them are acting as the hypnotherapists for the tension-ridden society. These tensions are peculiar to the World today, as it is witnessing the polarisation of countries and people into rich and poor in most blatant fashion. The two Indias, the one shining and the other whining is the reality of today's society. The rich nations, like U.S. and the poor nations like those of Africa, South Asia are again a reality.

The role of Godmen seems to be very complex. On one hand they act as the soothing balm for some, at the other they ensure the perpetuation of status quo, status quo of social relations and intra-society-social equations. No doubt most of them are affluent to the core amassing millions in their lifetime, and at the same time talking subtle language of status quo laced in the syrup of spirituality. The medieval times saw the divide between divine and human, the concept of Human agency in the matters of society has been the biggest gain of the modern times. The Godmen essentially are trying to undo the same. Their divinity is not meant for eradicating the poverty and social ills, their divinity helps the vested interests to fix their problems in the worldly affairs. Their divinity is a mask to create-promote opaqueness, to take them away from the gaze of critical questioning. It is an attempt to get the sanction for whatever they want to achieve and help their cohorts in the business and politics of the world.

One is puzzled as to where are the saints in today's society? Does this category exist today? Saints, the one's close to the deprived people, the one's destitute themselves and genuinely articulating the pains of the deprived. Not much can be said on this score. The service missions at places are filling some gaps in this direction. The language of anguish seems to have been mainly been used only by human rights groups and many of those who work closely with different deprived sections of society.

The veneer of religiosity is the best guarantee for getting away with whatever one does. The question is, can the *mutts* and Godmen's empires be subjected to social audit? The profane business done by the Godmen is cloaked under the veil of divinity, acquired through the rituals and many worldly circumstances. Interestingly the saints of medieval times, mostly from low caste kept away from the rituals and concentrated more on listening, sharing the pain of the people.

# Section–II

# Hindutva

Hindutva is the political ideology of the Hindu Rashtra. It is around this that the values of freedom struggle, the one's related to democracy and secularism are being questioned, opposed and humiliated. Though this word gives the impression of being a religion, as such it only uses the identity of religion for achieving its goal. It rouses the sentiments for political mobilisation, serving the agenda of Sangh combine. There are no parallel words in other similar political streams. The politics of those using Islam as a cover for their agenda can be called as being Islamism, and for the Orthodox Christian groups, the word available has been Christian fundamentalism. The general impression is that it is only the Islam, which has backward orthodox fundamentalist values but as a matter of fact fundamentalist politics made its first appearance in Christianity in early twentieth century in United States. The other common trait shared by these diverse political streams is that they stand opposed to democratic values but do make use of democracy to achieve their social and political agenda. In a way they also share the basic values with fascism, which emphasizes more on racial identity.

There is a deeper connection between the politics in the name of religion and the colonial powers. In last two and a half decades one can see the hand of imperialism at places where fundamentalism has reared its head. Colonial powers did leave behind a legacy of religion-based politics also. The practitioners of religion-based politics in India were in alliance with the colonial powers. Many a fundamentalist streams are directly promoted by the imperialist powers, Al Qaeda for example.

Hindutva is unique in many ways. To begin with it has been articulated very cogently by its ideologues, these ideologues have also paid tribute to the fascist powers then on rise in Europe and they have given the ideological justification for the attacks on minorities, and presented the caste and gender subordination in a very sophisticated veneer, giving the impression that these are the core values of Hindu society. It is no mean task to present the obscurantist values as humane values of the current times, and that's what these ideologues have attempted.

The relationship between the imperialist powers and Hindutva has always been congenial. They were not a part of freedom struggle; their main ire was not against the colonial powers but against the national movement and Gandhi in particular. RSS has the dubious distinction of supporting the attack of U.S. on Vietnam and later against Iraq. Currently it is the merry time for RSS, the progenitor of Hindutva ideology today, as its target Islam and Muslim matches so much with the world emperor, U.S. administration and industrial-military complex.

# 4

# Hindutva: Religion or Politics?

During last two decades India has witnessed a strange political scene. The language of political interaction has been made to shift away from the struggles and travails of the poor and exploited, i.e., those revolving around bread, butter, shelter, housing, health and education (the problems of this world). It has been made to take up the issues supposed to be related to 'faith'. We are witness to newer dangers to society, to democratic and secular values in the form of communalism, communal violence and rise of new social political forces basing themselves on 'Religion' in the political arena.

We have been hearing a new word called Hindutva from last two decades or so. Though this Hindutva ideology was rooted in certain social segments from last many decades, its social visibility has been much more in the last decade. On first thought it gives the impression as if it is some sort of religion. As we will see it derives its name from Hindu religion but it is a political ideology akin to the Islamist political ideology. This political ideology has raised afresh, the questions of nationality, community, identity and host of other issues in the social space. The Hindutva movement presents itself for building a strong nation based on the tenets of 'Hindu Dharma', Hindu Rashtra (Hindu Nation). There are many notions attached to this word and we need to understand the meaning of this. But this is a newer set of value system, which has found sympathy amongst a section of population. We need to understand as to which segment of society is behind this political movement.

While pursuing its political agenda, the Hindutva movement has brought to fore a number of precepts, which have found acceptance amongst some sections of society. It has popularised a new version of History, which looks at the past through the parameter of religion alone. Also the major political force, which is the vehicle of Hindutva politics, the RSS has been spreading this version of history from last many decades. Today large section of media does accept this version of History. It in a way has become part of 'social common sense'.

**Rashtriya Swayamsevak Sangh**

Hindutva movement is being spearheaded by a plethora of organisations, the patriarch of which is Rashtriya Swayamsevak Sangh (RSS), the real controller of all other organisations. It was founded in 1925, in the backdrop which needs to be understood in detail. In 1920 with the entry of Mahatma Gandhi into the political arena, the dynamics of the anti-British movement got tremendously galvanised. He brought in to the struggle people of all religions, castes and creed. The Brahminical domination in the Congress started declining. At this time the upper castes, and the Brahmins, supported by *Zamindari* elements and *bania's*, in order to reassert their hegemony on the social political and social scene came up with the idea of a religion based national organisation, the RSS.

**Hindutva: Fascism as the Source of Inspiration**

'Slightly prior to this Savarkar put forward the idea of Hindutva as the basis for politics, which stood for nationalism based on Hinduism' (Puniyani, 2000, 51). At that time the non-Brahman movement was peaking itself and was threatening to shake the very social power of Zamindar-Brahmin nexus. At international level the race based nationalism of Nazis (Germany) and Fascists (Italy) was on the ascendance. This was the main inspiration for the ideas 'Nationalism' of RSS. "German National pride has now become the topic of the day. To keep up the purity of the nation and its culture, Germany shocked the world by her purging the country of the Semitic races—the Jews. National pride at its highest has been manifested here. Germany has also shown to the world how well nigh impossible it is for races and cultures having differences going to the roots to be assimilated into one united whole, a good lesson for us in India to learn and profit by." (Golwalkar, 1938, 27)

Marzia Casolari, an Italian researcher who has done work on roots of Hindu nationalism concludes that "(a) the main historical organisations and leaders of Hindu nationalism had a distinctive and sustained interest in fascism and Nazism; (b) fascist ideological influences on Hindu nationalism were present and relevant; (c) to a certain extent, these influences were channeled through direct contacts between Hindu nationalists and members of the Italian fascist state"(Casolari, 2000, 37). RSS decided to keep aloof from day to day political struggles and began to train the young boys into the doctrine of Hindu Rashtra. As per this core ideology of RSS "Hindus and Hindus alone, constitute the Indian Nation, since they are the original inhabitants and sole creators of its society and culture. Hinduism is uniquely catholic and tolerant and hence superior to other faiths, ...The subsequent entry and takeover by foreigners created an illusion that India was a land of many different and equal cultures....Only a 'truly secular' Hindu Rashtra will afford protection to non-Hindus"(Basu, 1993, 37).

**Sangh Parivar**

Bharatiya Janata Party (BJP) is its political wing, Vishwa Hindu Parishad (VHP), is the organisation translating Hindutva political agenda on the emotive, religious ground, Bajrang Dal is a group of youth, who are active on the streets. Vanavasi Kalyan Ashram is engaged in promoting 'Hindu norms' amongst Adivasis, and Rashtrasevika Samiti is its women's wing. In addition there are other organisations like Saraswati Shishu Mandirs, which inculcate the young minds with its social, cultural and political understanding. These all are collectively called as Sangh Parivar (SP).

The initial concern of Hindutva movement (RSS and Hindu Mahasabha) was to counter the politics of Muslim League and to influence the Congress in pro-Hindu direction. RSS was mainly focusing on Shakhas, training volunteers for Hindutva movement and Hindu Mahasabha was taking part in electoral politics. After independence the number of cadres of RSS increased, Hindu Mahasabha gradually went into oblivion. One of the ex-pracharak of RSS, Nathuram Godse, murdered Mahatma Gandhi in 1948, following which RSS was banned for some time. Meanwhile RSS volunteers kept on infiltrating in army, bureaucracy, media and educational institutions. The number of RSS volunteers went on increasing and multiple RSS controlled organisations started coming up.

RSS mainly undertook the campaigns of ban cow-slaughter in earlier period (1960s) but the response was lukewarm. It became very visible with its anti-communist noises during India-China war and projected 'Nationalist, Patriotic' fervor. Its political wing Jan Sangh undertook the campaign 'Indianise Muslims' (late 1960s). Meanwhile the ideology spread by RSS and the increasing urbanisation process were the key factor in the increasing intensity of communal violence.

RSS gained higher respectability JP movement (1974), its political wing joined Janata Party, and came to power, got vital ministries (External Affairs, Information and Broadcasting etc.) and used the opportunity to further enter the bureaucracy. It left the Janata Party on the issue of duel membership, there was a demand from other components of Janata Party that former members of Jan Sangh leave the RSS. And so either they should leave RSS or the Janata Party. It did not want to leave the RSS, Janata Party broke and Jan Sangh re-emerged as BJP on the plank of 'Gandhian Socialism'.

**Ascendence of Hindutva Politics**

The period of early 80s saw a great turmoil in the society. Initially the event of conversion of some Dalits to Islam was given a great projection as the threat of Islam engulfing India. In 1984 the Operation Blue Star (Indian army entering Golden Temple to evacuate the temple from the occupation of Khalistani militants was followed by the assassination of Indira Gandhi by her bodyguards. This was followed by massive anti-Sikh pogrom in which many a Congress workers lead the assaulting mobs. During this pogrom the RSS ideologue wrote a document subtly supporting Rajiv Gandhi's turning blind eye to the ongoing anti-Sikh pogroms (Nanaji Deshmukh, 1984). Later to appease the Muslim fundamentalists Rajiv Gandhi got a bill passed in the Lok Sabha to reverse the Shah Bano verdict granting maintenance to her by the Supreme Court. In the same superficial and opportunist style he went on to get the locks of Babri Masjid opened. Both the fundamentalist streams, Hindu and Muslim were on the ascendant. The opening of the locks emboldened the Hindu fundamentalists and now the sections of Muslim leadership started feeling insecure on the Babri Masjid issue. Opening of the locks of Babri Masjid gave a fillip to the SP (Sangh Parivar) and BJP decided to take up the Ram Janmbhumi issue.

In 1990 due to his own compulsions vis-à-vis the politics of Devi Lal, V.P. Singh cleaned the dust of Mandal Commission report and decided to implement it. This implementation of Mandal Commission recommendations intensified the backlash of upper castes, who rallied around SP in a big way and the Rath Yatra got a tremendous response from these sections of society. With the Kar Seva of Dec. 6, the SP's political wing became politically more powerful, getting more seats in the Lok Sabha and also coming to power in various state assemblies.

The presence of religion in social and political space was not significant in first few decades of India's independence. RSS is the political formation of religion in politics, "... which was conceived primarily as the egalitarian vanguard of the 'Hindu Rashtra' (Hindu Nation), its leaders' conception of ideal society continued to be based on the varna (caste) system" (Jaffrelot, 1998, 23). RSS remained a fairly insignificant formation till quite late. Through its 'quiet' work it did keep on training young boys into the Hindutva doctrine. Hindutva doctrine is the crystalised ideology of Hindu communal politics. Historically development of concept of Hindutva... comes in succession on the construction of Brahminism as Hinduism and this Brahminical Hinduism then forming the base for Hindutva politics. Savarkar began to articulate the ideology of Hindu elite (Zamindars and Brahmins, Kings) by integrating Brahminical Hinduism with nationalism, calling it Hindutva which further showed the way to building the Hindu Rashtra. His key sentence was 'Hinduise all politics and militarise all Hindudom'"(Ram, 1998). This ideology asserts that India is a Hindu Nation and here Christians and Muslims are aliens. There is no place of 'Western' concepts like secularism and democracy in Hindu nation as Hinduism itself is the most 'secular' and tolerant religion. This ideology aims to bring in Hindu Rashtra in India and so far it has been consolidated on the hatred of Muslims, Christians and 'Western concepts'.

It did go in to create a number of 'children' organisations, meant to bring in the Hindu Rashtra by working in different fields of society. Before independence this ideology was the rival to Muslim communal ideology. After 50s it kept communalising the social space, receiving due provocation's from either the remnant Muslim communalism here or from the assertive postures of Pakistan on Kashmir issue, from across the border. The communalisation of society resulted in the communal riots, which began in a big way from 1960's and these riots went on assuming more menacing proportions over a period of time. The most ghastly of which were to be seen in the decades of 80s, post-Babri demolition riots being amongst the worst as far as their impact on the psyche of minorities is concerned. Talking in the same breath one has to take note of the 'new' enemy of this ideology. From 1996 this ideology's followers have been paying 'special' attention to another minority about which they were 'just theorising' so far, the Christians.

**Social Base**

The 'real' strength of this ideology started picking up in the social and political arena after the development model pursued so far resulted in the rise of vast sections of middle classes. The lopsided development on one hand resulted in the rise of rich farmers and on the other of vast mass of landless peasantry totally bereft of any support system. In cities it got compounded due to the rising unemployment and under-employment because of the rise of small-scale industries, which act as suppliers and subcontractors to the main industries. These type of industries result in the proliferation of small but prosperous industrialists on one hand and that of the workers whose living conditions are abysmal and wages are very close to the poverty line on the other. It also results in the rise of affluent professional groups. These middle sections have the peculiar type of existential anxieties; they are the one who have been the strongest supporters of the communal ideology. This is the sector, which has shown strong presence in the social space since the 80s.

**Hindutva's Goal**

Hindu Rashtra is not a religious state; it is a 'modern' phenomenon to impose the pre-modern social hierarchies on all sections of society. It is the goal of a section of society, which is the major beneficiary of current social privileges, the section of society, which have gained in the process of development of last few decades. It was the goal of section of society which was threatened by the social changes in pre-independence times (zamindar-brahmins) and who were champions of status quo and were allies of British at economic and political level. The Hindu Rashtra, which is threatening to engulf the society from last two decades is the battle cry of the sections who again are upholder of a status quo vis-à-vis social position of women, workers, Dalits and Adivasis. It is the offence of the section of society, which has benefited maximum by proliferation of middle classes—small industries, petty business and agriculture of the 'Green Revolution' type and, section of the professional and bureaucratic cadres. Indian nationalism as an encompassing concept based itself on secular grounds and attempts to strive for formal liberty equality and fraternity supplemented by the liberal space to struggle to convert these formal concepts in to reality. Indian nationalism is a positive concept, incorporating different religion's, ethnicity's and culture's and is an integral part of world economy and emerging global village.

The chronicity, i.e., slow speed of this movement has its inherent problems. Whereas on one hand it can capture the social space, on the other it can also elicit a reaction to itself. This reaction to it from Dalits, workers, women, section of middle class that is secular, is a big obstacle to the march of Hindutva. Big capital, the major industrial houses have a unique relation with Sangh Parivar. Whenever faced with crisis to their own existences the socially terrorising atmosphere created by Sangh Parivar helps the bourgeoisie to wriggle out of the compulsions of liberal ethos. The conservative movement of Sangh Parivar helps the needs of capital to keep thriving in an uninterrupted way. Thus this, chronic, resilient, thriving fascism, expressed through the vehicle of Sangh Parivar continues to throw up different shades of its existence, sometimes terrorising (to the poor and the minorities) sometimes aggressive (to the neighbouring 'enemy' countries), and sometimes even appearing to collapse under the weight of its own contradictions. But the march, at the moment is on. The social roots of Hindutva are all for the support and continuation of the repressive capitalist regime; sustaining the bourgeoisie aspirations, while continuing to pursue its own project.

**Fundamentalist Streaks**

Hindutva onslaught draws some support from fundamentalist concepts also. It culls out from the past-selective values to impose them on present. It uses religious imagery, glorifies the 'golden past' of rule of Hindu kings, sees women primarily under patriarchal control dictating their way of life, dress code etc. It co-opts all and sundry religious professionals and personnel to strengthen its political base and it uses religion in a very effective way to create the nationalist hysteria. At present the situation is fairly in balance. The onslaught has achieved mammoth proportions in the north, but south and east are comparatively unaffected by its paranoid aggression. The reaction of Dalits, though fragmented is definitely going to retard the march of the *rath* (chariot) of Hindutva.

The apparent target of Sangh Parivar, the Muslims are in a bind. On one hand they have been battered so much by Hindutva that they cannot afford to lie quiet any more.

Secondly unlike the Dalits they lie in sub-critical zone of backwardness where they find it difficult to come out of the grip of their own 'religious leaders', 'the Muslim obscurantists' posing to be speaking on behalf of their community. Thus, they face a double attack from both Hindu fascism and Muslim fundamentalism. Probably the suffering of the 'poor Muslims' is so great that they will be forced to come out and resist the 'bear hug' of Sangh Parivar and by side-tracking their 'obscurantist leaders' will pose definite obstacle to the march of 'Trishuls of Hindutva'. How Sangh Parivar overcomes this 'problem' which new 'velvet gloves' it discovers to remove this obstacle remains to be seen. The response of Christian community though mixed, to a great extent has been that of responding in a strong secular manner, to defend the human rights of different sections in general and to defend the human rights of minorities in particular. This is an ongoing phenomenon set into motion due to the attacks on Christians by different wings of SP directed by the ideological formulation of the RSS.

**Core Agenda**

The core agenda of fascist movement is to suppress and suspend the rights of the oppressed. It is a social agenda of shaken, threatened middle class in the service of big bourgeoisie. It is a mass movement. Hindutva is the political agenda of petty industrialists, sections of middle classes and rich peasantry blessed by capital. Hindutva aims to create new ghettoised untouchables, the poor Muslims, a la the shudra of the olden times and keeping this goal in mind it wants to suppress/sidetrack the social and political aspirations of Dalits, workers, minorities and women.

Last two decades have seen the intensification of communal politics. This is being spearheaded by Sangh Parivar (RSS, BJP, VHP, Bajrang Dal etc.).This fascistic communalism has been provided regular provocation by

Muslim communalism. In current times core support base of this onslaught is the neo-prosperous middle class; petty industrialists, business groups, traders and rich peasantry. This section of society wants to impose pre-modern structural hierarchies (unchangeable social relations of inequality sanctioned by social norms-Feudal Lord-Serf; Bramin:Kshatriya:Vaishya-Shudra, Man-Woman cf: the fluid hierarchies of democratic society where these relations can be questioned and changed through struggles) laced in the language of Hindutva, cultural nationalism and the like. Their basic project is to continue their dominant social position vis-a-vis workers, Dalits, women, minorities and adivasis. The democratic polity, by providing a liberal space gives an opportunity to these groups to struggle for their rights. This is something, which these middle classes find inimical to their social status. As we have seen above, the beginning of the Hindutva movement was an expression of the then declining classes of feudal lords, Rajas of Riyasats (princely states), Brahmins (Hindu clergy), Baniyas (Traditional business groups), the groups which again wanted to sustain the declining pre-modern norms of structural hierarchies. The politics of Hindutva provides the most refined way to impose the rigid hierarchies, and the semi-secularised society becomes the fertile ground on which this poisonous weed can proliferate with gay abundance.

**Post-Mandal Assertion**

The strengthening of this onslaught especially in the aftermath of Mandal Commission implementation, the polarisation of middle classes around SP is the expression of the existentialist anxieties of the middle classes. They have been the base of fascist movements in Europe and other secularised societies, and base of fundamentalist onslaughts in the semi- and pre-secularised societies. The SP has in a way caught the society in a pincer. Even before access to total state power it has 'succeeded' in gripping the society by an alround attack through various aspects of social and political life: culture, education, media, bureaucracy, police and other arms of state power. Coming closer to and occasional occupation of seats of power at states and centre has given it an added advantage; in the form of unrestricted abuse of democratic institutions of society and state.

It has changed the language of social discourse, and rights of oppressed and exploited, the real problems of society have been put on the backburner. The naked imposition of elite/upper caste culture is the mask under which the subjugation and exploitation of oppressed and exploited is being intensified and legitimised. In this direction the 'review' of constitution is one more mechanism, which will be activated at appropriate time. SP is a peculiar type of onslaught: it combines features of slow growing fascism with fundamentalist characteristics. Its base is the middle class. Like fascism it targets a particular community/ies, preferably one at a time to consolidate its aggression, projects the glorious past, aims at expanding empire (Akhand Bharat), assigns to women the primary role of mothers/wives, exhorts workers to work for 'nation' (industrialists) and not to bother about their rights and dalits are straightjacketed through social engineering like Samajik Samanvay (social harmony). Like fundamentalism it evokes religious imageries and the glorious rule of Hindu Kings, asserts the concept of Hindu Rashtra, is built around Ram, Geeta-Ramayan-Mahabharat, and Acharyas and Mahants. Both these phenomenon are basically against democracy and the accompanying liberal space.

## References

Basu T., Datta P., Sarkar S., Sarkar T. and Sen S., *Khakhi Shorts, Saffron Flags*, Orient Longman, Hyderabad, 1993.

Christophe Jeffrelot, *The Hindu Nationalist Movement and Indian Politics*, Penguin, Delhi, 1996.

M.S. Golwalkar, *We or Our Nationhood Defined*, Bharat Prakashan, Nagpur, 1939.

M.S. Golwalkar, *Bunch of Thoughts*, Jagaran Prakashan, Bangalore, 1966.

Marzia Casolari, *Hindutva's Foreign Tie Ups in 1930s: The Archival Evidence, Communalism Combat*, March 2000, p. 37.

Nanaji Deshmukh, *Moments of Soul Searching*, Pritipaksh, Delhi, Nov. 25, 1984.

Ram Puniyani, *Fascism of Sangh* Parivar, Media House, Delhi, 2000.

# 5

# RSS and Agenda of Imperialism

Decades ago M.S. Golwalkar, the then RSS Sarsanghchalak, supremo, had supported the America's aggression on Vietnam. That was the time when most of the world was condemning the U.S. offensive, its use of inhuman weapons on the unarmed citizens of Vietnam. The pretext for U.S. was that the emerging Vietnamese nationalism is a threat to freedom and democracy, as the flag, which Ho Chi Minh held high was a communist one. While most of the world had problems with the U.S. agenda, RSS chief complimented U.S. as the one, leading the forces of Dharma (moral-ethical values)! (V.D. Chopra, *Religious Fundamentalism in Asia*, p. 79). It is another matter that RSS certified forces of Dharma had to bite the dust and retreat in a most disgraceful manner. Neither was U.S. trying to protect freedom and democracy nor did RSS supremo mean to defend morals and ethics.

### America's Aggression and RSS Response

There have been multiple responses to the present attack of U.S. (March 2003). The ruling NDA coalition led by BJP opposed the U.S. aggression, under the compulsions of alliance. Meanwhile Mr. Pravin Togadia of VHP another progeny of RSS tried to test the waters by condemning Iraq as the Muslim country and so deserving the punishment.

There was not much support for Togadia line and probably he was asked to keep quiet on this count. The reigning RSS chief went on to embarrass the BJP Government by defending the U.S. aggression on Iraq, apparently to liberate the Iraqi people and to install the democracy, which is supposedly the divine mission of Uncle Sam. Mr. Sudarshan is upholding George Bush on two grounds (*TOI*, March 29, 2003). The first one being that it is a clash of civilisations and the backward, retrograde, Jehadi Islamic culture is a threat to the world as a whole and to the advanced, 'humane' Western civilisation in particular. Iraq as Muslim country is the home of world terrorism and so is a threat to the world peace. The second one being that Mr. Bush is only defending his own country, as Iraq is a threat to U.S. security. Iraq as per this argument is having weapons of mass destruction and being Muslim, it will support all the terrorists who any way are Muslims so the U.S. action is justified. As if to remind its earlier support of the civilising mission theory of colonialists, Mr. Sudarshan defends the U.S. imperialism by stating that U.S. first encourages the rogue states and then enslaves them to civilize them. Nobody could have defended the U.S. tyranny better!

At one level the hollowness of these arguments of Mr. Sudarshan is too obvious. By now most of the world with some humanism left, knows that neither is U.S.'s aim to eliminate WMD (very little discovered by the U.N. Inspectors anyway) neither is this tyrant, U.S. imperialism, interested in Democracy being there in other parts of the world. U.S. regime has not only supported and encouraged the despots and dictators all around, it has also installed such butchers by overthrowing legitimate democratic regimes, time and over again. Mr. Sudarshan as the major apologist for George Bush also argues that U.N. has failed to appreciate the U.S.'s concerns so Mr. Bush is within full 'moral' authority to attack Iraq.

**Colonialism and RSS**

RSS, the proponent of Hindutva, Hindu Rashtra has a very complimentary ideology to the one of colonial powers and imperialists. It has a lot to do with the ideology of status quo and suppression of the rights of workers, Dalits and women at deeper level. It is exemplified right since the beginning of the rise of Hindu Right wing ideology in late nineteenth century. With the arrival of British this section of Hindu elite accepted the British propaganda that they have come here to liberate the Hindus from the tyranny of Muslim rule and also to civilize the country (White Man's burden). This precisely was the culmination of the events in the famous novel *Anand Math* where the heroes of Bankimchandra's novel, 'Santans' (offspring's), overthrow the Muslim rule and celebrate the coming in of British rule. These anglophiles also went on to argue that our ancestors, Aryans while coming from arctic zone split into two streams, one going to Europe and other coming to India. So the coming of British to India is like meeting of the parted cousins, so we celebrate the arrival of our own parted brethren. Now of course this Aryan arrival thesis itself has been put under question by ideologues of Hindu right because if this is to be accepted than Aryans and thereby the Hindus are also "invaders" like the Muslims so how can the idea of Hindu Rashtra be asserted?

Anyway, the Hindu Right wing stream later on went on to form various organisations, Punjab Hindu Sabha, Hindu Mahasabha and RSS. The agenda of these organisations has apparently been to build the strength of Hindu society in the face of Muslim aggression. In reality the agenda of Hindu Right wing, Hindutva, has been to oppose the transformations, leading to caste and gender equality.

**RSS and Anti-Colonial Struggle**

So in a way it should not be surprising that the Hindutva votaries never opposed the British rule. United India Patriotic Association (UIPA), which incidentally had Muslim elites also as the members, which was the most initial organisation of Hindu and Muslim Right wing (1880's) went on to proclaim that Congress is talking against the ruler (Queen Victoria) and this way of opposing the ruler is against our religion, which teaches us to be loyal to our King (Queen in this). Accordingly, UIPA resolved to cultivate the loyalty of Indian people to British Crown. Later UIPA paved the way for the communal organisations, Muslim League and Hindu Mahasabha. Savarkar was an anti-British revolutionary before he became the major ideologue of Hindutva. After he assumed the leadership of Hindutva outfit, Hindu Mahasabha, he never opposed the British rule. And that is the mild way of putting the reality.

RSS came up with the goal of Hindu Rashtra and since the freedom movement was striving for secular democratic India and was opposing the British rule, so RSS kept aloof from the freedom movement. Efforts are on to dig out an occasional jail term by a RSS swayamsevak to prove that RSS was also for freedom struggle, but such incidents if any, are there, by default or for some other motive. Dr. Hedgewar the first RSS supremo joined the Non-Cooperation Movement in 1930 and went to jail but he clarified that it was to get in touch with Hindutva minded workers who at that time might have been a part of freedom movement. Mr. Vajpayee, wrote *Hindu Tan Man Hindu Jivan* (Hindu body and soul, Hindu life) when the majority of nation was singing, living and dying for Indian body, soul and life. Incidentally Mr. Vajpayee was also put in jail for a couple of days, a case of mistaken identity. This was rectified soon as he gave a written statement that he had nothing to do with the Quit India and associated movements and that he was a mere onlooker in the village when the local people were going to break Forest Law as a part of Quit India movement.

## Social Base of 'Religion Based Political Ideologies'

Both Muslim communal politics and Hindu communal politics came up in opposition to the rising Indian nationalism of industrialists, educated sections and workers. The revenue system shows the deeper social alliance of British on one side and Hindu and Muslim nationalists on the other. Indian Nationalism as a vehicle of democratic aspirations of industrialists, educated middle classes, workers and women had to develop against the British repression. While the communalists were in deeper social alliance with British powers and the association got reflected at political level in the form of these.

Rather than aberrations it should be seen as to why and how could Hindutva or Pakistan votaries be a part of freedom movement as both these were having a deeper social alliance with the British rule. British were having revenue alliance with the landlords. And in a way the base of Pakistan Movement was in the landed aristocracy and so was the case with Hindu Mahasabha and RSS. Anyway they did not oppose the British rule or one can go to the extent of saying that British ruled India in alliance with the ideological followers of Muslim League and Hindutva. The political alliance of colonialism was with the votaries of Hindu Rashtra. A votary of Hindutva murdered Gandhi, as the Father of Nation was the biggest obstacle to the agenda of Hindu Rashtra. After his murder RSS was banned and Mr. Golwalkar was jailed. From jail also Mr. Golwalkar requested to be released and promised that RSS will collaborate with the Government to eliminate the Communist 'menace'. Incidentally that was the era when American Imperialism was unleashing McCarthyism and hunting communists. U.S. agenda and RSS agenda matched exactly.

## RSS Progeny (Jan Sangh, BJP) and Political Orientation

RSS and its progeny Jan Sangh adopted the U.S. agenda in economic and political matters to the last comma. With collapse of Soviet states the U.S. imperialism has projected Islam as the main enemy of human kind (clash of civilisation etc.). RSS and its progeny have also chosen this time to sharpen its Trishuls against Islam and Muslims precisely at this juncture in global politics. Imperialism always props up the retrograde politics and social relations in countries where it controls. Its projection of itself as spreading civilisation or defending democracy is a cover for plunder and exploitation at all levels. Colonialism aligned itself with landed gentry who were adherents of pre-modern hierarchies of caste and gender. Imperialism similarly aligns with the most retrograde social forces. RSS fits into the bill of U.S. designs more than perfectly. BJP's coming to power at the centre has opened the floodgates of U.S. grip on India. BJP foreign policy has been to be subservient to the U.S. designs in toto. No doubt the RSS sponsored swadeshi is a bit like fly in the ointment in its subservience to the imperialism. But no social phenomenon can be without some contradictions in their gambit. Overall colonialism was OK for RSS, and imperialism is also OK for RSS. That's the major support for forces standing for arresting the transformation in social relations of caste and gender the central goal and agenda of religion based politics, and this is what Hindutva and Hindu Rashtra is all about. So at one level we should not be surprised that RSS is all for supporting U.S. aggression of Iraq, that is its agenda, to be complimentary force to imperialism.

**Imperialism-Clash of Civilisation as the Fig Leaf**

White Man's burden thesis came up with the colonisation, Defending freedom came up while suppressing the rising nationalisms and now the clash of civilisation is being put forward when U.S. is trying to control the taps of oil resources. There are many an Islamic countries in and around these resources, who had to be rubbed the wrong way, in order to maintain and extend the flow of oil towards fuel tanks of the powerful countries of the West. Keeping in mind this projection, which exploiters have generally kept for their own interests some ideological cover has to be maintained. If colonial masters are usurping the resources of colonies, it is White man's burden to civilize the people of the colonies, if imperialism is crushing the nationalist sentiments to be able to continue its hegemony on the world; it is fight for freedom of the world. Here both these have been used as a cover for the proactive deeds of imperialism. Now the 'Clash' theory is there to explain the 'reaction to the injustices' done to the section of Arab world. One knows that most of the Muslim nations are with the U.S. in its efforts to control the Afghan territory through the new puppet, which will be pro-U.S. One also knows that the Muslim dominated countries like Indonesia, Malaysia and many significant one's are with the U.S. for its 'sacrifices to save the freedom' in the world.

**Imperialism and Democracy**

Imperialist powers always invariably ally with despots and dictators. Not only that they actively crush the democracies wherever they want to control the raw materials and enslave a particular country. Second World War also saw the formation of Israel in the heart of the Islamic Nations, surrounding the oil resources. Here the democratisation process was quelled or counter-revolutions managed to push back the secularisation and democratisation process. America in particular not only tried to suppress emerging Vietnamese Nationalism, it actively uprooted the democratic regimes in Iran (1953), Chile (1972). In effect it supports the pre-modern social relations, pre-democratic norms wherever it has the designs on the raw materials of the particular country or wherever it aims to control the market.

**Why U.S. and RSS Goals Match Today**

Currently in its lust for oil the U.S. has been encouraging the clash of civilisation thesis and also been demonising Islam. RSS at home is the patriarch of the organisations aiming to bring in Hindu Rashtra as a state where pre-modern hierarchical relations of caste and gender can be imposed in the newer garb. In an attempt to bring in this politics it has demonised Islam, this is where RSS finds solace for its efforts. In a way RSS ideology is supplementary to the colonialists and imperialist designs as at social level the groups it represents were in alliance with colonial powers in yesteryears. Today subservience to imperialist goals at one level is reassuring to RSS as the U.S. hegemony will retard the process of democratisation and social transformation to a great extent. And this is what the social base of RSS is looking for. So it is no coincidence that most of the times the U.S. policies and RSS policies run parallel to each other and are supplementary to each other barring a few minor irritants like swadeshi, etc.

As per the U.S. claims and Sudarshan's defense of the democratising mission of the U.S., it is clear that democracy cannot be brought from the top, that is anathema. Democracy begins from roots. It cannot be exported, even by the well-intentioned powers, forget the lustful U.S.-U.K. axis. In a way Iraq had good chances of bringing in democracy prior to the earlier U.S. onslaught on Iraq. Even the worst of tyrants cannot last long enough. They get a shot in the arms when they are attacked from outside as at these times they can decrease the democratic space by pointing out the external threat. Even the theocratic state of Iran is showing good bit of progress in this front. Democracy is not a black and white affair. There are degrees of it depending on the situation.

In pursuance of its communal agenda RSS is demonising Islam and Muslims at home. In pursuance of its lust for oil U.S. is targeting one or the other Islamic country. It has propagated and projected Islam as the threat to civilisation. Imperialists always need a cover for their lust for material wealth and power. Centuries ago spreading civilisation was the ideology under which colonial powers enslaved the colonies and plundered them mercilessly. In yesteryears this fig leaf was provided by the ideology of "defense of freedom and democracy". It was under that banner that U.S. attacked Vietnam and Chile. It is under that ideology that it trained the Jehadis to fight in Afghanistan. And after the demise of Soviet Union the appeal of defense of freedom and democracy is fading. So the new fig leaf, protecting the Western civilisation from the evil effects of Islamic civilisation. And it is here that ideologies of Mr. George Bush and Sudarshan are thick as thieves.

# Section–III

# Hindutva and Minorities

As such in a democray no body should need a minority identity. But as the democracies have evoloved from complex backgrounds there has been prevalence a certain sections of citizenry, which belongs to this category on the grounds of religion and culture. In order that they feel free and non-intimidated various provisions have been set by the United Nations conventions to take care of their special needs and feelings. A society can be judged by how free the minorities of that country feel. The religion-based nationalism has the primary agenda of suppressing the inner groups, caste and gender, and they project the external group, minority, as the real culprit for the ills of the country. In a way the minorities are collateral victims of the onslaught of the religion based nationalism. This type of nationalism relegates the rights of minorities to secondary position and through browbeating them tries to seek their submission and ghettotisation through violence.

The majoritirian politics achieves this by spreading myths and stereotypes against them. These form the base on which communal violence rides, this in turn creates the feeling of insecurity and other consequences follow the major of which is emotional alienation.

In India Hindutva politics has identified Muslims, Christians and Communists as the internal threats to the Hindu nation. It is no coincidence that Muslims were the first targets, Christians are coming under the chopping block from last one decade and communists have been painted black all through. One does not know what lies in store for them in the future.

All minorities do not have a similar social and national situation. The Muslims are a discriminated against lot, and Christians are currently being hauled to the coals for the 'sin' of conversions. It is the sign of times that during the ascendance of Hindutva Party BJP some governments came up with anti-conversion laws. Tamil Nadu's Jayalalita is an interesting example; she came up with anti-conversion legislating during BJP regime and scrapped the same once BJP lost power at the centre. Currently some other states, where BJP is ruling, anti-conversion legislations are being contemplated. Gujarat, which is called the Laboratory of Hindu Rashtra and currently is the example of 'Hindu Rashtra in One-State' came up with the census monitoring of minorities for the purposes, which are anti-democratic. It also came up with norms for monitoring inter-religious marriages.

This section deals with the plight of minorities during last couple of decades.

# 6

# Minorities and Human Rights

This study deals with the status and rights of minorities in India. Beginning with the backdrop in which this problem is being addressed to, it goes on to define the minorities from different angles, than takes up the U.N. declaration of Rights of Minorities, and the provisions for minorities in Indian Constitution. It also deals with the status of minorities in India: their formation, socio-economic status and the obstacles they are facing in today's situation.

## The Political and Social Backdrop of the Minority Problem

India inherited the problem of minorities right since Independence. The whole partition process was seeped in the majority-minority discourse. The process of partition was outcome of the interaction of the three major forces: Muslim communal politics, Hindu communal politics and British policy of divide-and-rule, while the process of Pakistan formation had the patronage of the Zagirdari and salaried class of Muslims. The discrimination against the Muslims in jobs was prevalent right from the beginning and the anti-Muslim riots became a regular phenomenon. The culmination of these resulted in the demolition of Babri Masjid and after sometime the focus of majoritarian communal forces shifted to persecution of another minority, the Christians. The anti-Christian violence is currently being witnessed in a sustained fashion.

**Modern Democracies: Melting Pot or Mosaic Model**

The very concept of democracy is based on liberty, equality and fraternity. The state grants equal status and citizenship rights to all its citizens irrespective of their caste, creed, colour, gender or religion. The initial idea in the democracy was that since people interact on different facets of life the societal interaction will act as a melting pot bringing in uniformity in the language, dress code, social values and different other aspects of life. But the experience of most of the democracies has shown that this is only partly true and the mosaic of different shades persists for long time. This pluralism is healthy as it encourages the values of tolerance. Accordingly most of the good constitutions have endeavoured to incorporate this in their statuettes.

Despite these provisions, the reality of the situation has not been very satisfactory. "An ideal pluralist society demands that all citizens irrespective of their caste, creed, class, ethnicity and sex shall enjoy not only equal rights, but also security of life, property and avenues to promote their religion, language and culture while enjoying the fruits of economic development in an equitable manner. The Constitution of India does guarantee all this but there are serious and complex problems as far as their implementation is concerned." One of the main reasons for eruption of resistance to the pluralism is from the vested interests who fear that the democratic processes will change the status quo, which will go against their interests. This brings into the open the conflict of interests of different social groups disguised as communal, ethnic or language conflict. And if one of the communities is too dominant it is likely that it can trample on the rights of others.

## How to Define Minorities

Generally minorities are defined by numerical weakness or socio-economic vulnerability. But this term requires lot of qualifications. Also modern state has to deal with individual rights and group rights and with internal democratisation in social communities. Another catch is that the reform process in the communities is to be expedited without hurting the sentiments of the people of the community. This is one of the goals of the state, which has to be executed in a very balanced way.

The problem of minority-majority crops up due to the vested interests in the course of which the elite of numerically dominant community assert and try to usurp the social privileges for themselves. "Generally it is used to denote those non-Hindu minorities whose members are for one reason or another inclined to assert their distinctiveness in relating to Hindu community. Members of the Scheduled Castes and Tribes whose members are in many ways more severely disadvantaged, are hardly ever characterised as minorities. On the whole therefore the word 'minorities' seems to have been narrowly defined and denotes religious communities whose members project themselves as being different from majority community." Apart from the popular notion of minorities the minorities can also be on the basis of language, ethnicity and race.

## Formation of Minorities

Minorities have been formed in the history due to multiple reasons. As the world is interacting more and more through transmigrations it results in different communities locating themselves in far and distant countries. Large number of Indian communities have emerged as minorities in America, South Africa, Britain, Canada and many other countries as these communities emigrated in search of work and business. Migration of labour force in plantation and other types of work has been one of the most important factors in the initial part of 20th century. Spread of religion has been another major cause, because of which Muslims, Christians and Buddhists are minorities in different places.

It is worth recalling that all minorities are not disadvantaged. Jews in Germany, Parsis, Jains and Christians are a good example of this. Amongst these Jews were targeted in Germany and Christians are being targeted in India in pursuance of the political agenda of the fascist-fundamentalist forces. In India Nepali's have a very different status, while Sikhs are also not regarded as minorities per se!

In this presentation for the sake of brevity we will be focusing only on Muslims and Christians as the minorities.

### State and Minorities

The democratic constitution of ours' gives equal rights to all the citizens irrespective of their caste, creed or religion. Since minorities are disadvantaged in these societies they are provided with affirmative actions to strive towards substantive equality. State is committed to protect their social and political rights. Despite the provision for protection of minorities, the state apparatus is heavily infiltrated by the communal elements who ensure the protection of the violators of the human rights of minorities.

### Indian Constitution and Minorities

Indian constitution's being secular gives right to freedom of conscience and religion and it is also duty bound to preserve the composite culture of the country. Article 15 ensures that there is no discrimination on the grounds of religion. Article 29(1) gives the right to preserve language, script and culture. Article 30(1) gives the right to establish and run educational and other institutions, while Article 30(2) ensures that there should be no discrimination against minority institutions. Also Article 25 gives the freedom of conscience, free profession, propagation and practice of one's religion.

**Rights of Minorities Under the Constitution of India**

Article 29(1): "Any section of the citizens residing in the territory of India or any part thereof having a distinct language, script or culture of its own, shall have the right to conserve the same."

Article 29(1): "No citizen shall be denied admission into any educational institution maintained by the State or receiving aid out of the State funds on grounds only of religion, race, caste, language or any of them."

Article 30(1): "All minorities whether based on religion or language, shall have the right to establish and administer educational institutions of their choice."

Article 30(1A): "In making any law providing for the compulsory acquisition of any property of an educational institution established and administered by a minority, referred to in Clause (1), the State shall ensure that the amount fixed by or determined under such law for the acquisition of such property is such, as would not restrict or abrogate the right guaranteed under the clause."

Article 30(2): "The State shall not, in granting aid to educational institutions, discriminate against any education institution on the ground that it is under the management of minority, whether based on religion or language."

**U.N. Declaration of Human Rights of Minorities**

This declaration is based on democratic, humanist model. Thereby it prescribes multi-ethnic states with equal rights to all. It prescribes all the member states to protect the existence and identity of minorities. The member states are obliged to create conditions for promotion of their identity. India is a signatory to this declaration.

## The U.N. Declaration of Minority Rights

### *Article 1*

1. States shall protect the existence and the national or ethnic, cultural, religious and linguistic identity of minorities within their respective territories, and shall encourage conditions for the promotion of that identity.

2. States shall adopt appropriate legislative and other measures to achieve that end.

### *Article 2*

1. Persons belonging to national or ethnic, religious and linguistic minorities (hereinafter referred persons as belonging to minorities) have the right to enjoy their own cultures, to profess and practice their own religion, and to use their own language, in private and in public freely and without interference or any form of discrimination.

2. Persons belonging to minorities have right to participate effectively in culture, religious, social, economic and public life.

3. Persons belonging to minorities have right to participate effectively in decision on the national and, where appropriate, regional level concerning the minority to which they belong or the regions in which they live, in a manner not incompatible with national legislation.

4. Persons belonging to minorities have right to establish and maintain their own associations.

5. Persons belonging to minorities have right to establish and maintain, without any discrimination, free and peaceful contacts with other members of their group and with persons belonging to other minorities, as well as contacts across frontiers with other citizens of other States to whom they are related by national or ethnic, religious or linguistic ties.

**Problems of Muslims in India**

Muslim community has been the victim of different biases and prejudices because of which they have been kept out of the government and private sector jobs. Their representation in these has been very low. Also the 'social common sense' has been against them and regular and repeated violence against them has taken a heavy toll of their psyche. After partition the elite of Muslim community left India for Pakistan, and mainly poor Muslims and only few professionals and traders were left behind further worsening the status of Muslims. Muslim fundamentalist leadership came to the fore, unconcerned about the 'real' material problems of community, and today the community remains poor, backward and in the grip of orthodox elements.

It is propagated for political goals that successive governments have pampered and appeased the community. The facts are in total contrast to this. Their status in employment and other parameters are a good index of their social status and appeasement.

In government. sector in higher cadres their representation is very small (Class I: 3.19 per cent, Class II 4.30 per cent. In Class IV is just 8.16 per cent, while in private sector this figure is much lower).

In High Courts out of 310 judges as on 1.4.1980, only 14 were Muslims. In All India Services (IAS): In decision-making posts Muslim representation was (1984 figures) 2.14 per cent, in Indian police service 3 per cent, Central Secretariat Service 1.43 per cent, and only 0.72 of them were Section Officers.

In Industry: Among the country's top industrial houses, not one is owned or controlled by a Muslim barring the one owned by Azim Premji. As to participation in fresh growth of industries, the situation of industrial licenses issued for units between Rs. 3 crore and Rs. 20 crore during the year 1979 is as follows: Total No. 260, Muslims: 5 (1.9 per cent), 1980 Total 386, Muslims 6 (1.5 per cent).

Muslims are predominately in the handicraft sector as skilled artisans. A countrywide survey, which covered 31 districts, from 12 States indicates that out of 12.68 lakhs artisans employed in the Sector, 51.89 per cent were Muslims. But Muslim ownership accounted for only 4.4 per cent. In terms of financial assistance, Muslim borrowers were 4.3 per cent, and the volume of loans paid out to them was 2.02 per cent. The total financial sector disbursed only 3.76 per cent differential interest rate credit to Muslims. The average per capita income of Muslims is 5 per cent less than average of Rs. 4,247.

In the field of education their backwardness is appalling. According to the survey of the Planning Commission, 87-88, the average literacy rate among Muslims was 42 per cent, which is less than the national average of 52.11 per cent. In the case of women, only 11 per cent Muslim women were literate compared to the national average of 39.42 per cent.

This has occurred due to the biases against them. The popular myth that Muslims Kings destroyed Hindu Temples (truth is that both Hindu and Muslim kings destroyed temples and mosques sometimes in pursuit of gold and sometimes for political motives), Islam spread on the point of sword (Islam spread mainly under the influence of Sufi saints, who were away from the seats of power, and primarily Sudra's embraced Islam to escape the tyranny of Brahminism), Muslims are polygamous (as per the census figures the percentage of polygamy amongst Muslims and Hindus is more or less same), they produce more number of children and that shortly Muslim population will overtake the Hindu population has been the major propagation of the communal politics (the Muslim population has shown a minor increase during last nearly fifty years;1947-11.4, 2001-12.6). These myths have been the foundation on which the anti-Muslim violence stands.

**Christians**

Though different type of biases were spread against Christians even earlier, from last four years the anti-Christian campaign has been accelerated to the high pitch, because of which anti-Christian violence has picked up to a great extent. The attacks on Christians have begun especially from last 1997onwards. These attacks are being orchestrated by different organisations linked to Sangh Parivar (SP) and a general hysteria is being created against the Christian Missionaries in particular. During this year (1998-99) many a priests were humiliated (Fr. Christudas being paraded naked in Dumka), one of them Pastor Graham Stewart Stains, being burnt alive along with his two sons aged 9 and 7, many a churches have been damaged in these attacks, Bibles have been burnt and nuns have been raped in interior places.

This has occurred in the backdrop of anti-Christian propaganda as per which Christianity is a foreign religion, their missionary activities are a mere ploy for inducing people for conversions to adopt Christianity, their schools and hospitals are mere tools for the same. The CIA is planning this process and the Pope and Christian agencies, which are out to evangelize the whole country, where by Hindus will become a minority. Most of the inquiries by social activists, National Human Rights Commission, National Minorities Commission have shown that different organisations affiliated to SP are behind these attacks, and the attacks are taking place most in the BJP ruled states Gujarat, in particular.

Christian missionaries have been setting up churches, seminaries and schools wherever and whenever possible. They learnt Indian languages, set up printing presses and published religious as well as secular literature, to spread literacy and their faith. In the process they adopted Indian languages for their communication and the church adopted number of native practices. Despite 2000 years of Christian presence, and 200 years of British rule the population of Christians in 1971 was 2.6 per cent, which in 1991 stood at 2.32 per cent, 2001-2.30 per cent. Even in Manoharpur district, where the Bajrang Dal activist Dara Singh burnt Pastor Stains on the ground that he was converting Adivasis to Christianity, Justice Wadhava Commission did not find any evidence of conversions nor of the rise of Christian population.

Despite this the threat of 'their' population overtaking the Hindu population has begun only from one year or so. This anti-Christian bogey began at a time when the anti-Muslim pogroms have more or less achieved 'the target' of permanently intimidating and ghettoising them. Also SP realizes that if it has to break the electoral jinx to be able to come to power on its own it needs a newer vote bank and for this Adivasis have been seen as the one's having best potential. There is also a growing realisation in SP that after conversion to Christianity the Adivasis become more educated and aware of their rights, and this is a big threat to 'status quo', which is the base line of SP politics. These two factors seem to be the major one's in the current SP strategy of intimidating the missionaries. The calculation is that after this type of 'treatment' missionaries will be reluctant to go to the remote places and that will make the SP's job of wooing Adivasis to its fold comparatively easy.

### Minorities in India Today

The onslaught of communal politics is intimidating the minorities while the state is extremely insensitive towards the protection of minorities. As we have seen above the ghettoisation of Muslim community is very strong. Also the present intimidation of Christian community has reached intolerable limits. The provisions for their protection are on paper but the ground reality is something else. The rise in social power of SP has been the bane for the human rights of weaker sections of society in general and those of minorities in particular. State as it itself is infiltrated by communal elements has been unable to protect the minorities and has been fairly insensitive to their plight. It is only through the struggles for their rights and alignment with the struggles of other weaker sections of society that they can try to preserve their democratic and human rights.

## References

Asghar Ali Engineer, "Some thoughts on Pluralist Model of Nation Building", Minorities in India, Conference Papers, Rajiv Gandhi Institute for Contemporary Studies (RGISS), 1996, p. 27.

Imtiaz Ahamd, 'Indian Minorities', Minorities in India, RGISS, 1996, p. 27.

Iqbal A. Ansari, Readings on Minorities: Perspectives and Documents, Institute of Objective Studies, New Delhi, 1996.

Vinayak Damoar Savarkar, 'Hindutva, Who is a Hindu?', Nagpur, 1923.

M.S. Golwalkar, 'We or Our Nationhood Defined', Bharat Publications, Nagpur, 1939.

Chritophe Jaffrelot, The Hindu Nationalist Movement and Indian Politics, Viking 1996.

# 7

# Ayesha and the Head Scarf

## Alienation of Muslim Minorities

While walking down the pavement a few days after the 25th August (2003) blasts in Mumbai, I got a bit of a shock when I saw Ayesha covering her head with a scarf, *dupatta*. I have known her from her childhood and her father happened to be well acquainted to me. She is the only child of her beard-sporting father. She grew up as a bright young child in the English medium school. One could never see any typical Muslim identity from her dress. This was probably the first time I saw her after the Gujarat carnage and I presume this way of putting the *dupatta* has been a post-Gujarat carnage phenomenon for her.

While seeing her like that I was reminded of some more incidents. It was during the Mumbai riots of 92-93 that my doctoral student Salim, who earlier was indistinguishable from any other student, started sporting a typical Muslim beard and walked into my office one of the days telling me that if we have to die like this why should we not kill few before dying. It was a very traumatic experience for me to be unable to convince my student that violence is no answer to the ongoing anti-Muslim pogrom. It was during this period only that one of my friends born in a Christian family, who essentially was an atheist, told me to my utter surprise that in the aftermath of the Mumbai riots he has started going to the Church regularly, searching for his community association, which may be the only savior in current times. I was also reminded of one more incident at personal level. One of the activists of Muslim women's rights group confessed that their movement got serious setback in the wake of Mumbai riots. This movement of Muslim women essentially had been demanding abolition of triple *talaq*, end of polygamy and opposition to *burqa*. This had started picking up slowly in mid-eighties, had a setback post-Mumbai riots, came up a bit later and again was pushed back seriously in the wake of Gujarat riots!

Of course, Mumbai riots were a severe jolt to me as well. But initially it was difficult for me to comprehend as to why Salim has to grow beard, why he has to go to the level of insanity in talking the language of an eye for an eye, knowing fully well that in this case it is the whole body and not just the eye which is at stake, knowing fully well that this is not going to compensate for the lives of coreligionists who have lost their lives. It gradually dawned upon me that a life lost in violence sets in chain of socio-cultural thought process and makes the holes in the feeling of security of the community and that of the person.

In the times when Osama bin Laden and Kashmir centred terrorism is stalking the globe and the country, one can only feel the heat through the expressions of communities and people in their lifestyles. Narendra Modi demonstrated the limit of this when without naming the local Muslim community he could give a clear message that Muslims are terrorists and so need to be given a punishment. How could Mr. Modi give this message? How could the average common sense accept that the neighbouring Muslim deserves the same treatment, which should be meted out to the criminal terrorists? In a way the process of demonisation of Muslims community, which has been, going on at social level found its culmination in the Gujarat carnage. Now when one talks of terrorists it is not even necessary to use to prefix Muslim, as terrorists has become a synonym of Muslims.

One wonders as to what must have been the plight of an average Sikh during the Khalistani movement. One wonders what must be the image of an average Tamil in Sri Lanka where LTTE has been indulging in the acts of terror at mega scale. What impact Dhanu's acting as a live bomb to kill Rajiv Gandhi, must have had on the image of Sri Lankan Tamils in India. It is fortunate that these acts of terror have not crossed the critical level where the whole community continues to be branded in that stereotype.

Coming back to Muslims, Islam and Ayesha, one is struck by the critical levels having been crossed many times over. Multiple factors have contributed to stereotypes about Muslims. To begin with the continuation of pre-Independence communal politics of Muslims surfaced in the decades of 80s to play the retrograde role in the Shah Bano case in particular. The more assertive Hindu communalism kept going up and up all through again getting its critical mass in the decade of 80s when it used the Meenakshipuram conversions of Dalits to Islam, the Shah Bano case, and the rising Dalit presence in the social space, to launch the Ram Temple campaign. This campaign took the anti-Muslim propaganda, spread through RSS Shakhas in a consistent manner from decades, to the higher levels. And from this time on every incident served to increase the heat of communalism. The riots, which accompanied this politics, saw that the number of victims from Muslim community is proportionately much large in numbers. Also it was successfully propagated that Muslims start the riots and then Hindus just retaliate. This has no grain of truth in it whatsoever, but in a polarising society this formulation found an easy acceptance. This was further compounded by the problem of adverse Indo-Pak relations on the issue of Kashmir and alienation of Kashmiri youth.

The phenomenon of "Islamic terrorism" emerges from three major components. The first one is the formation of Israel. The plight of Palestinian refugees needs no recounting. This is closely associated with the U.S. lust for control over oil resources. Its intervention in Afghanistan through Jihadi Muslims to evacuate the Communist occupation set the jehadi trend into motion. Its alliance with the despotic rulers and curbing of democracy in this region has been with the overall view that it is easier to manipulate the Sheikhs and dictators than the democracies. The unresolved Indo-Pak relations getting manifested in the Kashmir imbroglio is another major factor contributing to the triad of reasons contributing to 'Islamic terrorism'. One has to slightly introspect as to what is primary. Terrorism or U.S. imperialist policies of control over oil resources? What is primary, Palestinian militants or the Israeli highhandedness in controlling vast lands or Palestine? What is primary, the terrorism of Kashmiri militants or the alienation of Kashmiris? The Gujarat Muslim revenge group or the Gujarat carnage? In a nutshell, whether terrorism is a disease by itself or whether it a manifestation of the deeper diseases needs to be understood.

The Gujarat carnage has many a lessons to learn from. Two of these stick out in prominence. When an affluent and socially prominent Ahsan Jaffery is killed after being mutilated what message it sends to millions of less privileged Muslims? When the Muslim women's being is violated, what signal it sends to millions of women of that community? And to top it all who then gives the shelter to these hapless survivors of the violation of their democratic rights? As witnessed in Gujarat, it was the mosque or the Muslim run charity, which gave shelter to the survivors. What message it sends for the whole community except increasing the hold of obscurantist mullahs and orthodox elements in the community.

My atheist friend born in a Christian family started going to Church when he witnessed the violence against another minority community. My research scholar Salim grows the beard to show his Muslim identity in the face the Mumbai riots, can Ayesha be far behind in succumbing to the pressures of the same elements to start putting the *dupatta* on her head? Will Salim's progeny take to terrorism or will they come to take the path, which their father had taken before the 92-93 riots in Mumbai? Will Ayesha graduate into a *burqa* clad women in due course or will she revert to the earlier carefree self of pre-pogrom phase is a question which has no clear answers today!

# 8

# Anti-Conversion Legislation

Tamil Nadu Government has passed a legislation banning the conversions by force, fraud and allurement (2002). Earlier Orissa Government had also passed a legislation on similar lines and one bill by Anant Geete of Shiv Sena is pending in the Parliament for discussion. This bill calls for a ban on conversions and also equates free education as allurement! As per these proposals a prior permission/intimation will be needed to be given to the authorities who will sit on judgement whether the conversion is 'legal' or not. In a way most of these legislations violate the fundamental rights of citizens, the right to personal freedom affecting profession, practice and propagation of faith (Article 25).

Just a month ago 150 Dalits in Kootharanbakkam village of Tamil Nadu had converted. Similarly on November 4, last years thousands of Dalits had converted to Buddhism under the leadership of Udit Raj and this set the trend for conversion in many places. As such in recent memory the conversions in Meenkashipuram in 1980, where many a Dalits had converted to Islam was the major event which was projected as the invasion of petro dollars for conversion to Islam in India. The issue was used to consolidate the upper caste-class reaction against the social changes especially related to the aspirations of Dalits. The same issue was raked up again from 1997 when the anti-Christian violence was orchestrated. It was alleged that Christian missionaries are converting by force and allurement. It was also alleged that these are being sponsored by the foreign money, courtesy the Pope. Thc major victim of this propaganda was Pastor Graham Steward Stains who was burnt alive along with his two sons when the trio was sleeping in the jeep. During this period churches begun to be attacked, Bibles were burnt and Christian priests were attacked. The very suddenness and countrywide spread of the phenomena came as a bolt from the blue.

The attacks were accompanied by the intercommunity divide on the ground that new followers of Jesus are abandoning their old communitarian norms and so the conflicts are coming up. The most surprising part of the 'forcible conversion' story was that this took place when the percentage of Christian population is declining. The census data, and the data from Justice Wadhava Commission of Inquiry gave the 'truth' of conversions away.

In Manoharpur in Keonjhar district Pastor Stains was doing his work amongst the lepers. Justice Wadhava report gives an interesting statistics. As per this report there is a rise of Hindu population by 2.52 per cent, and that of Christian population by.008 per cent between the years 1991 to 1998. These figures totally demolish the foundation of the argument that massive forced conversions are on. The point to be noted is that the conversions are projected to be a purely passive process in which the poor Adivasis are converted by inducement and allurement. This again is a point which gives the image that those converted are mere passive beings bereft of intelligence just because they are poor and so susceptible to the 'anti-National' activities of the missionaries.

A slight peep into history of conversions in India will make the matters clear for us: whether conversions are active or a passive process? If we recall a while ago the major component of anti-Muslim propaganda was that Muslim Kings converted the Hindus by the sword, and this construct formed the base of the anti-Muslim sentiments in the social common sense. Before we go into the historical process whereby Islam spread in India lets have a look at the opinion of Swami Vivekanand on the issue (Collected Works, Vol. VIII, p. 330). Says Swamiji, "Why amongst the poor of India so many are Muhamedans? It is nonsense to say that they were converted by the sword, it was to gain liberty from Zamindars (feudal lords) and priests." Islam, contrary to the popular belief came to India through the Arab traders who used to visit the Malabar coast for trade, and it were the Hindu Kings who built the initial mosques to sustain the trade. Also there are still communities in the coastal areas who practice mixed, Hindu and Muslim, rituals.

The major spread of Islam in India took place through the Sufi saints whose spiritual strength and attitude of being close to the people attracted the lower castes to embrace Islam in the hope of escaping the Brahminical oppression of which they were the victims. There is no doubt that some conversions also took place out of fear of the invading Muslim Kings and also out of the anticipation of reward from the Muslim Kings, but surely this number is inconsequential. Similarly even today there are some insignificant boisterous Christian groups who blow their trumpet and propagate in an aggressive way. Again their impact is insignificant.

It is interesting that Sikhism, which drew heavily from Islam as well as Hinduism, attracted more of low caste untouchables in big number. Many of them converted to Sikhism in the early part of twentieth century despite stiff opposition from the Arya Samaj and other elite Hindu streams. The case of Ambedkar and his followers embracing Buddhism needs a bit of recounting. Dr. Ambedkar tried his best to have a place in the Hindu social order. In this direction he led the Chavdar Talav movement, to have access to public drinking water, he led the Kalaram temple agitation, to gain entry to Hindu temples. The violent reaction of the upper caste Hindus to these agitations made him to say that that though I was born a Hindu I will not die as a Hindu. Further he went on to burn *Manusmriti* and later decided to convert to Buddhism.

Dr. Ambedkars' trajectory is the classical example of low caste Hindus adopting a different religions by choice. And this is what has been the phenomenon all through-attempts by the low castes to escape the Brahminical Social Order by embracing different religions. Be those the religions of 'Indian origin' or be they of 'foreign origin', what is important is that, the oppressed have been active partners in the process and not the mere objects for the conversions.

Using this as a tool for communal politics is a favourite weapon all through. As such Hinduism is based on caste system and Brahminism has been its dominant factor. It is not a religion based on the teaching of any prophet, and thereby spreading, preaching it to others is not the norm. Earlier Brahmin groups, being the elite, insisted more on 'exclusion' of others rather than on proselytisation. As such the Dalits, belonging presumably to the same religion were untouchables and had to live in the ghettoes outside the village. Other 'Indian' religions, which are based on teachings of prophets (Jainism, Buddhism and Sikhism), did believe in propagating and that's how Buddhism in particular spread far and wide, to other countries.

Hindu and Muslim political forces in early part of 20th century did undertake conversions (*shuddhi* to Hinduism nor *tanzim* and *tabligh* to Islam). The *shuddhi* was more to attract those low castes' that had adopted Islam or Sikhism as their religion. The current *Gharvapasi* campaign of VHP draws its legitimacy from the assertion that Adivasis are

Hindus. If ones' belief systems, deities, holy books, and communitarian practices determine religious functions than in which way they are the Adivasis Hindu? They many a times have been beef eaters, are unaware of Ram and other deities of Hindu religion, are oblivious to the Hindu holy books, i.e., *Gita*, *Ramayan*, *Mahabharat*, and Vedas, and are practicing the animism in their own way. As per the obligatory criterion of religion they cannot be called as Hindus. But they are being labeled as Hindus as a part of the phenomenon of political will and for the necessities of Hindutva (not Hinduism, and they are different categories) onslaught, which is trying to match Islamic fundamentalism in its pernicious methods. *Gharvapasi* is a proselytisation in a cleverer garb. The Adivasis are being baptised in newer ways (holy baths, washing their feet with sacred water etc.) and this being backed up with teaching them the Hindu ways, i.e., making them aware of the Hindu deities, Hindu holy books, Hindu festivals, etc. Today, despite the claims to the contrary many a Hindutva outfits are indulging in proselytisation.

The spread of Hinduism is always a problem. Politically Hindutva needs to assert that all those except Muslims and Christians, are Hindus. Here, the criterion applied is the nationalism of religions. One is doubtful if religions can be tied to any nation. Buddhism, which originated in India is the religion of majority of people in Thailand, Sri Lanka. Christianity, originated in Jerusalem but today it is major religion of U.S., Europe etc. While in Gharvapasi campaign the new caste of Adivasis remains a vague issue. What is remarkable is not that conversions as a marginal phenomenon have been a part of Indian reality from ages but the fact that political phenomenon of intolerance has made it a political issue today.

# Section–IV

## Hindutva's Threat Projection-Islam, Terrorism

September eleven gave one more pretext in the armamentarium of the Sangh combine to use it as a whipping cord against Islam and Muslims. It has been popularised that all terrorists are Muslims and that there is something in Islam which breed's terrorism. While the central focus of this compilation is to understand the threat of Hindu Rashtra, we cannot remain aloof from the global situation. The prevalence of terrorism in the Middle East has been attributed to the Islam, the terrorism in Kashmir has been associated with that and it has added further to demonisation of Islam. As we understand that fundamentalism is a by-product of the policies of imperialism, the Hindutva has deep association and appreciation for the policies of U.S. Also the goals of U.S. imperialism and Sangh combine have always been matching, e.g., anti-communism of U.S. in late forties and anti-Islamism in current times. At both these junctures RSS politics finds itself on the side of U.S. policies.

Terrorism is because of Islam or is an outcome of imperialism needs to be looked at. The general view that Islam is the cause of terrorism is the inverted reality. It is the U.S. policies, which have created discontent and the terrorism in turn.

At times the extreme intimidation and violence against the Muslim minority has caused the frustrated response in the form of bomb blast etc. have also been presented as those being to Islam/Muslims. We need to examine this in a slightly deeper way. The intimidated threatened community can come up with responses which are perverted and do result in further worsening of the situation.

# 9

# Terrorism: Symptom or Disease

The bombing on the Parliament has shaken us all to the core. This coming in the aftermath of WTC bombing is still more frightening. While words are not enough to condemn these heinous crimes by the terrorists, a new dimension has been added up in the tragic scenario, and that pertains to its association with Jihad, Islam and Muslims. On the one hand the social common sense is being subtly doctored to believe that Islam as a religion gives rise to terror and Jihad, which is an integral part of Islam, means violence and aggression. On the other hand the means to tackle terrorism have been defined, which essentially focus around tightening of security, intelligence etc. A prescription to harden the nation and society is being dished out as it is being said that we as a nation are victims of the terrorism as we have become a soft society and soft nation. Also some talk is in the air to launch an aggression on the neighbouring country where the terrorist camps are located.

Myopia at its worst is on the display. Can violence originate from any religion worth its spirituality? Does Jihad mean violence? Is there terrorism because we are a soft society and nation? These understandings have serious flaws, as they do not look beyond the nose of those promoting these ideas.

How is Islam related to terror, or for that matter how is any religion related to the cult of violence? Were the crusades undertaken by Christian Kings to promote Christianity? Did Muslim Kings undertaken Jihad to promote Islam? Were the Dharmayudhas by Hindu kings undertaken to promote Hindu religion? By no stretch of imagination any war related violence could be attributed to these religions. It is the kings whose basic goal was to expand their kingdoms, who undertook these wars and misused the names of their religions to get more people involved in the same. Timothy Mc Viehg, Oklahoma bomber was not serving Christianity, neither Dhanu was serving Hinduism when she acted as a live bomb killing Rajiv Gandhi and innocents around him, nor was Bhindranwale serving Sikhism when he promoted the cult of violence which led to murder of Indira Gandhi and then the butchery of thousands of Sikhs, nor was Osama bin-Laden serving Islam when he thanked Allah in the wake of the WTC tragedy, nor are the Kashmiri militants serving Islam when they maim and kill innocent Hindus and Muslims in the Valley of Kashmir. Terrorism is the product of social and political discontent, discontent, which flows though the barrel of the gun or explodes with the bomb of terrorist when the democratic channels are not available for its expression for the victims of injustice. People belonging practically to all the religions under the sun have resorted to terror in the name of their religions. It is not that only one religion has the 'distinction' for this misuse.

In Indian context the terrorism of Khalistanis could be contained when the dealing with the militants could be combined with winning over the hearts and minds of people and by making available the effective democratic options to the people at large. The present terrorism by the self-proclaimed Jihadis is definitely a slightly different ball game. The role of Pakistan in this is very discernible. But here our myopic vision stops and fails to see the imperialist designs in promoting the terrorism and routing this through the conduit of Pakistan. We are unable to see the deeper imperialist goals of control over oil resources, which has nurtured Talibans. Our policy makers are eager to jump to the softness thesis so that POTO or the worse forms of violations of civil liberties can be brought in with ease. So that they can get away with their other hidden agenda of creating a religious fascist state. It is surprising that our government is prostrating in front of the very power, is touching the feet with reverence of the very imperialist power, which has promoted the cult of violence, the cult of Jihad to ensure its control over the oil resources by controlling the political power in the subcontinent.

Right since the formation of Israel and its being backed by U.S. the signals were around of its designs in the Middle East and then in the subcontinent. Israel went into violate all the U.N. resolutions, attack Arab world repeatedly, to capture the Palestinian lands and to cause the loss of home and hearth of close to a million Palestinians. In due course U.S. started tightening its grip on the resources of the region. First it helped in the ouster of Mossadegh (Iran), who was planning to nationalize its oil wells and replacing that by a puppet Raza Shah Pehlavi regime to ensure the cheap flow of oil into its tanks. Later it went all out to promote the fanatic groups in the Afghanistan to fight the Russian occupation. Since then the base for the fanatic camps was laid in the region. Pakistan as the handmaiden of U.S. imperialism kept acting as the conduit to promote the U.S. interests by all possible means. U.S. to keep its hegemony in the region was playing different game. With Ayatullah Khoemeni replacing the U.S. stooge Raza Shah Pehlavi; U.S. backed Iraq, in Iran-Iraq war for long years. Later it turned its barrel against Iraq itself on the pretext of rescuing the Sheikh of Kuwait and his sovereignty. With the Russian occupation being pushed back, the fanatics, basically products of U.S. training, started intruding into Kashmir, in the process worsening the Kashmir imbroglio, where due to weak democratic institutions the alienation of Kashmiri people acted as the base for the terrorist game and the green valley turned red with the bullets flowing from the barrels of militants and the Indian army.

The dissatisfactian in the Arab world initially got manifested through the terrorist attacks on Jews. The terrorism here had two dimensions, one anti-Israel-U.S. and later anti-Soviet occupation. U.S. encouraged the later through the conduit of ISI. Now after 9/11 the cycle has turned full circle giving further pretext to U.S. to interfere more in the affairs of the region. The end of Socialist block has also marked the beginning of the demise of the role and power of U.N., whatever it was worth. With U.S. acting as the super cop and super bullly rolled into one, the problems do not seem to have any respite. So contrary to U.S.'s own attitude vis-a-vis 9/11, a blind reprisal and aggression on the Afghanistan, it is advising restraint to India on one hand and increasing its own grip in the region on the other.

No amount of hardness of Indian society and state, as if it is not violative of civil libertarian norms already, can be solve the problem in the present set up where U.S. hegemonic designs are on their naked march. While on one hand the intensification of military vigil and intelligence can act as a short term measure, the region cannot breath in peace unless it is left to itself sans the U.S. interference. Removal of U.S. hegemony in the region is a must for any possibility of peace. The regional confederation of Middle East and South Asian countries on the line of European Commonwealth should not be a goal meant for dreams but an urgent necessity. Along with U.N., the movement, which has suffered a serious set back is the non-aligned movement. Its a tough task to restore and further strengthen NAM and to expand the SAARC in to an Asian Commonwealth, but that seems to be the only base around which we can think of sidetracking the U.S. designs in the area and bring an end to the symptom of terrorism in the region. In a way this symptom is the secondary to the primary disease of imperialism. Terrorism is not a disease, it is a symptom of the underlying disease, the disease which manifested first in the form of colonialism (projected as white mans burden) then went on to crushing the nationalism in different countries, Vietnam, Chile etc. in the name of defense of freedom and now is further continuing its agenda in the name of clash of civilisations, the economic lust of more advanced countries to control the resources of weaker countries and to create market for their goods in these countries.

The choice before us is either to buy the logic promoted by these powerful countries and focus on the superficial symptom of terrorism and to demonize one religion, or to have some vision and prepare to chart out a long-term goal of Asian Commonwealth.

# 10

# Terrorism as Revenge

The recent bomb blasts in Mumbai (August 25, 2003) shook the whole city. It has been a long series, Mulund, Ghatkopar and culminating in the worst one at Jhaveri Bazar and Cuffe Parade. The reaction to these dastardly acts has been diverse. While the City of Mumbai kept moving with some hiccups, the opinion and reactions of politicians revealed a lot about their mind set. The Shiv Sena supremo Bal Thckeray called for the help of LTTE in tackling terrorism, while Mr. Advani, came up with his oft repeated convenient accusation that Pakistan is responsible for these acts. In this simplistic explanation one can effortlessly conceal the causes of genesis of terrorism, which his own brand of politics has unleashed. In a related event the Muslims of Ahmedabad went on for a day's Bandh in response to the simple leaflet, which stated the truth that the Muslims are being regarded as terrorists. The simple leaflet was innocuous but the hurt psyche of Muslim community found an expression of their anguish. They suffered pain and sorrow not only during the carnage but their misery continues in various forms as the 'Hindu state' of Gujarat is on the way to fascisisation with abolition of the citizenship rights for minorities. The Best Bakery case has transcended all the limits of democracy and there is nothing an average person of minorities can look forward to for one's rights of living as a decent citizen. The investigations of the Mumbai blasts have been starkly revealing. In contrast to Advani's attempts to hide the real reasons of the terrorism, the truth seems to be coming out. The Gujarat carnage, which led to the loss of lives of around 2000 innocent victims, which resulted in thousands families being rendered homeless, which witnessed the violation of the being of hundreds of women and on the top of that which saw the child in mother's womb being subject to brutality, did result in the anger which has taken illogical directions. One understands the existence of Gujarat Muslim Revenge group, one is shocked to learn that many a Muslim youth battered by the inhumanity perpetrated on their community have been recruited in large numbers by the existing terrorist outfits.

Just a decade ago the Mumbai riots in the wake of Babri demolition had seen the bloodshed, which was coordinated by Bal Thackeray, a close ally of Advani and Co. During the bloodshed it became clear that the victims are mainly from the minority community, despite Congress rule the then Chief Minister of Maharashtra surrendered to Thackeray (incidentally he later joined Thackeray's party also) and let the Shiv Sena goons go on rampage. This one-sided cruelty kept going on and on. Then one bad afternoon a series of bombs exploded killing a large number of innocents. And it seems that after this incident the simmering violence took some respite.

During the Gujarat genocide many a perceptive commentators did point out that this violence will also give birth to terrorists. Of hundred of youth who see their kith being killed for the only crime of being a Muslim at least a couple may take this insane path. Of the hundred of young children who saw their sisters and mothers being molested some may grow to be the terrorists, goes without saying. In Mumbai blasts the new feature is involvement of women, in the blasts. One knows that when millions of Palestinians were exiled due to the by the highhanded tactics of Israel duly supported by United States. The terrorism sprung up. And one name, which sticks in the memory, is that of Liala Khalid, a young Muslim girl who took to this insane path. One also recalls a girl named Dhanu, a part of LTTE set up, who blew up Rajiv Gandhi for his supporting the Sri Lankan government in restraining the LTTE.

So who is responsible for the genesis of terrorism? Is terrorism a religious phenomenon? Is it due to the members of a single community? How come some people come to take the steps, which surely are suicidal for them? Terrorism is basically a political phenomenon. People belonging to different religious communities have resorted to it. The prerequisite of this is of course an intense injustice perpetrated by the dominant group. Be it Israel, or Sinhala ethnic politics or the sense of alienation felt by the people in Kashmir or North East. The sustaining factor for this phenomenon is the abuse of democratic norms. Terrorism is an act of extreme desperation where the victims do not see any light at the end of the tunnel. One remembers the plight of Kashmiri Pundits at this point. Comparing the miseries of Kashmiri Pundits with Palestinian refugees will not be fair. Both are sipping their own cups of woes and these are not of the same quality or quantity. The three major points due to which Islam and Muslims are demonised, are scattered all over. The problem of Palestine is the major one. It is a mere coincidence that the regions, which are rich in oil wealth, also happen to be the regions where followers of Islam are more. These are also the areas where American Imperialism wants to control the oil wealth and prop up despotic rulers in these countries who have nothing whatsoever do with democracy. The issue of Kashmir has been a matter of great anguish for the country at large. The initial policies due to which the dictum of Do Pradhan Do Vidhan (Two Prime Ministers-Two Constitutions) was violated resulted in the alienation of large sections of

Kashmiri youth, making them fertile ground for terrorist ideas and actions.

The rise of Hindutva, the communal violence has again resulted in the violence in which minorities are the big victims. The lack of justice mechanism, the failure to implement the inquiry committee reports and the communalisation of civic society has given a deep sense of hurt to the Muslim minorities. The demonisation of minorities is by now complete due to the continuous efforts of RSS and its progeny. the doctoring of mass consciousness has gone to the extent that average person has come to believe that Islam is the religion, which promotes violence, and that Muslims are devils incarnate.

In a way the Islam worldwide is demonised in pursuit of the Imperialist ambitions of U.S., more so after the demise of Soviet Union. Islam has been projected to be the backward religion. This has been backed up by the ideologues of imperialism like Samuel Huntington who see the present obstacles to America's ambitions to control the world's oil wealth as a clash between the advanced Western civilisation and the backward Islamic civilisation. Can any civilisation be totally dictated by religion in the current times? What is the similarity between the civilisation of an Islamic country like Indonesia and Saudi Arabia? What is common between the Muslim population of Japan or U.S. and the believers in the cult of Osama bin Laden?

Kashmir is another sore point but it is hardly an issue related to Islam or for that matters to the Indian Muslims. Hindutva surely has made great strides and the original proclamation of the RSS Sarsanghchalak that Muslim and Christians don't deserve even the citizen's rights is being implemented by the saffron eyed boy of Sangh Parivar, Narendra Modi, with great admiration from the top rulers of the country as a whole.

So what is primary—does terrorism give rise to Israel-U.S. policies or U.S.-Israel atrocities result in Osama bin Laden and his clan? Has Kashmir terrorism its roots in Islam or in the unresolved Indo-Pakistani relations and using the people of Kashmir as the hostages to two supra-nationalisms of Pakistan and India, is the cause of problem in the valley? Does terrorism give rise to Gujarat carnage or Gujarat carnage gives rise to Gujarat Muslim Revenge Group? In this case they're an interesting twist. Mr. Modi will like us to believe that Godhra 'terrorism' gave rise to Gujarat carnage. A deeper analysis will show that Godhra was projected as the terrorist offense to legitimize in advance the carnage which was planned much earlier. The Hindutva and for that matter all narrow nationalisms do create an enemy to ensure that their planned actions are projected as revenges to the original acts. And that's where the evil genius of Bal Thackeray and Modi comes in handy to implement the anti-minority pogroms.

Today the reality has been inverted fully. The causes remain hidden, subtly glorified, presented as the solution of their own effects. The victim being projected as the culprit is the key of those perpetrating the cult of violence for their narrow goals of power, social privileges and accompanying hegemony?

# 11

# Combating Terrorism

In recent times (2002) the country has witnessed a long list of acts of insanity, attack on Sabarmati train, Parliament, Kashmir Assembly and Akshardham. Since this violence is supposedly being perpetrated by the 'International terrorism', which derives its legitimacy from Islam, all the Muslims have become suspects and the slogan goes that "all terrorists are Muslims". It is in this backdrop that Bal Thackeray's magic solution to solve terrorist problem is dished out for the benefit of the nation. First get rid of four crore Bangladeshis who have infiltrated, the pro-Pakistan Muslims should leave the country and "Hindu suicide squads should be formed". With this triad of solution coming from Hindu Hridaya Samrat (Emperor of Hindu Hearts), as some of his followers call him, the nation will be rid of the menace of terrorism and this Hindu Rashtra can relieve the great glories!

In normal times the utterances of the likes of Thakeray deserve to be put in the waste paper basket. But unfortunately since this 'mini fuehrer' does represent the most vocal part of the Hindutva politics, and has been joined in by a new Hindu Hriday Samrat, Narendra Modi, he cannot be ignored. Before we go further we do need to take note of a point that both these (Thackeray and Modi) have been 'accorded' the prefix of Hindu Hriday Samrat in the aftermath of their roles in two of the worst violence's which the whole country saw painfully, the post-demolition Mumbai riots and the riots in Gujarat.

Thackeray's prescription that Hindu suicide squads are the answer to the Islamic terrorism is not only flawed but it also labels the acts of political motives as having their roots in a particular religion only. It totally betrays the basic unwillingness to understand the causes of violence, terrorism etc. One can add that it is not only an unwillingness to understand the basic causes but also it is a deliberate ploy to instigate the aggressive sentiments, to provoke the violence in the society. One knows that the ilk of Thackeray have political motives in ensuring that communal violence continues. It is only on the chariot of communal hatred; that the parties like BJP, Shiv Sena are able to gain electoral mileage. Be it the case of Mumbai riots in 92-93 or be it the Gujarat violence, the basic agenda of Thackeray-Modi combine is the same.

During post-independent India the riot victims, the unfortunate lot, have mostly been from the poor community. This statement has to be qualified by the addition that this was so prior to Gujarat 2002. In Gujarat the earlier observation that it is only poor who are victims of communal violence has been upturned and now even the affluent can be the recipient of the wrath of the politics, the one called Hindutva, in this country. Again in the similar vein one will add that though the percentage of Muslims in the population is around 12, the same percentage amongst riot victims is 80 per cent, and that too is as per the pre-Gujarat statistics. That the observations in Gujarat will change this for the worse, is sure. This violence derives its legitimacy from the stray acts, which are either provoked or occur due to insecurity of the community under the battering ram of the violence. The agenda of majoritarian politics projects the battered minority as the threat to the majority and in order to 'protect' the majority' the pre-emptive' strikes are undertaken. And that's how the butchers and violators are accorded, or get themselves accorded, the prefix 'Emperors of Hindu hearts'.

To add to the good fortune of Thackeray-Modi, George Bush has provided the international ideological support. Now the equation of Osama Bin Laden-International terrorism-Pakistan and Indian Muslims being together in their mission to attack the virtuosity of Western civilisation globally and the glorious Indian traditions here has been combined into a single combination pack. Why and how the likes of Osama and Kashmiri terrorist came up, what is the role of American imperialism in promoting the same is forgotten in the process. When and who trained the Osma group into 'Jihad' techniques, why only in oil rich zone, the terrorism originates and prevails, is also forgotten. It is also forgotten that the most initial act, which prompted the terrorism to come up on the big scale in the Middle East was violation of international norms by Israel, fully backed up by the mighty U.S.. The suppression of democratic aspiration in this region, starting from overthrowing the Mossadegh regime by the U.S., the previous aggression of U.S. on Iraq and the forthcoming violation of Iraqi sovereignty by U.S. are again understated. The merry alliance of Sheikhs and despots with Uncle Sam, who is crushing democracy in a ruthless manner wherever possible, is a matter of deep concern for all the conscientious citizens of the World, be it Vietnam where America unsuccessfully tried to crush the Vietnamese nationalism or be it Chile where a democratic government was overthrown and a butcher of the status of Pinochet was installed by U.S., all has been forgotten from the public memory. As a matter of fact the self-proclaimed upholder of freedom is the biggest suppressor of democracy all over the world. And this, of course, is done to pursue its imperialist designs. In a way Palestanian militancy was a reaction to Israel's highhandedness, Osama, himself a product of CIA training, turned against its mentors for their dominating presence and intervention in the Middle East. What is the cause and what is the effect. The popular perceptions, thanks to the 'Manufacturing consent' by the dominating states and the 'doctoring of mass consciousness' by the domination social groups, ensures that the likes of Thackeray and Modis can 'merrily' conduct pogroms to support their political agenda favouring social status quo. One can undertake an exercise of seeing the parallel between the agenda of Uncle Sam and Hindutvavadi's breathing down our neck. One recalls that during Mc'Arthy era when communists were being hunted down our own M.S. Golwalkar, the ideologue of RSS was writing to the Indian Government offering all his support to eliminate the menace of Communism. Five decades later when Uncle Sam has unleashed a 'crusade' against 'Islamic Terrorism' the inheritors of the legacy of Golwalkar are busy actually wiping out the followers of Islam. So some progress there as far as 'our' own dealers of hate politics are concerned.

Closer home, post-Babri demolition the anger of Muslim youth can be used as a pretext to unleash the pogrom. Similarly the acts, which have no religious motive, like murder of Mathadi workers or the burning of Bane family (Mumbai) can be projected to be the attack of Muslims (since the victims were Hindus) to annihilate the Hindus and so the mini-fuehrer can take over the streets and his minions can supply arms to the marauding mobs to do their job. In this background the polarisation of communities keeps going on and the electoral chickens hatch soon enough for the leaders of the pogroms. Thanks to the painstaking work of Shrikrishna Commission one can confidently state this a decade down the line. But damage has been done. Popular perception has no time for such commissions, they can well be fed with the soup that Muslims attack first and so we have to... That the violence is not spontaneous, neither non-avoidable has been more than proven by a comparison of projected post-Godhra carnage and post-Akshardham calm.

But here again the popular perception has no time to introspect. One, people have enough problems on hand and two, the 'doctors of mass consciousness' are working overtime to ensure to enforce the message that Godhra has links with international terrorism, Osama Bin Laden, Pervez Musharraf and the Muslim next door. By the time the reports of inquiry commission will bring out the truth, the ilk of Chote Sardar, the newly anointed Emperor of Hindu Hearts, will en-cash the resulting polarisation into the electoral arena. By the time the inquiry commission report comes out, if at all in this case, the graves of those who perished in the carnage will be submerged deep down. After all, all is fair for the assertive propagators who swear and kill in the name of their virtues of tolerance.

The suicide squads in a way already exist. The impoverished Adivasis and Dalits, who can be made handmaiden of the communal agenda, are already willing to risk their lives for a price. And this is the new acquisition of the perpetrators of the cult of politics in the name of religion. The march of the present policies are already creating fertile ground for the squads, who for mere biological survival will be coming in handy for further suppression of democratic ethos and norms. Thackeray and Modis are writing the script, which wants to eradicate the gains of freedom struggle, the Indian Constitution. The only caution exercised is that the attack is projected as the self-defense and the victim is projected as the biggest culprit. And the better one plays this game taller one rises in the Sangh Parivar hierarchy.

Is Mr. Thackeray concerned about eliminating terrorism? No way. This terrorism is his best support. So he wants to see that the terrorism 'flourishes', and so he gives the call for suicide squads. The proposed squads can be the best incitement to the feeling of insecurity, which promotes terrorist acts. Surely Balasaheb is on the right tract for his political agenda.

# Section–V

# Communalism-Violence

As such the word communal stands for the issues and concerns of the community. In Indian context it has come to mean the use of religious identity for political mobilisation with a social agenda in the backdrop. It begins with the idea that all those belonging to one religion have similar political and social interests and goes on to assert that those belonging to different religions have interests, which are hostile to each other. This has been the foundation of the politics of Muslim League, Hindu Mahasabha and the RSS and its progeny.

This communalism rides on the base of communal violence. The observation that communal violence precedes the strengthening of communal parties has been put forward by most of the scholars of communalism. The case of BJP demonstrates it times and over again. Even before the decade of 80s the areas witnessing communal violence saw the rise of communal parties in the aftermath. In middle and late eighties we see the rise in communal violence in different parts of the country more so in the north. This was a major outfall of Ram Temple movement. This decade also saw that a non-descript communal party went on from strength to strength in the wake of communal violence unleashed in the aftermath of Ram Temple movement. In 1984 Lok Sabha elections, it had two MPs. By the time Babri demolition and

Mumbai riots stalked the country, the number of these went on rising 2 to 89, to 171 and there by leading to its coming to the seat of power in the centre.

Communal violence is not just a spontaneous process. It begins with the spread of hate ideology, takes advantage of some stray incidents, accidental or sponsored. The events are so planned that the minority community is cornered and sometimes is forced to throw the first stone. This pretext comes in handy for those who are bent upon unleashing violence and later to en-cash on it politically. The violence in the immediate aftermath leads to polarisation of communities and in the long term leads to ghettoisation of minorities, the ghettoisation of minorities and the accompanying consequences. The role of state machinery in the riots has been abysmal, more so that of police personnel who abandon their responsibilities to take on the role of assisting the perpetrators of violence or themselves playing that role. There are honourable exceptions to this as well. Communal violence is the most visible part of the communal politics and it in turn results in deeper societal repercussions.

# 12

# Communalism and Collective Violence

## Issues and Interventions

### *Communalism*

Communalism, communal politics, assumes that people belonging to one religion have similar interests and these are opposed to the interests of the people belonging to 'other' religions. In its milder form it asserts that interests of the people belonging to one religion are similar. In moderate form it goes on to state that these interests of one community are different from the interests of the 'other' community' and in its severe form it asserts that these are opposed to the one's of other community.

During our freedom struggle these communal trends, manifested in the form of Muslim League and Hindu Mahasabha, RSS. Muslim League, with this understanding wanted an Islamic state (Pakistan) and the Hindu Mahasabha-RSS stated that it is a Hindu Rashtra.

## Communal Violence

Communal violence is the superficial manifestation of deeper communal politics. It targets the 'other community' as the object of hate. Here the values of one's religions humanism are contrasted with the practices of the 'other' religion and the hate is created for the other. It is on the basis of this hate that violence can go on in the streets. It is because of the doctored mass consciousness that this violence sustains itself. The doctoring of mass consciousness is also accompanied by religion based group identity, which consolidates sections of society for this politics and the violence.

2.1 *Group Identity*: The group identity, which rules the streets, paints a uniform picture of the other communities, Christians-Hindus in Pakistan or Hindus in Bangladesh or Muslims-Christians in India have been painted in the uniform evil colour. This process, which has been going on from last many decades has picked up tremendously during last few years. The 'others' being projected as demons occurs through complicated social mechanism in which the social psyche is doctored, the ideas are manufactured, based on some aspects, which have roots either in History or in the societal patterns related to community life and demographics.

2.2 *Communal Violence in India*: Communal violence is the festering wound on the body politic of Indian society. In pre-independence period the communal riots were a sort of reciprocal violence between Hindus and Muslims with the police (mainly British officers) intervening to restore peace. The nature of these riots after independence has changed in a significant way. First, the number of victims are more from Muslim community, second, the loss of property is also more of Muslims and third, police plays a heavily partisan role in favour of the majority community. Initially it used to be mainly the poor Muslims who were the major victims, but lately even the middle and upper class Muslims have also been drawn into this vortex.

The post-partition riots were followed by a period of comparative calm, in the decade of 50s, barring the one episode in eastern India in 1950. This calm was broken in 60s when in 1961 and 1964 Jabalpur, Jamshedpur and Rourkela riots broke out. "Of the bloody pogroms in sixties, the ones at Ranchi, Bihar (1962) and Ahmedabad, Gujarat (1969) stand out as the major events. In seventies the Turkman Gate massacre of 1976 perpetrated by police..., the riots in Moradabad (1980), Nellie, Naogaon, Assam (1983), Bhiwandi (1984) and Meerut (1987) have been the major ones in which more than a thousand lost their lives" (Khalidi, 1995). The Ramjanmabhumi campaign left a big trail of blood in which more than thousand people lost their lives in 1989. The massacres of Bhagalpur, Hyderabad and Aligarh heralded the onset of bloody 80s, which has seen the peak of communal violence. Advani's *rath yatra* and post-Babri demolition riots were one of the worst, the country has suffered so far. The post-demolition riots gripped Mumbai, Surat, Bhopal in a major way and many other places in a significant way. From 1960 to 1995 the incidences of riots have been on an upswing. A big proportion of these have been taking place in six states—UP, Gujarat, Rajasthan, Bihar, Madhya Pradesh and Andhra Pradesh. So far these riots' occurrence is mainly in cities, but involvement of villages is also there and has been in the rise but lately even the small towns and villages are also being drawn in the vortex.

2.3 *Communalisation:* This communalisation process goes through various levels, beginning from 'the Muslims are aliens', 'responsible for partition of the country', 'have spread Islam on the strength of sword' and 'are loyal to Pakistan' to the last and one where the slogans like *Musalman ka Do hi sthan, Kabristan ya Pakistan* (Muslims can have only two places to live : Pakistan or Kabristan), *Pahle Kasai Phir Isai* (first Muslims and then Christians) etc. In between these two there are various subtle conveyor belts, which ensure the translation of this ideology into the action. Which in this case means a violence in which poor Muslims are the biggest victims and a section of poor Hindus, mobilised by activation of communal identities also loose their lives and properties. It goes without saying that Hindu communalism (expressed through Sangh Parivar : RSS, BJP, VHP and Bajrang Dal) is the main player in this game in today's scenario. It keeps getting stimulation and provocation from the remnants of Muslims communalism whose acts of commission, though feeble in social intensity are pretext enough for Hindu communalism to pounce on the Muslim community with full intensity.

2.4 *Pre Riot Mob Psychology*: Build up of group psychology occurs on the communalised social space, which has been actively vitiated by Hindu communalists, duly provoked by Muslim communalists. The group or mob is mobilised on the communal ground and systematic projection of 'fear' of impending attack from the other side. The 'forth coming attack on our temple', 'build up of weapons in the mosques' are few of the major rumours employed by the communal forces. In most of the riots the majority communalism is well-assisted by the state and police machinery and on occasions the police itself takes over the total execution of riot. Religious frenzy is the fodder of such a group and rumours, communalised media are the major forces in broadening the extent of violence. Apathy of state administration thoroughly infiltrated by the Hindutva (incidentally Hindutva is not religion, it is a politics a la Islamism, the one based on elite version of Hinduism aiming at suppression of human rights of Dalits, women and workers) elements comes in as a big help to these forces. The communal build up is aided by slogans, some of which have found a permanent place in the dictionary of communalism and some of which are manufactured and propagated as the contingent measures.

Mob psychology is built upon 'projected fears', 'Bangladeshi infiltration' and the like. Organised activities like processions (Maha-Aartis), inflammatory speeches, writings etc. fan the flames. As pointed out before from here on the rumours take over as the engine of mass psychology, 'cow slaughter', chopping of the breast of Hindu/Muslim women. 'They' have poisoned the milk, 'Huge number of arms are being accumulated in the Masjid as the preparation', 'Temple is going to be attacked', 'Pakistanis are landing on the shore with the arms' are the commonly employed rumours with great effect. Riots break out with the processions raising provocative slogans, desecration of temple/mosque, music before mosque, throwing coloured water, *gulal* on mosque, elopement of Hindu woman with a Muslim or vice-versa. Lately international terrorism is projected as the main offender in alliance with local Muslims. Involvement of few criminals from one community is projected as the involvement of all the people belonging to that religion.

2.5 *Who starts the riots* : Teesta Setalvad (Who Casts the First Stone, Communalism Combat, March 98) by citing the extracts from five commissions of inquiry shows the truth behind the start of communal riots.

1. Ahmedabad 1969 : "There was deliberate attempt to suppress the truth from the commission especially the active participation in riots of some RSS and Jan Sangh leaders" (Jana Sangh is the previous political *avatar* of present BJP) (from Justice Jagmohan Reddy Commission).

2. Bhiwandi, Jalagaon 1970 : "In his report to his superior the SP, Thane district has stated, "I found that a section of Hindu elements, particularly RSS and some PSP men, were bent upon creating mischief. Their idea in accompanying the procession was not so much to pay respect to the Great Shivaji but to establish their right and, if possible, to provoke and humiliate Muslims.

The villagers shouted provocative anti-Muslim slogans, behaved aggressively, threw on the Moti Masjid at Bangad galli Hyderi mosque situated at the junction of Dargarch Road and Sutar Alli aided by passive police." (Justice D.P. Madon Commission).

3. Tellichery 1971 : "In Tellichery Hindus and Muslims were living as brothers for centuries... It was only after RSS and the Jana Sangh set up their units and began activities in Tellicherry that there came a change in situation. Their anti-Muslim propaganda, its reaction on the Muslims who rallied around their communal organisation, the Muslims league.... the communal tension that followed prepared the background for these disturbances".

(Report of Justice Joseph Vithyathil (Commission)

4. Jamshedpur 1979 : From Report of Commission of Inquiry : "In the run up to the communal

build up before the elections prepared by the Intelligence branch, Jamshedpur (March 23, 79) there was a special mention made to the divisional conference of the RSS scheduled to be held on March 31 and April 1, in which among others RSS Sarsanghchalak was to participate.

The dispute on route of the procession became sharp and agitated reactions from a group of persons who called themselves Samyukta Bajarang Bali Akhara Samiti, who systematically distributed pamphlets to heighten communal feeling and had organisational links with the RSS. A call for defiance of authority and administration when it refused permission for one of the routes led to violent mob protesting and raising anti-Muslim slogans. Thereafter incendiary leaflets doing rounds of Jamshedpur (issued on behalf of Sri Ramnavmi Kendriya Akhara Samiti), that is nothing short of an attempt to rouse the sentiments of Hindus to a high pitch to distort events and show some actions as attacks on Hindus that appear to be part of a design".

5. Kanyakumari Riots (1982): Justice Venugopal Commission : "RSS methodology for provoking communal violence is:

   (a) Rousing communal feelings in the majority community by propaganda that Christians are not loyal citizens of this country.

   (b) deepening the fear in the majority community by a clever propaganda that the population of minorities is increasing and that of Hindus is decreasing.

   (c) training young people of the majority community in the use of weapons like daggers, swords, spears;

(d) spreading rumours to widen the communal cleavage and deepen communal feelings by giving a communal colour to trivial incident.

### *2.6: A Police Officer's Research*

V.N. Rai, a fellow of National Police Academy has dealt with this point very well (Combating Communal Conflicts). He breaks the myth of Muslims starting the riots by analysing the riot data and demonstrates that in the riots between 1968 and 1980 (Govt. data 3949 incidents occured in which out of 2289 victims 530 were Hindus and 1598 were Muslims. Let us keep in mind that Muslims are 12 per cent of the population but in the riots around 80 per cent victims are Muslims. The police machinery is extremely biased and all the police action during and after the riots is also concentrated against the Muslims. The preparation for communal violence goes on for a long time before it erupts and a trivial incident sparks off deep lying hatred to the surface. Many a times business rivalry and land disputes are also made to be solved through such a violence. The 'first strike' may be made by the frightened community which is anticipating the attack from the other community. In a very perceptive observation Rai adds "very often the way in which the first stone is thrown or the first hand is raised in aggression, suggests an outside agency at work, an agency that wants to create a situation in which members of the minority community commit an act which ignites severe retribution for themselves. In order to guard themselves against external criticism and to preserve their self righteousness, violence is projected to be started by Muslims. It is as if a weaker person is pushed into the corner by a stronger, forcing him to raise his hand so that he may be suitably punished for his 'attack'. Before the punishment is meted out a suitable hue and cry can be made about the fact that because the person cornered is naturally wicked and violent, he is bound to attack first" (Pg. 56-57).

**Independent India**

During first three decades of free India these forces were miniscule in proportion and Religion based Nationalism had to take the back seat, though it kept itself alive through different communal riots. From the decade of 80s the sections of upper caste and affluent middle caste/classes, which in a way share the basic ideology of religion based nationalism came back to reassert its opposition to the social transformation through anti-reservation riots. These were transformed into anti-minority riots by a clever maneuver and this politics started asserting itself through Rath Yatras etc. The major onslaught of this politics manifested through the Babri Masjid demolition and post-demolition riots. It also brought to fore the communal party into the fold of power. Lately it was seen that the appeal of this politics was declining, as manifested in the results of elections in the northern states. And that's when Godhra came in handy. And communalists used this pretext for their nefarious designs. What took place was the process of killing and maiming, burning of people and violating the being of women. The central aim of all this is to polarize the society along the lines of religion. That is what the communalists want. Akshardham did come in as an aftermath of the massive anti-minority pogrom and it was not followed by any 'spontaneous Hindu hurt' as post-Godhra events were projected to be.

Today nation is sitting on the volcano of communal hatred, this can burst into communal holocaust as and when needed by those for whom it is politically beneficial. So what should be done to stall the march of politics of hatred, the politics deriving its legitimacy from religion?

**'Secular' Parties: 'Secular' State**

The political outfits, the secular one's have shown tremendous weakness in the face of communal onslaught.

Many of them have compromised with the communal politics, directly or indirectly. Some of them have shamelessly allied with them. The state apparatus has also been infiltrated to a great extent by the trained communalists. In addition due to overall pressures of the communal offensive at all the levels, different wings of state machinery cannot be relied upon to protect the secular constitution and the accompanying social values. That leaves the civic society, which has to take the whole responsibility of the protecting and nurturing the principals and values emerging from our freedom struggle, the values of secular democracy, values of Liberty, Equality and Fraternity.

# 13

# State and Violence

### BJP-Ruled Gujarat State's Naked 'Glory'

In the worst ever communal flare up Gujarat has lost over 2000 of its citizen's, over 3000 crores worth of social wealth, most of it belonging to Muslims, and has witnessed the decimation of religious places, Dargah's and Masjids. It is not for the first time that we have seen state not playing partisan role but here the matters are qualitatively different. The demand that state administration should be transparent has been fulfilled in the wrong direction, the participation, compliance and encouragement of state personnel in supporting the rioters was transparent and no alibis were used for breaking the laws, in twisting the meanings of the clauses. The state apparatus was a mighty tool in the hands of the pogrom conductors coming from the stable of Sangh Parivar.

To begin with one of the civil servants, Harsh Mander was so aghast with the role of his peers and colleagues from the administrative services that he could not overcome his disgust and resigned from the administrative service. Then 'Super Cop' Julio Reibero was equally ashamed as his colleagues in the Khakis who were supposed to be manning the 'riot control' were behaving in a way that it was difficult to distinguish the rioters from the one's who are supposed to control the riots. One also recalls many a ministers operating from the police control rooms and directing the anti-minority operations. Most of the human rights reports like Human Rights watch report stated that State officials of Gujarat, India were directly involved in the killings of hundreds of Muslims since February 27 and are now engineering a massive cover-up of the state's role in the violence. When approached many of the police officials told the approaching victims that we have no orders to protect you. (http://hrw.org/reports/2002/india/). One of the researchers from South Asia watch pointed out that what happened in Gujarat was not a spontaneous uprising; it was a carefully orchestrated attack against Muslims. And that the attacks were planned in advance and organised with extensive participation of the police and state government officials.

The seventy-five-page report from the Human Rights watch documents some of the attacks against the Muslims and concludes that the police were directly implicated in nearly all the attacks against Muslims. The standard response was 'We Have No Orders to Save You': While in some cases they were passive observers in other instances the police officials led the charge of murderous mobs, aiming and firing at Muslims who got in the way. At times, on the pretext of offering assistance, some police officers led the victims directly into the hands of their killers. And the phone calls made to the police and other support agencies did not bring in the dutiful responses.

The acme of the degeneration of the duties of the state has been reached. When Hitler was on rampage against the Jews, other weaker sections of society, and against those who were opposed to his policies, it was state, which implemented the programme of annihilation of the Jews and others. Probably the hairs breadth difference still lies between what we witnessed in Gujarat and what happened in Hitler's Germany. Here though the Sangh Parivar is controlling the state apparatus it itself is not the state apparatus.

The trajectory of communal violence has come a long way since they first began in the last decade of 19th Century. These riots provoked by the communal politics (Muslim and Hindu both) came up in response as a reaction against the rise of Secular Indian National Congress (INC). British had a two-pronged strategy as far as the communal politics was concerned. At the political level they did promote the communal outfits of Muslims and Hindus both to pursue their policy of Divide and Rule. At the level of communal violence they were fairly neutral. After independence before seeing the role of state in communal violence as such we must remember that due to the Partition tragedy most of the Muslim communal elements had left for Pakistan and Muslim League's impact became very weak. Right since the beginning the Hindu communalists, in addition to having their own outfits (Hindu Mahasabha and RSS) had also infiltrated in the INC. Also the trained swayamsevaks of RSS started entering all the wings of state machinery right from the beginning. One notable example is that of district magistrate of Ayodhya, K.K. Nayyar in late forties, who came forward in helping RSS in laying the foundation of a dispute of Babri Mosque. Such characters were there in all the walks of administrative machinery, media and the armed forces.

In most of the riots, which have pained us since the first Jabalpur riot of 1961 one sees a common pattern. While the bureaucracy soft peddles the offence of wings of RSS, police plays the partisan role. While the administrative machine is sympathetic, to the 'Hindu sentiments' (read Hindu Communal politics), the communalisation of police has been blatant. There are instances (Meerut-Malyana, 1987) where the Provincial Armed Constabulary lined up around 300 Muslims besides the canal and shot them so that the bodies gets disposed off in the canal. There are instances (Bhagalpur 1989) where the police along with the rioters killed 180 Muslims, buried them in a paddy field on which cauliflower was grown. Most of the inquiry commission reports have shown the partisan role of police in the riots. The Shrikrishna Commission also indicted the police especially its Addl. Commissioner R.D. Tyagi for his shooting of the innocents in the Suleman Bakery.

One also recalls the communal virus seeping in the various state sponsored institutions, right under the nose of the government which is supposed to be protector of secular values as per the constitution. After the demolition of Babri Mosque, Lal Bahadur Shastri Academy students, the future administrators etc. celebrated the event with unusual gusto.

So the rot is set all around. And its qualitative transformation in the Gujarat is a dangerous portent to the values, which emerged from the Indian Freedom struggle and got enshrined in the Indian Constitution. Where did the things go wrong? Why the infiltration of RSS swayamsevaks in state machinery could not be checked? Why did the nation adopt a complacent attitude towards the proliferation of communal virus in the police stations and other offices? Did most of us think this 'outdated' ideology will die its natural death and does not deserve to be fought in a proactive way? We need to answer all these if we want to restore the democratic ethos and secular values in our political and social life. What needs to be done to stem the rot, the polity is seriously ill. A serious effort and careful nurturing of values is more than called for to promote the plural democracy which celebrates differences as what matters at political level is not one's religion but one's citizenship, which is supreme and non-negotiable.

# Section–VI

# Political Chessboard

Communal politics comes to power through various routes. Since in India it has been trudging along for long and the chances of its clear cut electoral ascendance had not been there for long it kept using all the mechanism and tactics to come to the centre stage. Using the democratic space to abolish the democracy has been the underlying strategy of Hindutva. In the process it has been promoting some as icons (Savarkar), has been striking alliances with some parties, which had not been principled enough to stick to the democratic ideals, at times it has also been trying to project itself as the democratic player of the game. All these require a fairly acrobatic stance, which Sangh combine has in abundance. It also has the advantage of having multiple different organisations as its progeny, which amongst them undertakes and implements different facts of its politics, some of which may be contradictory to each other at times. At times they may also take positions, which are opposed to each other.

It also has the responsibility to uphold the 'Golden Past', a particular interpretation of history of Ramayana. One realizes there are umpteen interpretations of the story of Ram, but Sangh combine will having nothing of that and will try to stifle the interpretations which are not very eulogising to the Lord. It also has the onus of promoting cow as 'Mother' irrespective of the fact that during its 'ideal Vedic period' it was essentially meant to be food and sacrificed accordingly. Taking the things too far in that direction sometimes some of their ideologues and leaders comc up with the cow based economy.

The Gujarat carnage saw the many hues of the Sangh combine, from orchestrating and coordinating the pogrom, to providing the umbrella to those perpetrating the crimes of commission and omission, to shedding tears on the violence, quite a job! While supporting the carnage by, looking the other way when one could put a brake it, some of their leaders went on to offer apologies, which had neither substance nor credibility. This balancing act is needed for many a reasons. On one hand they have to provide protective umbrella to those doing this duty for the Parivar, at the same time tears and apologies are to be proffered so that international image is kept up and also the future electoral prospects are safeguarded.

Since the present constitution, is committed to democracy and secularism, attempts were made to tamper with it in a very clever move, which are aimed to change it. It is noteworthy that there was a severe protest from people all around and so the move to change constitution had to be dropped.

Matters are further compounded when one sees that many other electoral outfits have also indulged in communalism, riots have taken place under their regime and they had not been principled enough in these situations. So what distinguishes the communalism of BJP from the rest is another question dogging the socially oriented people.

# 14

# Veer Savarkar : Brave by Half

The film on Savarkar is due to be released shortly (2001). The film even before its release has created lot of ripples of excitement. It may be probably the first major venture eulogising the pioneer of Hindutva ideology. One is aware that any objective discussion on Savarkar is filled with lot of emotional outbursts as he has been iconised amongst sections of population as the brave freedom fighter. He also gets the prefix of 'Swatantra Veer' (Brave warrior for Freedom), which is only half true. One needs to look at the trajectory of his life to understand this transition from anti-British revolutionary to the ideologue of Hindutva.

Savarkar's life underwent major transition during his confinement in Andamans. He was a changed man after the period of his jail life. He was a committed anti-British revolutionary prior to his deportment to Andamans but later he never associated with any thing even remotely sounding as anti-British.

He had gone to study law in London and for his anti-British stance he was denied the barristership. In England Savarkar formed 'Free Indian Society' committed to overthrowing British rule in India. That time he rejected the British proposal to give the undertaking not to participate in politics. His group had learnt the art of bomb making from a Russian revolutionary in Paris. One member of the group killed a top-ranking official in India Office (London) and was sentenced to death. For involvement in this and for another charges on him in Indian courts, Savarkar was arrested, sentenced and was to undergo life imprisonment. He was deported from England. The ship carrying him stopped at Marseilles, where he jumped into the sea and swam to the shore to claim asylum on French soil. He was captured back and was transported to Andamans for life imprisonment.

The conditions in Andman jail were very painful and he was tortured severely. It seems that conditions of jail life broke his spirits. Incidentally from 1920 Indian National Congress was asking for his unconditional release, but due to reasons best known to him Savarkar preferred to give a written undertaking to get released from the jail-"I hereby acknowledge that I had a fair trial and just sentence. I heartily abhor methods of violence resorted to in days gone by and I feel myself duty bound to uphold law and constitution (British, added) to the best of my powers and am willing to make the 'reform' a success in so far as I may be allowed to do so in future" (from facsimile of Savarkar's letter to British authorities, *Frontline*, April 7, 1995, p. 94).

The reforms he is referring to here are the Montague Chelmsford proposals of 1919, which did not satisfy the nationalist movement's demands. In response to this, as a trade off, the British Government released him under the condition that he will stay in Ratnagiri district in Bombay province and will seek permission of the government to leave the district. Also that he will not engage in any public or private political activities without the consent of the government. The period of conditions lasted till 1937, when the Congress ministry was sworn in. Subsequent to this he assumed the office of the President of Hindu Mahasabha. This aspect of his total surrender is totally hidden by the

Hindutva forces, they confer on him the epithet of 'Veer (brave) Savarkar'.

Why did British government release him? How is it that after his release the track of his politics totally changed and he came to adorn the mantle of ideologue Hindu Rashtra? How is it that later he never undertook any anti-British agitation? How is it that he never joined and supported the major movements of those times like Quit India movement? How is it that instead of being the part of freedom struggle, he chose to help the British in recruiting Indians for their army?

One can have ones' own inferences but his compromise with British hides lot of messages about the nature of his politics from then on. He did emerge as the undisputed leader of Hindu Mahasabha. In most of the times, post-1937, his politics was the polar opposite of national movement led by Gandhi and 'no support to Congress move' was his basic dictum. This can be best exemplified in the 1942 Quit India movement, when Gandhi gave the call for the people to leave the government jobs. Instead Savarkar issued the edict-"I issue this definite instruction to all Hindu Sanghathanists in general holding any post or position of vantage in the government services, should stick to them and continue to perform their regular duties". (Quoted in A. G. Noorani *Frontline*, Dec. 1, 1995).

Also working committee had passed a resolution on August 31, 1942 asking all Mahasabhaites to remain at their jobs. Savarkar does have the 'honour' of brewing Brahminical Hinduism with nationalism, and he was the first exponent of the doctrine of Hindutva.

Savarkar's initial anti-British struggles were very impressive but after assuming the role of the proponent of Hindutva his major energies were channelised in strengthening the politics of hate, formation of communal Hindu Mahasabha and helping RSS from distance.

Savarkar's work 'Hindutva: Who is Hindu' (1923) became and remains the basic text defining this political concept. With the simultaneous rise of Muslim communalism, in due course most of the Hindu consolidations took place by showing the fear of Muslims. This nationalism consolidated itself on the ground of the 'threatening other', but this threatening other was not the British imperialist colonizers whose rule the country was suffering but was the Muslim.

As an aside we should note here that Savarkar's anti-British struggles and anti-British activities totally ceased after his release by the British, and from then on all his guns were to be targeted against the Muslims. Savarkar argued (later on this became the ideological base of most of the Hindutva organisations)-"the Aryans who settled in India at the dawn of history already formed a nation, now embodied in the Hindus.... Hindus are bound together not only by the tie of the love they bear to a common fatherland and by the common blood that courses through their veins and keeps our hearts throbbing and our affection warm but also by the tie of the common homage we pay to our great civilisation, our Hindu culture." (*Hindutva*, p. 108).

Thus Hindutva according to him rests on three pillars: geographical unity, racial features and common culture. He further went on to elaborate the criterion for who is Hindu? According to him all those who regard this land as their fatherland and holy-land are the only ones who are Hindu and thereby the people to whom this land belongs. This led to the automatic interpretation that the Christians and the Muslims, whose holy places are in Jerusalem and Mecca are not on par with the 'Hindus' who 'own' this country. Initiating the theorising of the 'doubting of patriotism of Muslims', Savarkar states-"but besides culture the tie of common holy-land has at times proved stronger than the claims of a motherland. Look at Mohammedans: Mecca to them is a sterner reality than Delhi or Agra."

Savarkar's politics was rival to Gandhian politics. Gandhi-the representative of Indian Nationalism was branded by Savarkar as conciliator and appeaser of Muslims. Savarkar propounded that struggle for supremacy would begin after British left and that the Christians and Muslims were the real enemies who could be defeated only by "Hindutva". He maintained that this land belonged to Hindus and so by implication Muslims with holy land in Mecca and Christians with holy land in Jerusalem cannot have equal status to 'Hindus'.

It is also worth remembering, that murderer of Gandhi, Godse was his ardent follower. Savarkar himself was the co-accused in Gandhi murder, but was let off as Godse took the whole responsibility of this murder totally on his ownself.

While the film and the present projection of Savarkar is going on, one has also to assess his role in second half of his life. An honest assessment of our past will show us the different versions of nationalism and their political stance. The present hysteria of paying blind obeisance to Vinayak Damodar Savarkar should not come in the way of objectively assessing his changed role in later part of his life.

# 15

# History as the Battleground

History writing as an enterprise has gone through different phases. The struggle over different methods has become a major point of debate in our country, especially since the coming to power of BJP led coalition. It has been projected that the present (NCERT) history books are insensitive to the feeling of some communities; they have leftist orientation, they are 'one-sided' and so they need to be changed. Already process has begun and 'Historians' whose identity is being kept a secrete, are already working on new version of History, which is to be introduced in our schools and colleges. Professional history bodies have opposed this move. The tempers have risen to the extent that the then Prime Minister Mr. Vajpayee (*Indian Express*, 25 Nov. 2001) had to say that 'If History is one sided it should be changed', while President K.R. Narayanan had to caution that, 'We should not change History' (*Mid-Day*, 30th Dec. 2001), and the Minister in charge came down scathingly on the Historians who had written these books. Dr. Murli Manohar Joshi (*Hindu*, 30th Dec. 2001) said, "there are two types of terrorism facing the country. One, "intellectual terrorism", which, had "spread like a slow poison" because of the "wrong presentation of Indian history" by Left historians and was "more dangerous" than the "cross-border terrorism".

Why so much heat over this issue? Why is Dr. Joshi so incensed with the present NCERT History books? Why he could not even wait for the new History books being written by new 'Historians', which will be out in the market soon? Why certain portions from the prevalent books have been deleted in the middle of the year on an emergency basis?

In a way what is going on is shadow boxing. Two views of looking at society are clashing on the battleground of Historiography. J.S. Mill was the first who periodised Indian history into Hindu, Muslim and British (not Christian) periods. This kept being taught for long times. In this way of looking at the past religion is the sole marker of society. It is a communal view as communalism basically stands for looking at social phenomenon through the eyes of religion alone. It is another matter that Mill did not characterize the British colonial period as the Christian period. Here the predominance is given to the Kings and rulers and their motives are derived from their religious faiths. It leaves lot of events unexplained as to how Muslim Kings allied with Hindu nobles and Kings? (eg. Akbar+Mansingh against Rana Pratap+Hakim Khna Sur, Aurangzeb+Raja Jaising against Shivaji + Siddi Sambal) Why there were battles between Kings of same religions? It also does not explain as to why Mahmood Gazani had Tilak and Sondhi as his Generals and his army which attacked Somnath temple had good number of Hindu soldiers. It also does not explain as to why a Hindu King Raja Harshdev of Kashmir appointed an officer called Devottpatan Nayak (an officer who uproots the images of Gods). It goes without saying that Kings did not take up crusades, *Jihads* or *Dharmayudhas* for the spread of their religions but for the expansion of their empires. Barring post-Kalinga Ashok not many rulers used the state machinery for the spread of their religions.

This view of History glorifies the Kings belonging to the ruling communal outfits and denigrates the Kings of 'other' religions. Like if the King belonging to 'our' religion wins over new territories. He is valiant and brave. If the king belonging to 'other religion' comes to 'our ' territory it is projected as an act of cruelty and oppression. This view also cleverly hides the prevalent social hierarchies, the oppression of Shudras, landless peasant and women etc. This view of History goes very well with the colonial policies, which harped, on the divide and rule to prolong their rule here. This way of looking at history goes well with society where status quo is actively promoted by state authorities. In Pakistan, plagued by domination of Mullahs in state policies, more so from the era of Zia Ul Haq, the basis of colonial Historiography has not much changed and the History begins with Harappa and then takes a straight jump to the Muslim rule in Sind centuries later, period belonging to Hindu kings has been deleted from the books presumably because it hurts the sentiments of the Mullahs ruling the roost.

In India, post-colonial period, attempts were made to change the communal orientation of History. The process of change has not been complete. But the direction was towards introducing rational view of History as far as possible. In this attempt the best efforts were after the formation of NCERT in 1961. Amongst rational historians, professional historians, the attempt is to look at the history and society from multifaceted angel, religion not being the only determinant of analysis. Here the emphasis is on the sources and the interpretation of sources is done in conjunction with other parallel information's, literature of the time, evolution of language etc. It is not that this science of History has reached its acme, what is important is that the attempt has been in this direction. Many a professional Historians who emerged and earned reputation and name in their disciplines had largely been sympathetic to progressive and left orientation, but surely there are an equal number of non-left rational historians. But as far as their Historiography is concerned their contribution has been a landmark in professional excellence by any standards. Some of these are Romila Thapar, Irfan Habib, K.N. Panikkar, Arjun Dev, R.S. Sharma, and Bipan Chandra, etc.

So where is the problem. Why Dr. Joshi thinks that these historians are worse than the terrorists? Why he thinks that this Rational History has poisoned the minds of society? The answer to this question lies in Dr. Joshi's commitment to the ideology of Hindutva, which aims at Hindu Rashtra. In contrast to Secular Democratic India, the outcome of our freedom struggle and enshrined in our constitution, Hindu Rashtra aims at a society which is inheritor of the social values and social structure of pre-modern times. It is upholder of social relationships outlined in the Holy Hindu books like *Manusmriti*, etc. Here is the basic conflict. On one side a process of social transformation towards liberty, equality and community, a breaking of the birth based hierarchies and on the other the aim to have a society based on birth-based hierarchies of caste and gender as reflected in the Hindu Holy scriptures. A rational view of History as attempted in the NCERT books aim to raise the questions of caste and gender hierarchy, it tries to look at the society beyond the religion of rulers and so promotes a way of thinking which is capable of questioning the social relationships. This view is dangerous to the monolithic projection of religious communities, held by communal view.

That's why the history as taught in Pakistan has adopted the communal view, that's why the attempts are on to undo this rational method in India. The effort is to introduce and adopt the 'model' of RSS shakha history to be as the 'national' view. In this view the pages of Hindu warriors winning and demolishing other's land and kingdoms are golden pages. In this, the period when caste system was at its peak, the gender injustice was at peak is golden. In this view the society is one homogenous mass and rivers of milk and honey are flowing, the kings are great because they respect the Brahmins and give them generous gifts. The source of King's wealth, the sweat of shudra peasant is not to be registered as it will upset the applecart of status quo. In this view the nation building has been done by the glorious RSS and Hindu nationalists like Hedgewar, Golwalkar, Savarkar and Godse (the last name is not projected assertively but should be a logical continuation of the Hindu Rashtra politics), here the modernizer of India, (which resulted in breaking of status quo to some extent), Nehru, is a villain as he brought in 'western' values in our society, and as per this partition of the country took place due to Gandhi's appeasement of Muslims, here the RSS and Hindu nationalists got us the Freedom while the Indian nationalists were in jails to enjoy the five star luxuries offered to them by the British. So why wait till the new books on these lines become our new Gita's or Bible's?

We cannot tolerate that the then beef mention in Vedas that was eaten in Vedic times, as it weakens the emotive appeal of our Hindutva movement. Here we can not tolerate the mention of the fact that caste system was oppressive to Shudras. In this we cannot permit the pages in the books, which mention that around the place of Ram's birth, Ayodhya, there is no evidence of human habitation during the period when he is supposed to have lived. So along with these we have also to tear the pages of books, which mention about the plundering acts of Hindu kings, as Hindu kings can do no wrong, contrary to the fact that plundering other kings territory was a 'normal' operation for kings armies irrespective of their religion.

# 16

# Many Ramayana's

Recently, (Feb. 2001), in one of the less publicised incidents in Mumbai, one roving bookseller was roughed up by Sangh Parivar (Parivar) activists at a meeting to commemorate the birth anniversary of Dr. Babasaheb Ambedkar. The charge against the bookseller was that he was selling books, which are offensive to the Hindu gods. One of the books to which they objected strongly was Periyar Ramasami's, "True Ramayan". As per the SP activists this book insults Lord Ram and other revered figures of Hindu pantheon.

It is not long ago that in the aftermath of Babri demolition Sahmat exhibition on different versions of Ramayana (Story of Ram) was attacked by Parivar goons as one of the panels based on Jataka (Buddhist version) showed Ram and Sita as brother and sister. Also the fellow travellers of Parivar politics, the Shiv Sainiks of Mumbai's mini Hitler Bal Thackeray, adopted their usual strong arm techniques to protest when Dr. Ambedkar's book 'Riddles of Ram and Krishna' was published by the Maharashtra Government.

It is known that there are hundreds of versions of Ramayan, Buddhist, Jain, Brahminical (Valmiki). And again there are different interpretations of the prevalent Valmiki Ramayana, which are not to the liking of the currently offensive politics of Hindutva in whose service the vandals of Parivar break the poster exibitions or rough up the booksellers. Here one is not going into the issue of liberal Hindus of SP variety who criticize the fanatic Muslims on the ground that they become charged up whenever someone insults Prophet Mohammad, while as the Hindus are inherently liberal they do not indulge in any violent protest.

Ram Katha (Story of Ram) has various versions and surprisingly one can see the correlation between the class-caste aspirations of the narration-interpretation. In post-Brahminical Buddhist Dashrath Jataka, Sita is projected both as sister and wife of Ram. As per this version Dashrath is King not of Ayodhya but of Varanasi. The marriage of sister and brother is part of the tradition of glorious Kshtriya clans who wanted to maintain their caste and clan purity. This Jataka tale shows Ram to be the follower of Buddha. Similarly in Jain versions of Ramayan's project, Ram as the propagator of anti-Brahminical Jain values, especially as a follower of non-violence. What do both Buddhist and Jain version have in common is that in these Ravana is not shown as a villain but a great soul dedicated to quest of knowledge and as a spiritual soul, with majestic commands over passions, a sage and a responsible ruler. Popular and prevalent 'Women's Ramayan Songs' (of Telugu Brahmin Women), keep the women's concern as the central theme and present an alternate perspective. These songs present Sita as finally victorious over Ram and in these Surpanakha succeeds in taking revenge over Ram.

In recent times Jotiba Phule who stood more with the interests of Dalits and women, was amongst the first ones to interpret this mythological tale from the perspective of those subjugated by Brahminism. Phule's interpretation of the Ram story in a way forms a partial base of the Ramayan interpretations of Ambedkar and Periyar also. Phule points out that Brahmins were descendents of conquering Indo-Europeans who overturned the original egalitarian society and forbade the conquered from studying texts. His mythology is woven around King Bali, who could invoke the image of peasant community. Needless to say his murder by Lord Ram from behind is condemned and is seen as an act of subjugation of lower castes by the upper castes. And Ram is seen as an avatar of Vishnu out to conquer this land from the Rakshasas for establishing the hegemony of Brahminical values of caste and gender hierarchy.

Dr. Ambedkar and Periyar's commentaries are more an alternative reading of the Valmiki's text rather than a separate version. There is a good deal of overlap in the interpretation of both. Dr. Ambedkar focuses his attention on the issues pertaining to Ram's killing of Shambuk for violating the prevalent Brahminical norm where a low caste has no right to do penance, *tapasya*. Like Phule he also castigates Lord Ram for murdering the popular folk king Bali. He questions Ram's act of taking Sita's *agnipariksha*, trial by fire, and his attitude towards her. After defeating Ravan he tells Sita that he had done all this battle not to get her released but to restore his own honour, and his banishing her in response to the rumours about her chastity when she was pregnant comes for severest criticism from Ambedkar.

Periyar is basically taking the same line but in his interpretation the North Indian Brahminical onslaught-South Indian low caste resistance becomes the central theme. Periyar the initiator of Self Respect Movement was the pioneer of secularisation process in Tamil Nadu. In one of the movements, which is less known, on the lines of Dr. Ambedkar burning *Manusmriti*, he planned to burn the photo of Ram as for him Ram symbolised the imposition of Brahminical norms on the South Indian low caste. This was a part of his campaign against Brahminical Hinduism, (which is the base of the current Hindutva onslaught), for assertion of Tamil, Dalit identity. According to him the Ramayan story was a thinly disguised historical account of how caste ridden,

Sanskritic, upper caste North Indians led by Ram subjugated low caste South Indians. He identifies Ravana as the monarch of ancient Dravidians, who abducted Sita, primarily to take revenge against the mutilation and insult of his sister Surpanakha. Ravana is practitioner of Bhakti, and is a virtuous man,

The latest version of Ramayan to be popularised, and this one sends bouquets of roses to the Parivar followers, was that of 'Maharshi' Ramanand Sagar's tele serial Ramayan, which went many steps further than the Valmiki Ramayan in glorifying Ram and the accompanying values. As an example here Sita herself is keen to be banished to jungle by her Lord and master to ensure that people don't talk ill of Him. And currently this is the bottom line, and any deviation from such blind obeisance comes for severe reprimand from the Parivar. This selection of Ram and this version of Ramayan is no coincidence for the Parivar. It is very clear that this icon best conveys its agenda of subjugating the rights of Dalit-Bahujan, women, and adivasis. So starting from Savarkar who called Ram as the Monarch of Great Hindu race down to the Ramjanmbhumi campaign, which acted as the electoral goldmine for Parivar, Ram has to be its central figure.

And thus any other version, any different reading of Ramayana will be opposed tooth and nail by the 'tolerant Hinduism', as that stands opposed to the political message of Sangh Parivar.

# 17

# Political Wine in a Cultural Bottle

Recently (Jan 2000) Gujarat government lifted the fourteen-year-old ban on the government employees on joining the RSS. As such government employees are barred from joining the political organisations. As per one of the orders issued in 1966 RSS and Jamaat-e-Islami both were treated in the same category and the government employees were barred from being a part of these outfits. Since then UP government has also lifted this ban and RSS functionaries are going hammer and tongs on getting this ban lifted at all India level. While some opportunist secular politicians are keeping deliberate mum on the issue being more engrossed on the issue of their political survival some other like Karunanidhi, belonging to a party which began as an anti-Brahmin movement, are willing to play the power game and are issuing the good 'social' certificate to the father of their political ally at the centre. RSS products like Advani are facilitating it, to ensure that their alma mater expands further through the legal and other assistance, which at present can be extracted due to the fact of their being in power in the central government.

### Rashtriya Swayamsevak Sangh—The Organisation

As is well known RSS began as a vehicle of the ideology of Hindutva with the goal to establish Hindu Rashtra in

India. For achieving its goal it preferred to train its recruits on an ideological ground and kept aloof from the freedom struggle and politics of Indian nationalism that aimed at the Independence of the country from the clutches of British colonial powers. Its central theme was that this country belongs to the Hindus. Muslims, Christians and the Communists are the internal threat to the country and so the Hindus should get organised under the RSS to achieve the goal of Hindu Rashtra: a nation state based on Brahminical Hinduism. The ideologues of RSS drew heavy inspiration from the fascist ideology of Mussolini and the Nazism of Hitler. Their nationalism is based on the hatred of other religions like the nationalism of Hitler, which was based on hatred of other races. RSS projected itself as a cultural body but was most visible around the events related to communal violence.

Its first foray in to the electoral politics began when it helped in floating Bhartiya Jana Sangh, the previous avatar of BJP. It also went on to float many other bodies like Bharatiya Majdur Sangh, Vishwa Hindu Parishad, Bajrang Dal, Adivasi Kalyan Ashram, Rashtrasevika Samiti and a hoard of others. Lately it and its progenies singly and jointly have started floating different issue based organisations like Hindu Munnani, Hindu Jagaran Manch and Kashi Sanskratik Raksha Sangharsh Samiti, etc.

**RSS in Action**

The most striking part of its organising technique was manifest after the murder of Mahatma Gandhi by Nathuram Godse. Godse who had worked as a pracharak of RSS for long years was at that time secretary of Pune branch of Hindu Mahasabha. He was also editing a paper called as Hindu Rashtra. After Gandhiji's murder, followers of RSS distributed sweets and openly celebrated the murder of the father of the Nation. (*Outlook*, April 1998) There was a popular perception that Godse was a part of RSS and accordingly RSS was banned. At his trial Godse denied his being a part of RSS to protect this organisation from the wrath of legal action. In the interview his brother conceded that they were always part of RSS and Nathuram denied this fact in the trial to protect the RSS from the wrath of legal action (*Times of India*, 25th Jan 1998). RSS could get away with Gandhiji's murder, as it does not keep any written record of its membership. The ban was lifted on the ground that henceforth it would keep a proper record of its members. But apparently all those who follow the RSS shakha are not entered in the record as they are designated as deemed members only. This arrangement has been very convenient for this body as it helps to protect the parent body from the anti-legal acts of its followers.

The second ban on RSS came during the emergency when it joined the Jaya Prakash Narayan movement. The major ban on it came in the wake of Babri demolition when different wings of RSS went on the rampage to destroy the Babri Mosque, presumably to build a Ram Temple as according to their 'records' Lord Ram was born precisely at that spot millenniums ago. Apparently even now the record of membership is not kept properly, if kept at all, with the result that the clear association between the breakers and violators of law and this body cannot be proved. All the same it came out from the ban unscathed and with more venom in its activities.

**Communal Violence and RSS**

At least five inquiry commissions have indicated about the role of RSS in communal violence more than just spreading communal hatred, which is its 'core level' work. Jagamohan Reddy (Ahmedabad1969), Madon (Bhivandi

Jalgaon), Vithayathil (Tellicherry 1971), Venugopal (Kanniyakumari 1982) and Jamshedpur riot (1990) reports point out the complicity of RSS functionaries in the riots (Communalism Combat, March 98). One does not know what are the cultural activities (Culture as understood so far) as popularly understood in the field of art, literature, performing arts, theatre, cinema, music, painting, etc. in which this 'cultural organisation' is contributing. Of course this statement is partly wrong as one has witnessed their 'intervention' in the cultural arena in the form of attack on Husain's paintings, attacks on Sahmat exhibitions, attack on the film-sets shooting *Water* and so many such 'cultural expressions' by its 'militant' followers'. On the 'positive' side we have witnessed them doing 'promotion' of Taslima Nasreen's book *Lajja*. Also one has seen them spreading venom against others' religion, something which is not a part of 'Indian Culture' as understood by average Indian in the mould of Indian nationalism.

**Politics as Culture**

Of course RSS has been an active player of the politics, but with a difference. It operates through its 'progenies'; it influences media through its own publications *Panchjanya* and *Organiser*, leading the pack of its media intervention. One also remembers it offshoot Bharatiya Jana Sangh (BJS) pulling out of the Janata Party in late 70s when the BJS politicians refused to withdraw from their RSS affiliation. The Ram Janmbhoomi campaign, which brought BJP to power was initiated and sustained by it directly and also by its another progeny the VHP before the 'genuinely secular' BJP took it over and plunged the country into a new era of communal holocaust. Even its direct interventions in the day to day running of the government are visible to all and sundry. It has the 'real' control' even on the electoral process: distribution of tickets etc. RSS volunteers are active not only in relief and rehabilitation but also in active election campaigning.

It has a deeper politics, that of Hindu Rashtra. Hindu Rashtra is a concept of the nation, which derives its foundation from the narrow concept of religion and aims to abolish democracy and liberalism from the face of the country. Hindutva is its political slogan, which confuses the average person into believing as if it is some sort of a religion, which it is not. It is in pursuance of this deeper goal that RSS combines its activities through different organisations. It is all pervading virus threatening to engulf the hard won freedom and democracy. It is for this that it has devised the deceptive term cultural nationalism for its project of a Hindu Nation.

**RSS—The Politics as Deceit**

RSS has been the biggest player on the political arena from last two decades. One must 'admire' that it operates in such a way that even without direct political interference most of the time it can achieve the same through different members of it family, the Sangh Parivar. As and when convenient it does not hesitate to bring up new organisations to achieve its long term and short term goals. And in this respect its application of the 'division of labour', the fluid overlapping caste system (BJP, VHP, Bajarang Dal, Adivasi Kalyan Ashram etc.) takes it far ahead in the race for communalising the country and simultaneously eroding the democratic space by and by.

Currently the ban on government servants joining the body was on two grounds–one it being the major communal body and two it being the fountainhead of the Hindutva politics. By its clever mechanisms it has used the democratic liberties to work towards a society where democratic liberties themselves will be made to occupy the dark corner of the 'museum of the undesirable western values'. One presumes the ideologues of the Hindu Right, emboldened by their recent 'successes' of alliance politics might have started working towards that. And in this project of theirs they are being well assisted by the politicians of different hues especially those who were earlier claiming to be the torch-bearers of secularism.

# 18

# Looming Saffron Threat and Electoral Choices

The electoral arena in the decade of 90s has taken a qualitative turn for the worse. The earlier electoral equation Congress vis-a-vis the Janata Dal/Janata Party and its allies have been replaced by a triangle with BJP and later BJP and its allies as the base of the triangle. Of the two other arms of the triangle one is the Congress and other is constituted by the now declining Third Front. Barring the left parties, whose secular and democratic credentials are strong, and the other earlier constituents of Third Front who mostly stood by secular and democratic ground (though many of these have shown cracks in this lately), both the major constituents of the electoral battlefield are tainted with communalism of different varieties. It is in this context that the role of left in singling out BJP as the communal force, to be isolated and dumped on priority basis has come for criticism amongst different friends and groups on the liberal, progressive and left spectrum. These radical elements, bringing to our attention the gory deeds of Congress in subtly tolerating communalism, being the main agency of anti-Sikh communal violence and its role in colluding with the Sangh Parivar in demolition of Babri mosque and the anti-Muslim pogroms, have been advocating the maintaining of equidistance from BJP and Congress. What are the pitfalls of this equidistance thesis?

Right since its inception the main thrust of Indian National Congress has been to struggle for democratic secular India. At a formal level this central concern of the Congress stood on this ground with innumerable compromises and weaknesses. Though there have been major changes in the trajectory of the Congress during the last 11 decades of its existence, this single principle has been kept at the core of the policies, though at formal level. The same got enshrined also in the Indian Constitution, which accepted the principles of liberty, equality and fraternity, and also brought into the Constitution the concept of a secular state right from the beginning, though this word was added into the Constitution much later.

Despite this main current, there has always been a weakness to accommodate and tolerate the communal elements more so Hindu communal elements. Some of the major leaders of the Congress had strong streaks of Hindu nationalism, for instance, Lala Lajpat Rai, Madan Mohan Malaviya, and Munje (who was one of the founders of RSS also)! Many a leaders of Hindu Mahasabha were also members of the Congress. The first sarsangh chalak (supreme dictator) of RSS K. B. Hedgewar was formally in the Congress till 1934 after which he concentrated exclusively on building the fountainhead of Hindu communalism, the RSS.

The Congress in pre-independence time acted as a platform. The dominant part of the platform was secular and democratic as represented in the leadership of Mahatma Gandhi and Pandit Nehru. But undoubtedly the Hindu communal elements remaining within the Congress put pressure on it from inside to supplement the agenda of Hindu Mahasabha and the RSS, to act as the opposite and parallel of Muslim communalism which was represented predominantly by Muslim League.

With partition, the formation of Pakistan and migration of the Muslim elite to Pakistan, Muslim communalism in a way got deflated. But it did continue to survive in the Indian polity, assuming stronger postures at crucial times like Shah Bano case, etc. to provide the much needed provocation to the Hindu communalism. The Congress underwent a major transformation in the mid-1960s. Though it continued to pay strong lip-service to the secular rhetoric, apart from appeasing the fundamentalist sections of Muslim community, it did not do much to ameliorate the conditions of minorities.

Also by this time the state apparatus was being infiltrated by Hindu communal elements, the RSS trainees, who started giving a Hindu slant to the secular state policies at the grass roots level. It is due to these factors that Muslims began to be discriminated against in jobs, etc. They also became victims of anti-Muslim violence led by Hindu communal organisations and supported and abetted by the state and exonerated by the Congress. A large section of Congress leadership was not very principled as far as the secular ethos was concerned and did not have any qualms in compromising with and promoting Hindu communalism.

During these years the principal project of the Congress was to build the Indian state as per the Indian Constitution. During this process it started subjugating ethnic and regional aspiration and imposed an 'Indian' identity and laws on many ethnic groups and regions by force. The Congress pursued the policy of relentless centralisation and intervened in state affairs at every minor pretext. This led to situations of insurgency in the north-east, Kashmir and Punjab. The anti-Sikh pogroms conducted by the Congress in 1984 can be characterised to belong to this category of repression of ethnic aspirations of Sikhs. They have to be contrasted with the anti-Muslim violence whose ideological roots lie in the concept of Hindu Rashtra. With intense repression in these states, the situation worsened and later in Kashmir and Punjab the situation was communalised with the Hindu-Muslim, Hindu-Sikh being the two poles of this move of the Congress government. Massive anti-Sikh pogroms took place after the murder of Indira Gandhi. Congress communalism is pragmatic and has been used by it times again to 'solve' some other problem, like suppressing the ethno-regional aspirations.

The BJP is the political arm of Sangh Parivar. By implication it is an offshoot of RSS. The internal dynamics of operation of Sangh Parivar is fairly uniform for all its organisations. The basic premiss of RSS is to work towards the goal of Hindu Rashtra. This just does not mean that since the majority of people living in this country are Hindus, so it should be or is a Hindu Rashtra. This concept emerged as the political project of the declining classes (Zamindars, rajas of riyas, etc. and the brahmins).

This concept was paralleled and opposed to the concept of Muslim state, which represented the political aspirations of Muslim jagirdars and the elite. Hindu Rashtra was defined as a political concept whose politics is Hindutva, first by Savarkar (Hindu Mahasabha) and later on refined by M S Golwalkar, the second sarsangh chalak (supremo) of RSS. This is a type of nationalism, which while giving the illusion of being based on religion, is based on the hatred of others' religion. This is akin to race-based nationalism of the Nazis (Hitler), fascists (Mussolini, Italy) or the fundamentalist states like Ayatollah Khoemeni's Iran or Afghanistan under the Taliban. These nationalisms are opposed to the principles of liberty, equality, fraternity, and the concept of liberalism. They are supporters of status quo and favour the unequal hierarchies which are prevalent in society. In addition the concept of this nationalism aims to impose the uniform elite culture on the whole society. As per the core ideology of RSS, India is a Hindu Rashtra since the time Aryans stepped into this land and the 'aliens' who came here, the Muslim and Christian British have brought ignominy to the Hindu society. Now under leadership of RSS/Sangh Parivar, the whole of Hindu nation has to get organised to restore past glory.

The previous *avatar* of BJP, the Bharatiya Jan Sangh was founded by Shyama Prasad Mukherjee, a leader of Hindu Mahasabha, and was totally taken over by the RSS trained volunteers. Its major agenda (1951) was induction of nuclear weapons, opposition to public sector and co-operative farming. The major campaigns it undertook were 'ban cow-slaughter' and 'Indianisation of Muslims'. Meanwhile RSS was actively communalising the social space leading to communal violence beginning from Jabalpur (1962) communal riot. These riots went of becoming more and more ghastly. In addition to intimidating and ghettoising the Muslim community they started consolidating the elite Hindus behind RSS/BJS. After joining the JP-led movement (1974) RSS/BJP gained social respectability and BJS emerged as the major component of the Janata Party formed in the wake of lifting of emergency. The BJS members refused to withdraw their membership of RSS leading to the collapse of Janata Party. BJS re-emerged as BJP in 1980.

From 1986 it took over the aggressive agenda of Hindu Rashtra through the Ram Janmabhoomi campaign leading to the demolition of Babri Mosque, post-demolition communal violence, etc. Most of the inquiry commission reports on communal violence (Jagmohan Reddy, Justice Madon, Vithayathil, Shrikrishna and Venugopal) have proved without any shadow of doubt that RSS/SP have been the major actors in anti-Muslim communal violence. Similarly the National Human Rights Commission, National Minorities Commission and the Human Rights groups have highlighted the role of most of the progenies of RSS in anti-Christian violence.

Lately, after realising that it cannot grab the power at the centre on its own (on the plank of communal issues), the BJP has 'cleverly' been talking of a national agenda of governance and a national democratic alliance to woo the regional parties, whose narrow regional interests and tubular vision does not permit them to see the core communal project of the BJP. This democratic posture of BJP is merely for the sake of gradually increasing its vote bank/social base to be able to come to power at centre on its own and that's when the agenda of Hindu Rashtra 'in toto' will be unleashed on society. Till then the decent looking agenda will keep getting sprinkled with the hidden agendas. In the long term this elite, middle class party will freeze society in the existent social dynamics, taking away the rights of the exploited, oppressed and those on lower rungs of hierarchy to struggle for social, economic and gender justice. The communalism of BJP is a cover for the slow growing fascism, with the aim of foisting brahminical Hinduism based politics on the country. In words of Aijaz Ahmed its is a programmatic communalism. A programme to bring in a different notion of state, in order to do away with democracy and liberalism.

Seen in this light amongst all the electoral parties BJP is the only party, which is a political wing of some other organisation (RSS). As seen in the past and as evident in its inner structure the RSS control over the party is complete due to the RSS-trained cadres being the main human agency of BJP. Despite contradictions the basic goal of Hindu Rashtra is not negotiable as far as SP is concerned. And that's what sets it apart from every other electoral outfit. It is not to say the other parties are desirable, ideal and capable of sustaining the secular democratic programme. We have seen that the Congress, with ease, could impose emergency and various anti-democratic legislations time and again. It has compromised and aided SP communalism a number of times; the other parties have also shown manifest inadequacies as far as perusal of democratic principles are concerned. But all said and done none of them is driven by the engine of a brahminical Hinduism based nationalism akin to race-based nationalism or Muslim religion-based nationalism. This is what makes BJP a different cup of tea (nay poison) setting it apart from other electoral outfits.

The SP movement is a fascist variant with a number of similarities to European fascism, which got strengthened after fearing dalit OBC assertion in 1990s (post-Mandal). It projects national interest over the interest of the people, has seeds of expansionism (Akhand Bharat), targets minorities to strengthen its social base (first Muslims then the Christians), glorifies the past as the sustaining force, is aggressive to the weaker sections of society and has a base mainly amongst urban middle class, upper caste and section of socially ascendant OBCs. It differs from the European variety of fascist parties in having a long gestation period, and having an ideologically self-sustaining organisation, the RSS as the controlling engine. In Germany, Hitler increased his social and electoral base in a quick fashion projecting the fear of strong workers' movement. The triangle there was communists, Hitler's national socialists (fascists) and the centrists, akin to the Congress here, the social democrats. In spite of seeing the methods and dangerous potential of Hitler, communists who were a substantial force, in a way followed the electoral policy of equidistance from social democrats (whom they called social fascists) and the national socialists (Hitler's party). They virtually ignored the Nazis and thought that it was a farcical force, which could be easily tackled even if they came to power. Hitler had his own version of VHP and Bajrang Dal (the storm-troopers) whom communists thought Hitler would monitor and control once he was in power. Though Hitler did not have a majority, he was able to come to power through negotiations as the opponents had shifting and divided aims and were unable to focus on the real essentials of power while Nazis had unwavering aims and had a firm grasp on 'real politics'.

We will not go into the economic policies where there is a lot of overlap in the Congress and the BJP policies barring two major differences. One, as witnessed during the 13-month rule of BJP-led coalition, is that BJP is more influenced by the traders who are its major support base. Second, BJP's version of swadeshi supports the petty industrialist, with their much more backward labour relations and advocacy of firmer repression of workers. This is at one level relative and even other electoral parties may not have anything much better to offer. As we have seen the Congress has appeased Muslim fundamentalist leadership ignoring the interests of a large mass of minorities. It has communalised the Kashmir and Punjab issues to 'build' the bourgeois nation state in its own way. Indira was particularly shrewd to begin the use of communal card from 1980s, Rajiv did the same in Shah Bano case and opening the locks of Babri Mosque, Narasimha Rao was merrily fiddling when Ayodhya was getting decimated and most of the Congress governments have been mute spectators of the anti-Muslim pogroms. These are grave 'lapses' which show that secular policies are the first victim when it comes to keeping power intact. But in contrast the BJP and the SP are communalism personified (see Aijaz Ahmed, *EPW*, June 1, 1996, p. 1329). Communalism is not opportunism for them, it is their very *raison d'etre*, their core programme. Its manifestation will keep changing as per the situation. It is political wing of RSS, which is pursuing the goal of Hindu Rashtra in pursuance of which violence has been used like 'surgeon's knife' (M. S. Golwalkar) and the concept is the mix of fascist and fundamentalist state as demonstrated above. So despite the apparent similarities, at the core, Congress communalism is opportunist, BJP communalism is programmatic. Congress communalism at times has been employed at the service of building 'bourgeois nation state', BJP communal violence has been/and will be 'dedicated' to the building of Hindu Rashtra.

Taking advantage of the fragmentation of polity and rise of regional parties the BJP is doing its best to ally with the short sighted regional parties who, to preserve their regional power equations are overlooking the fascist/ communal core of the BJP. The rise of the BJP in the centre has dangerous portents, as with every rise, its hidden agenda becomes the part of government programme. The slogan 'defeat BJP' apart from being negative in itself also gives an indirect message that the only other electoral outfit, which may benefit from this, is the Congress, whose 'compromised secularism' is there for everybody to see. So the policy of maintaining equidistance from the Congress and the BJP is a better one, argue some friends.

Just because there is a dearth of parties with better secular and democratic credentials does not mean that one ends up supporting a party, whose fascist potential exists without any shadow of doubt. What if the Congress which time and again has used communalism to fulfil its ambitions of power, benefits from it? Surely it is an evil whose magnitude is many times lower than the dangers of BJP being in power.

The way to build egalitarian, just society is through the painful path of struggles of the oppressed sections. In a way, the whole rightward shift of the political language is due to the weakness and apparent absence of strong social movements. These movements of workers, dalits, adivasis, women and minorities being scattered as they are, are not able to reinforce each other and in turn are unable to influence the direction of the centrist political formations. One of the byproducts of the platform for secular democracy will be warding off the threat of fascist danger, in whatever guise it comes, while pursuing its goal of social secular democracy. This building of the platform of secular democracy and social justice is the long-term goal towards which the efforts have to begin right away. Most of the electoral parties cannot properly hold on to the secular and democratic principles. It is only such a platform based on the struggles of exploited weaker sections of society, which can not only build the egalitarian society with social justice but also during the course of its struggle can ensure that the centrist formations are forced to adopt secular and democratic principles on firmer grounds. Thus the 'Defeat BJP' slogan is like a fire fighting measure. Real efforts have to be focused towards much neglected social movements, towards building the bridges among them. These bridges are the boosters, which can and will enhance the total strength not in an additive fashion but by qualitatively transforming the very nature and social role of these groups.

# 19

# The Politics Behind Attempt to Review Constitution

During last few years (1998) a number of opinions have been put forward to modify and totally change the Indian Constitution. In one of the major congregations of the VHP's *Sants* and *Mahants*, a resolution was passed in its *Dharma Sansad* (Religious Parliament). This resolution said that Indian Constitution is an anti-Hindu Constitution and so it should be done away with and be substituted by the one based on the Hindu holy books. They also constituted a committee to formulate a Constitution based on Hindu scriptures. As per some newspaper reports they recommended that the universal adult franchise should be scrapped and the power of voting should be restricted only to the educated people, teachers and the Hindu holy seers. They should be the ones who will not only elect the Parliament but should also constitute the law making and implementing bodies. RSS *Sarsanghchalak* (Supremo) Mr. K. Sudarshan on his anointment (April 2000) as the RSS chief stated that Indian Constitution should be scrapped and be replaced by the one based on Hindu *Dharma Granths* (Holy Books).

The BJP led NDA Government at the centre appointed a commission to review the Constitution the mandate of which was left vague. Earlier there was also a talk of examining the possibilities of doing away with the parliamentary system and to bring in the presidential form of government. There was also a debate to fix the term of the members of the Lok Sabha for five years and to do away with the provisions of mid-term polls. The provision to bar citizens whose birthplace is outside India from holding the high offices was also contemplated.

Before we come to present moves to curb the democratic spirit of our Constitution we should register that even Hitler went in for major constitutional changes before he could impose the Fascist rule and cause havoc in Germany and major parts of Europe. In the same way many amendments were also brought into the Constitution in the early 70's which laid the ground for the imposition of emergency in 1975. But even those changes were much mild compared to what is being asserted today by different communal and fundamentalist groups, the conglomerate called Sangh Parivar. These current proposals have the potential of undoing the very foundations of our democracy carefully articulated by the founding fathers and nurtured by the Indian people.

**Making of Indian Constitution**

Prior to the formation of Constituent Assembly various acts of British parliament and state councils were in practice. The first in the series was The Indian Councils Act, 1892, which was brought in to being due to the pressures of Indian National Congress (INC). It brought in the representative character in the legislative council and removed some of the restrictions on its functioning. In 1906 INC kept *swaraj* as the goal. Later many a reforms, which did not satisfy the aspirations of Indian people fully were brought in succession-Minto-Morley Reforms, 1906-1908, Indian Councils Act, 1909, Montagu's Declaration, 1917, Monford report 1918, Govern-ment of India Act, 1919, and Government of India Act 1935. This last named act is the most significant as it endeavoured to give the written constitution to the country, but Indian people had no role in creating this.

Indian Constitution was formulated by the Constituent Assembly, which was representative of all the people and it involved careful effort aimed at incorporating the most enlightened aspects of most of the constitutions of the world. The Constituent Assembly was mainly an elected body with representatives of all the political parties and most of the eminent legal stalwarts were a part of this. It had representatives from states and the provinces and was fully sovereign of all external authority. It could abrogate or alter any law made by British parliament applying to India.

This assembly appointed number of committees to deal with different aspects of framing the constitution like Constitution committee, Union powers committee, committee on fundamental rights, Minorities etc. Recommendations of these committees were considered by the drafting committee, which was headed by Dr. Baba Saheb Ambedkar. A 'Constitutional Precedent' was prepared as the reference; this gave the salient texts of constitutions of over 60 countries. It was finalised in the backdrop of the situation when many countries, princely states and colonies were becoming and aspiring to become a modern nation state. For this assembly it was a challenge to come up with a document, which could ensure the representation of diverse interests of different communities. It had to ensure that starting from colonial legacy we should be able to lay the foundation of a state which is not only acceptable to different sections of people but also is democratic down to the core. It had to ensure the incorporation of the principles of liberty, equality, fraternity, social justice and welfarism in the same. Its emphasis was to be on the democratic principles while consideration was to be given to the plural and diverse nature of Indian society. Its first major achievement was to introduce the universal adult franchise, the basis of democracy.

### Aim to Restrict the Franchise

Dr. Ambedkar said in constituent assembly "by parliamentary democracy we mean 'one man, one vote.'" In contrast, in most of the fundamentalist countries like Iran, Afghanistan, Pakistan etc. the democratic institutions are not only conveniently done away with, but the downtrodden sections are also marginalised from the mainstream of society. The Mullahs and other vested interests rule the roost in the name of religion. They derive legitimacy from the selected/narrowly-interpreted parts of scriptures and impose other practices suitable to the interests of the elite by keeping the weaker sections out of the political processes. The proposals of the Indian fundamentalist organisations to restrict the franchise to the educated and Sadhus and Mahants is fairly close to these retrograde tendencies. The current argument that poor and illiterate are not capable of exercising their democratic options and can be bought over by corrupt politicians and is the most elitist way of humiliating the deprived and weaker sections of society. They do exercise their options very judiciously as seen in the results of different elections. It is only the communal parties who reject the right of the poor and illiterate. What is needed is to increase the democratic rights of these sections through education and empowerment. The present tirade against the illiterate is a motivated one aiming to bring in a religion based nationalism where only the elite will dominate and hegemonise the powers and privileges. The educated and religious elite, whatever their intentions may be, cannot represent the aspirations of all the people.

### Presidential Model of Government

The current opinion to revise the Indian Constitution, so as to have the presidential system should be viewed in the light of its initial debates on the same issue. During the formulation of our Constitution this point did come up and the founding fathers did consider it in all seriousness before rejecting it. The argument was that ours is a diverse country having people with many cultures, religions, languages and ethnicity, living in different parts of the country. The elements of parliamentary system were already present in the rudimentary form as established by the British and that the parliamentary model avoids the arbitrariness of the presidential system. To recapitulate, the presidential form depends on the fixed term of the house (Lok Sabha). The President is close to irremovable and he chooses his executives (ministers) from the general citizenry who are not answerable to the house of the representatives in contrast to the parliamentary form where the ministers are generally the members of the either house, except for brief periods at the best. These members are much more answerable than the handpicked ones, chosen by the will of the President. Again the presidential form and the fixed term for the Lok Sabha is being demanded by those for whom 'stability' is more important than accountability to the people, who should be the sovereigns in a democracy.

Similarly there is a talk to bring in 'two party system'. Two party systems if it evolves as a part of democratic process will be a welcome phenomenon, but then it has to emerge out of the grass root realities. Its imposition on the people will be counterproductive. The present multiparty system is a real reflection of the ground realities. It represents the diverse pulls and pressures of different sections of society. As we have pointed out above, ours is a plural society in more ways than one. In such a society multiparty system is but natural till a time when substantial development and progress ensures the betterment of people of our country.

As a matter of fact what we need is an improvement in the representative character of our system. This can be achieved by ensuring the increased accountability of the elected representatives to the people. The present pattern is ensuring that the elected representatives can remain aloof from the citizens. Those who can get elected are the ones who have the vast sums of money at their command and who once having got elected can remain entrenched in their own world of manipulations and keep doing further politicking for enhancement of their own social, economic and political interests.

**Western Influence**

There is a difference between western and modern values, though there may be an overlap between the two. The concept of democracy and secularism began with the industrial revolution. The newer formations brought the concept of liberty, equality and fraternity to replace the Feudal values of birth-based social, economic and gender hierarchies. These were rigid and inflexible because of which the poor peasants, in our case the *shudras*, were tied to the land as semi-bonded labour with very little independent rights. They were under the political control of *Zamindars* and social control of priests, i.e., mainly Brahmins. Similarly patriarchal notions were deep rooted and the right of men over the lives of women was absolute. Women were also regarded as the property of men. The industrial revolution changed this scene totally. This phenomenon occurred first in many western countries. In India with industrialisation the same trends started occurring and along with the freedom struggle there went on a process of transition in social values from that of feudal times to the ones of industrial times. This transition is not complete and the present aspiration and longing is for the relations based on equality. And our Constitution is based on these modern values of formal equality, and gives us space for striving to achieve the real equality through democratic struggles.

The 'Hindu Constitution' as being demanded by the members of Sangh Parivar (SP) is the assertion for abolishing these values of formal equality and oppression. Hinduism as presented and projected by SP is the one based on inequality. Most of the ideologues of RSS and SP uphold the *Manusmriti*. The second Sar Sanghchalak of RSS, Mr. M.S. Golwalkar wrote in his book *Bunch of Thoughts* that Manu has been the first and greatest ever law-maker of the world and his laws are of eternal nature, which were applicable not only for that time but are and will be relevant for all the times to come. By now most of us are aware that *Manusmriti* forbids *shudras* to go in for study and if they do dare to go in for that they have to be suitably punished or have to face the fate of Ekalavaya, an Adivasi boy for whom archery was prohibited but he learnt the same on his own and as a punishment his thumb was cut. The status of women in this system is also very low and they are advised to serve their husbands in an unquestioning manner, and of course they too are denied education as for them, serving husband is equal to learning process. Though the present language of Sangh Parivar is fairly sophisticated the sum and substance of it remains the same. That's why the Chairman of the drafting committee of Indian Constitution Dr. Baba Saheb Ambedkar went on to burn the *Manusmriti*. The present chief of RSS Mr. Sudarshan is more forthright in his demand for re-imposition of the laws of Manu when he says that the present Constitution should be scrapped and the one based on Hindu *Dharma Granthas* should be brought in. Here the polar opposition between the value system of Dr. Ambedkar (burning *Manusmriti* and drafting the Indian Constitution) and the epitome of SP politics Mr. Sudarshan (calling for scraping the constitution and demanding for Dharma Granthas like *Manusmriti*, based norms) is more than obvious. The other ideologues of SP are cleverer and they say the similar thing with more attractive and modern looking language.

Sangh Parivar politicians and ideologues are the political forces, which in the wake of Babri demolition were openly asserting that their loyalty is more to Lord Ram than to Indian Constitution. One can very well see that this sort of play with emotions in the name of Lord Ram has nothing to do with the good of society but only for the sake of political power. These fundamentalist political formations like SP have no democratic aspirations. In the wake of Babri demolition they violated all the norms and rule in the Indian Constitution and broke the promises of protection of the Masjid given to the Supreme Court. As pointed out above fundamentalists across the countries have an agenda similar to each other in its retrograde values and pre-modern systems being brought in under the attractive garb of 'our glorious heritage' and 'cultural nationalism'.

**Indian Constitution: Anti-Hindu!**

Indian Constitution as we have seen above was made by the broad based principle of democratic representation. It was made by the constituent assembly, which had people from all the religions. The primary identity, which the founding fathers of Constitution emphasised, was the Indian identity and not the one based on this that or the other religion. It declared that India will not have a state religion and in the eyes of the law all the religions will have equal status. At social level people will have the liberty to follow their own religion or not to follow any religion depending on their own faith and belief. As a commitment to respect for all the religions, which our multi-cultural society has, equal status was accorded to all the religions. All in all the principles of a secular state were incorporated in an uncompromising manner. Also special provisions were made for the protection of the rights of minorities. This is not against any of the religion.

But then why SP members are saying that it is anti-Hindu. The ideology of SP is that India should be a Hindu Rashtra and should be based on Hindutva. Hindutva is not a religion but is a politics based on the values of Brahmanism, i.e., inequality and discrimination on the basis of birth. It represents the interests of the elite section of Hindus, the upper castes and the upper classes, to the exclusion of low castes and the minorities. For the elite this Constitution means a threat to their centuries long 'reservation' on socio-economic privileges, for them it means that the birth-based inequalities are no more recognised. On the contrary there is affirmative action in the Constitution, which this elite section feels as a pampering to low castes and minorities. Since the implementation of Mandal Commission this elite section has come out more aggressively under the banner of SP to reassert their hegemony and they see the present Constitution as an obstacle to their interests. And that's why they are projecting this secular Constitution, which respects all the religions equally, as an anti-Hindu religion.

**Indian Constitution has Failed Us!**

Indian Constitution represents the aspirations of Indian people in general and in its preamble it declares that India is a Sovereign, Socialist, Secular and Democratic Republic. Accordingly the goal of the state should be to secure for all its citizens social, economic and political justice; liberty of thought, expression, belief, faith and worship; equality of status and opportunity; and fraternity, assurance of dignity of the individual and the unity and integrity of the nation. Despite these provisions being there, our society is riddled with poverty, hunger, disease and misery. It is riddled with oppression of Dalits, Adivasis, minorities, women and workers. Even the founding fathers of Constitution were clear that Constitution on its own cannot deliver social justice and a lot depends on those who are in the seat of power in executive, judiciary and bureaucracy to ensure the deliverance of provisions of the Constitution.

It is precisely for this reason that when Mr. Vajpayee in pursuance of his agenda of Hindu Rashtra was calling for the review of Constitution in the joint meeting of the

Parliament to commemorate the 50th year of Constitution, the President K.R. Narayanan in a forthright manner reminded the nation that what is needed is not the review but proper implementation of the provisions of Constitution when he said, "it is not the Constitution which has failed us, but it is we who have failed the Constitution".

**Hidden Agenda Behind this Review**

It may be argued that since the BJP does not have majority, and the coalition does not have two-third majority there is no possibility of the recommendations of the review committee being implemented. So why suspect the motives of BJP?

The agenda to change the Constitution started becoming clear and obvious with the rising power of BJP. During its run up to the Babri Masjid demolition its leaders started saying that the opinion of Hindu Sants and Mahants for them are more valuable and that they will prefer to act according to their advise rather than the Supreme Court's decision on the matter of Ram Janmbhumi. Similarly over a period of time BJP has been realising its inability to come to power on its own. The frequent change of Government during the last few years has given it a pretext to bring forth various ideas like presidential system of Government and the fixed term of Lok Sabha. The fixed term of Lok Sabha will be at the cost of representation of the aspirations of the people. And it will be similar to the experiences we witnessed during the emergency of 1975. As the MPs know that they are secure in their seats their accountability to their constituency will become far less than it is at present. The politics of manipulation will be rule of the day.

In Presidential system the President has the power to induct non-representative 'experts' in the Government and that again reduces the accountability of the Government to the people. Though it may be a workable system in some developed countries, in a country as diverse as ours, it will stifle the aspirations of large sections and regions of people. BJP's long-term agenda is that of Hindu Rashtra. A nation state based on Brahminical values. Hindu Rashtra like its counterparts Islamic fundamentalist states does not have the place for the democratic polity. Though BJP knows it cannot get the recommendations of its 'illegal' review committee passed in the Parliament, it has 'cleverly' put the question mark on the constitutional process and paved the way for future illegal manipulations of the same. It has 'succeeded' in equating constitutional amendments, which are legal, with the illegal process of review in the popular mind. Also it is providing an efficient 'cover' to the deep designs of its parent organisation, the RSS, to inflict a fascist–fundamentalist state and the social system.

# 20

# Fire of Fanaticism

The incidents of Godhra (Feb. 2002) have shaken our conscience to no end. What can be more condemnable than the violence, violence against innocent human beings, violence in the name of religion, violence perpetrated apparently in and around the issues related to temple and mosque? Promptly it got propagated that those who committed the crime were 'Muslims' and as a reflex action 'Muslims' have been brought on the firing line, their households on fire in Ahmedabad with the state machinery obliging the rioters by looking the other way around. While Ahmedabad is being burnt state apparatus is merrily declaring that 'situation is under control'!

Yes it has been under control of those who have deeper motives in keeping the flames of communal hatred alive. The backdrop of the incident is very revealing. A party, BJP, which is part of the Sangh combine, (whose other members are VHP, Bajrang Dal etc. all whose controllers come from the same stock, volunteers, swaymsevaks, trained in the politics of Hindutva, with the goal of Hindu Rashtra in mind), looses its grip in many a states in the state assembly elections.

As soon as the exit polls start showing the doom of the Party of Hindu Rashtra, its family members, "'saints' and co." raise the pitch of their histrionics for building temple for Lord Ram. The 'saints' of the VHP and the Parivar soon realised that the emotive appeal built around the temple is not yielding the dividends as it used to do in the yesteryears. Barring the hardcore supporters of Hindu Rashtra all other fringe supporters who were brought in by the emotional appeal of Ram Lalla soon realised that what they need more than the Temple at Ayodhya is bread and butter, shelter and clothing, education and employment, health facilities and drinking water, and so they realised their folly of falling in for the party of Hindu Rashtra and vote with their tummies to stage its route in the elections. On the top of it even the 'holy Saints' were not able to draw the expected crowds to the 'Holy Yagnas' and other campaigns. So finally the communal politics meets its death! If these issues don't bring the votes to the kitty of BJP, it has no future.

One recalls that BJP's earlier edition; Jana Sangh had begun its politics on the slogan of cow protection. It asserted that the cow is 'equivalent' of our mother. But people at large, those who are unable to take care of their own mother who gives them life, did not fall in the trap and the support base of Jan Sangh did not take off. During eighties as if 'by a stroke of genius' Sangh Parivar discovered the need for Ram Temple in Ayodhya and by now since an elite, upper caste/class urban middle class was in for opposing the social transformation, the campaign clicked. And the rising communal venom got focused through the Ram Temple agitation.

Interestingly it got its real 'flesh and blood' after the Mandal Commission implementation and in due course the Babri demolition and post-demolition riots gave the party of Hindu Rashtra, what it needed desperately, power to eat into the very ethos of our harmonious culture, syncretic traditions and the values of Indian Constitution.

Now BJP's electoral success was based on its 'hard core' prepared by RSS shakha training and by drawing the fringe, novice populace who intermittently submit to the appeal of Lord Ram in the political area. So what are the 'lessons' to be learnt by the Sangh Parivar from this setback?

Number one that Lord Ram will no more be able to collect the votes for them.

Number two they have to carry on with the spoils of power by taking the allies along.

So with multi-speak in action, different languages are spoken, secularism by Vajpayee, threat of terrorism by Advani, and need to keep the facade of NDA agenda by many of them.

Coming back to Godhra. This writer has a feeling of deja vu while hearing the blame that 'Muslims' have done the dastardly crime. In case of Mumbai riots blame on this community was based on a very simple logic. Since the victims are Hindus, (Mathadi Workers in Dockyard or Bane family in Jogeshwari) so the culprits must be Muslims. Fortunately today at least after the Shrikrishna Commission report the mist is clear and 'Muslims' exonerated from the crime, but not from the popular memory? The retaliation or whatever that is, duly supported by the BJP Government, stalks the streets and the clear targets are Muslims. One believes that not controlling the riot when it can be controlled is connivance if not an outright support. Today one does not know who burnt the train for sure.

What were the incidents, which led to the mob coming together, getting armed with petrol bombs etc.? One has some reservations in believing outright that in the "laboratory of Hindu Rashtra", Gujarat, any 'Muslim' group can plan it so well under the nose of the most efficient Swaymsewak Narendra Modi. Surely there is more to the 'Muslim involvement' in Godhra train incident than meets the eye. But how does that matter. What is important is that in a society where the popular psyche is doctored against minorities, broad masses can jump to such quick conclusions and do the rest?

The immediate aftermath of this will be an increased flow of Kar Sevaks to Ayodhya. There again another swayamsevak will ensure that whatever is needed to keep the flames of politics of hatred aflame is done, even if one has to pay the price of that with human blood. After all 'unfair is fair' in politics of power and more so if this politics is projected in the name of God or religion. One can see the minor repeat of the post-Babri demolition scenario. With the violence spreading and those in power calculating as to what is more beneficial to control this mayhem or to let it go on, as that may be more profitable for one's politics.

Whosoever is the real culprit behind the incident, one thing is sure. Nothing would have served the Sangh combine politics better. With the waning of the appeal of the Temple the 'threat of terrorism' and in turn the threat of 'aggressive Muslim community' has to be brought up to keep the electoral base alive. As such this community, which has been ghettoised due to regular outburst of communal-violence can hardly be regarded as a threat to the highly muscular Sangh combine support. However one should note in passing that during last five decades, the percentage of the victims of communal violence have their own tale to tell. The 12.4 per cent of the Muslim minority has an 'enviable' 80 per cent representations in the riot victims! Whosoever says that they are not well represented? In most of the inquiry commission reports (Teesta Setalvad, Communalism Combat, March 98), have indicated that though it is projected that it is Muslims who start the violence, generally the events are so manipulated that either they are cornered to throw the first stone or simply blamed for it out of the blue. One does not know whether the present event has similar interpretation or something else. Only a proper inquiry will tell the truth but meanwhile those who wanted to bake their political bread have already achieved their purpose.

Where do we go from here? The popular psyche has been doctored by Sangh combine into believing that Muslims are the villains, terrorists and all that. It is that which sustains the violence in a deeper sense.

# 21

# Putting Crocodiles to Shame

## An Open Letter to the Mask of Sangh Parivar

Dear Mr. Prime Minister,

The nation watching your shedding the crocodile tears, sorry your performance is far superior to the proverbial crocodiles' shedding tears, has become a matter of routine by now. One wonders if as a measure of complimenting you in your skills, crocodiles themselves may adopt the term Vajpayee tears. Surely the faculty of your alma mater, the RSS, are overwhelmed with joy at the performance of one who can call the Gujarat anti-Muslim pogroms as a shame, a *kalank*, one who can pretend so convincingly that he is disturbed by the genocide of Muslims in Gujarat and is in grief, while celebrations are on in his patriarchal Parivar house. Incidentally your alma mater is also complimenting itself for the ease and efficiency with which Hitler's gas chambers have been given more innovative adaptations in their Laboratory of Hindu Rashtra, Gujarat.

How else does one explain the utter silence, apathy and just a mild reprimand, if at all, to the Chief Minister of Gujarat, another fellow swayamsevak, who is brusquely claiming his efficiency in controlling the riots in 72 hours, when even after three weeks, Gujarat is continuing to burn?

How else can one explain your not being able to find time for so long to wipe the tears of the haggard community whose back is being broken by destroying their source of livelihood? How else can one explain utter and total disregard in providing any relief to a community battered and butchered in the most heinous crimes ever committed in India?

One keeps being reminded of your frame of mind in these situations. You must be constantly memorising your Shakha Bible "We or our nationhood defined", where your Guruji gives instructions about dealing with the 'internal threats to the Nation' a la Germany which preserved its 'Nationalism' by wiping out the minorities in a physical way. You are not a good product of Shakha for nothing, you do remember the instructions given to you very well.

Except for those who have been gullible enough to be impressed by your 'shows' of being a 'good man', most of us have seen your mask slipping too often and seeing your real face as a 'swayamsevak', willing to pay any price to uproot the democratic values, wanting to pursue the agenda of Hindu Rashtra. One remembers the times of Babri demolition when you were supposed to be uncomfortable etc. and later the ease with which you asserted that this is what happens if the sentiments of majority are ignored for long. We also recall your call for national debate on conversions in the wake of anti-Christian attacks. We also recall your joy of being amongst your clan in Staten island in the dollar land and declaring your privilege of being a swayamsevak. We know where your real loyalties lie. We come to know at such occasions that it is not Indian 'Tan Man' (body and soul), which you are proud of but it is 'Hindu Tan Man, Hindu Jeevan' (Hindu soul and body; Hindu life), which keeps you ticking. It is at those times that your true credentials are reemphasised to your own ideological kith and kin, and your worth and importance to the 'peddlers of hate', the Sangh Parivar, becomes more obvious.

Your gentleness is projected to trap the power hungry allies like Fernandes, Mamata or Paswans into the net of NDA, which is a ruse to keep strangulating the plural culture and democratic ethos of the country. We remember that you fed Khichadi to the greatest Kar Sevak turned Ram Sevak of the present epoch, the one who 'used' Lord Ram to collect votes and bring your party to power, Mr. Advani. And later he duly complimented not only your ability to cook the Khichadi but also realised your indispensability to lead the Mahakhichadi coalition. He realised your capability and potential of creating secular illusions by genuine sounding expressions while hiding the iron claws of Hindutva in the maze of brilliant oratory. And correctly he proposed your name for the Prime Ministership, while he was in a position to nominate himself for this top slot. But he knew better and you were anointed to lead the Mahakhichadi.

Many a components of this Mahakhichadi, which you are using to spread the secular aroma, had to use your name, 'good man in a bad party' etc. so that they could shamelessly plunge to enjoy the spoils of power while dumping their old principles and values. You in your majestic style have since been making most of the 'correct' noises to ensure that they are kept in good humour while your Parivar members can keep digging at the democratic, plural and composite roots of our nation, can keep harassing the minorities one after the other to implement the hidden agenda, which any way is not so hidden by now, of Sangh Parivar in a subtle and manifest way.

If at all there is some RSS sponsored 'Hindutva Ratna' award you do deserve it many times over. Nothing has proved it more than the present Gujarat carnage being done right under your nose when you are busy touching the feet of mahants and acharyas and making the show of weeping into your handkerchief for the *kalank* of Gujarat. The 'beauty' of your '*kalank* strategy' is to kill many birds with one or two 'touching words', literally so. While your Parivar member, Modi is getting kudos from all the Khaki *knickerwallahs*, whole nation is watching helplessly the crimes against the humanity, crimes of commission and proactive omissions.

Your coining of terms of sorrow, one after the other is enough to keep your 'conscience' clear of the failure in doing your constitutional duties of providing security to the people of this country. But any way, deep in your heart you know you are doing no wrong, as swearing by this constitution is another play acting, as you know that this constitution is based on 'western values' so should be scrapped, (as your boss Sarasanghchalak Sudarshan enunciated so clearly), and the one based on Hindu Dharma Granthas has to be brought in. What better Hindu values we need with one of your alma mater killing Father of the Nation for his 'sin' of pampering the minorities and another one supervising the anti-Muslim pogroms in such a 'competent' fashion. Fortunately for you, the swayamsevak colleague doing his 'patriotic' duty in Gujarat is doing such a 'brilliant' job in your Laboratory of Hindu Rashtra that you just have to silently clap while shedding the crocodile, nay Vajpayee tears, for the horrific violence, which is shaking most of the nation barring you and your Parivar.

May Lord Ram bless you for providing oratorical velvet cloak to the Trishul shaped dagger of your own Sangh Parivar.

Sincerely

An Enraged Indian
(March 2002)

# 22

# Gujarat Carnage—Can We Halt the March of Religious Fascism?

The Gujarat carnage has shaken us to no end. The events of Godhra were followed by the violence in Gujarat. More than two thousand lives and close to two thousand crores of social wealth has gone in the gullet of the communal demon. The condition in Gujarat is hardly towards recovery, thanks to the motivated political leadership, coming from Sangh Parivar stable, for which the whole thing was an upsurge of Hindus and for whom it was passé due to various reasons. Tragically mainstream Gujarati society has not shown any remorse for this and that partly gets reflected in the attitude displayed towards relief efforts and also in the silent and subtle message that 'they deserve it'! Can Gujarat repeat itself? Can our civic and political structure ensure that such a ghastly event does not repeat itself? Can the political force behind the implementation of the Gujarat genocide be contained? Can the Indian electorate learn from French to boot out the fascist forces? Can the social and political formations stand up to dangers, which Sangh Parivar has erected during last eight decades? Can we as citizens care to see the difference between the Secular democratic principles and the religion-based nationalism (Hindu Rashtra)?

Too many questions accompany the agitated mind of society. Too many challenges are baying in the face of those who will like to preserve the gains of freedom struggle, the principles of liberty, equality, fraternity, and the Indian Constitution. The backdrop of Gujarat carnage is very revealing. Post-Babri demolition the Parivar got the shot in the arms and then a marginal outfit; its political wing BJP, started inching towards the reach of political power. It is not that Parivar depends on political power alone to flourish. Its work, which has intruded most of the aspects of our social life, goes on irrespective of being in political power or out of power. But being in power does help. Every stint of political power makes its social institutions more powerful. Every occupation of seats of political power gives it the opportunity to plant its swayamsevaks in the crucial and strategic seats of influence in society.

The 'effect' of Babri demolition lasted for close to a decade and lately it was becoming obvious that the communal polarisation brought in by Babri and post-Babri violence was declining. The polarisation levels were dropping and so were the electoral fortunes of BJP. All attempts were made to keep the communal fire burning; Shila Pujans, Yagnas, and more events around the Ram Temple issue etc. But nothing worked. Then Godhra came in as a 'Ram sent' opportunity. It is said that there were some other cards also up the sleeves of Parivar (like the video cassette of cow slaughter) but nothing could have been better than the act of some insane Muslims who burnt the coach of Sabarmati train! Our "leaders", more so from Parivar or those close to Parivar are experts in 'instant investigation'. One does recall the 'brilliance' exhibited by the 'Loyally Yours' of Parivar, George Fernandes, who along with two of his ministerial colleagues, could investigate Pastor Stains brutal burning just by sniffing the area for a little while, to declare that the burning of Pastor with his innocent sons was a part of international conspiracy to destabilize his Master, Vajpayee's Government. In the similar vein swayamsevak Modi could immediately discover the link between the local Muslim criminals, who burnt the train, with ISI and the international terrorists, who attacked the WTC. And the rest is horrific history, part of which is still going on. The ongoing cycle of 'retaliation' under the able leadership of the bright boy of Parivar, the 'Chote Sardar' has brought immense shame to the land of Buddha, Kabir, Nanak and Gandhi.

The ghastly events have awakened a large section of concerned individual to stand up for defending the Secular Democracy. The non-BJP-Shiv Sena, Non-NDA parties have firmed up their resolve to stand for secular values. Some of the sensitive individuals around this time felt that Godhra-Gujarat is the reaction of frustrated Parivar and that the communal fire is on the verge of getting extinguished, and this is the heightened flame before its being extinguished. It was part optimism and parts a commentary on the electoral defeats of BJP in Gujarat Panchayat elections and the state assembly elections in the northern four states.

In the aftermath of riots there are conflicting assessments and the assessment of Chote Sardar based on the feedback from BJP local units indicates that BJP will be winning elections hands down in the wake of carnage. The blood of innocents, stench of the dead bodies and smoke of burning houses is the 'offering', which the demon of communal politics needs from time to time. And once the level of 'these offerings' becomes less in the system of this demon, communal parties starts loosing out. And BJP and Parivar pundits know it too well. It is not for nothing that Godhra and Gujarat's are planned or happen at regular intervals, of course with increasing ferocity every next time. The deeper mechanisms, human and organisational are well entrenched to ensure that Parivar's electoral calculations are translated on the streets and into the ballot boxes.

The present impasse has also aroused a deep dislike for the politics being manipulated and imposed on the society.

What is desirable is that we learn the lessons from the recent French elections. Just to recall, the Parivar clone in France came very close to the Presidency due to voter apathy and due to the dislike for the non-performing Chirac, in the first round. The French electorate immediately realised its folly and a fortnight later rallied around Chirac to ensure that Le Pen does not come anywhere close to power. The electorate and the other political parties did not use their rhetoric power against each other and instead concentrated to ensure that country does not fall in the hands of an avowed non-democrat. Is such a thing possible here? The Mulayam Singhs, Sonias, and Sharad Pawars are ever keen to fight amongst each other, even if that means that Advanis and Vajpayees of the Parivar appropriate the political power despite being in minority.

In a scenario where the Dalit leadership like Mayawati is ever willing to ally with the modern Manus of BJP, can one hope that in the next election round, our Le Pen does not occupy the seats of power? Can there be alliances, which ensure that only those committed to democratic values, pluralism and Indian constitution are voted for. On this count BJP, the political son of RSS, the Parivar, can 'cleverly' talk in a democratic language while subtly talking of Hindu Rashtra. With forked tongue it can spell two contrary concepts in the same breath, democracy and religious fascist state. Unfortunately we do not have much choice of a 'good' secular democratic party. We do not have the luxury of selecting from the assortment of good, better and best. We are doomed to identify just the bad, worse and the worst. And reconcile to bad and reject the worse/worst. To the writer of these lines Parivar and its affiliates should not qualify even for the worst category. As they are not having faith and commitment to secular plural values and Indian Constitution they should not be considered at all as far as the choice for electoral purpose is concerned. Those, who belong to the Parivar for whom Indian Constitution should be replaced and the one based on Hindu Holy books (! read *Manusmriti*) should be brought in (a la K. S. Sudarshan) the patriarch of Parivar) do not qualify for consideration as the electoral oufits worth considering.

But that's just one part of the total spectrum of Parivar's exploits. We need to look at its schools, propaganda machinery, its cultural fronts, and its communalisation of society as a whole. Even without electoral success Parivar can sustain itself for a long time. And that's where the 'real challenge' lies. Its a marathon task. Communalisation of polity through rumours, myths and cultural fronts cannot be easily combated. New mechanism for secular culture, democratic values, syncretic practices are to be brought to the forefront. The version of Hinduism, which is currently being propagated by Parivar, is antithetical to the subaltern streams of Hinduism. The Shramanic Hindu traditions of Charvak, Tantra, Shaiva, Kabir, Tukaram have to be given their due. The Hindutva's Hinduism is based on Hate for other religions. The Hinduism of Shramanic traditions are based on the respect for humanistic aspects of other's faiths. The new practices and Brahminisation of subaltern practices, the Brahminisation of Saints has to be recognised and fought against. The 'community' has to be at the centre of the programmes taken up by the social groups committed to social, economic and gender justice. The cultural space left unattended by progressive forces has to be appropriated back to ensure any meaningful building up of a society based on plural ethos and democratic values.

# 23

# Fishing for Votes in the Rivers of Blood

In the wake of Gujarat genocide many a masks are falling one after the other. We are witnessing the 'naked glory' of those claiming to be secular, as it is ingrained in their 'glorious tradition'; new meanings are also being added to this word. The litmus test of this in a way was the response of BJP, Vajpayee and company, to the most elementary demand of dismissal of the architect-in-chief of Gujarat carnage, Mr. Modi. While defending his fellow swayamsewak our 'poet-prime minister', who is generally well covered by his mask, dropped not only his mask but all the guards to show his *khakhi-knickers* and the *trishul* well placed in the pockets of his *knickers*. Thundered the swayamsevak, wherever there are Muslims in the world there is strife. Islam has come to mean forcing their opinion through terror and fear, putting the blame of Gujarat genocide on the victims of genocide themselves, he went on to assert, Muslims provoke and then Hindus..."

He peaked his role as the RSS warrior by saying that what happened in Gujarat was deplorable but who started the fire? In a nutshell, the venom, which the RSS, VHP, Bajrang Dal spreads in the society, was neatly capsulated and delivered by Mr. Vajpayee in a 'masterly' fashion. While protecting the butcher of Gujarat, BJP also called for elections in the Gujarat, a move, which Mr. Shanta Kumar dubbed as doing politics on the corpse of the riot victims, a few days ago! Surely Mr. Shanta Kumar will have to pay in due course for not being able to keep some of his left over humanism, despite being a swayamsevak, under wraps.

With this, the path is open for the BJP to chart the course for electoral success by encashing the polarisation brought in by the ghastly events of a bleeding state. How come every time a riot occurs, the communal forces become strong? Why BJP was showing electoral decline during last many elections it faced? The survey sponsored by Mr. Modi did show the chances of BJP winning the elections in the wake of the violence. While many of us may simplistically believe that after getting its hands bloodied in the violence most of the people should shun this party like plague and how come the survey shows its confidence of winning? Surely its leadership is going by its time proven formula, riot-polarisation and thereby electoral success for communal forces!

Analysis of different riots during last 50 years has shown that while riots may invite disgust and repulsion amongst some people, a large section easily buys the story that it is the communal forces, which have protected them from the aggression of the enemy. During Mumbai riots we had witnessed the police-Shiv Sena complicity ravaging the streets and unleashing the violence while sections of community gripped by common sense in the spell of 'Manufactured Hatred' gleefully approving and following the saffron bandwagon and further than this many an elements taking advantage of the situation to fill their coffers or to control a piece of real estate. Many an immigrants wrote back to their families in the villages applauding the mercies of Lord Ram in providing Shiv Sena, thanks to whose efforts we are alive today from the organised conspiracy of the Islamic Fundamentalists. Many an undiscriminating amongst us might have been swayed by this but for the Shrikrishna Commission's brilliant work, which confirmed the findings of the public tribunal headed by Justice Daud and Justice Suresh who within few months of the riots came to conclusion that it was Shiv Sena organised anti-Muslim pogrom. The 'brilliance' of communal outfits lies precisely here. They did successfully propagate that the murder of Mathadi (who carry luggage on head) workers or burning of the Bane family by some miscreants was in fact a handiwork of the aggressive Muslims. It is worth recalling that Hindu Hriday Samrat (King of Hindu Hearts) Balasaheb Thackeray gave a call for the violence after these two acts by writing in his mouth piece *Saamna*, Hindunni Ata Akramak Vhayal have (Hindus should become aggressive now). Rest of the story is too well known to be recounted.

Similar pattern seems to be under play in the wake of Godhra tragedy. The coach was torched on 27th Feb., by the same evening the word is spread that ISI along with local complying Muslims have attacked the Hindus. The secularists as usual are not condemning the act so the Hindu souls are deeply pained. The next day the organised carnage stalks the streets of Gujarat and the warriors of Sangh Parivar well equipped with swords, maps of Muslim households, business houses and holy places, draws the rivers of blood on the streets of Gujarat and the survivors pitying their existence are forced into the camps, unattended by state and humiliated by their plight of living in the Hindu Rajya, the state of Chote Sardar, Mr. Modi. One knows that the aggressive communal forces need a pretext for their survival. The eclipsing electoral fortunes were too obvious to the wily strategists of Sangh Parivar, who were 'needing' a Godhra to happen for their own very existence. Bereft of such situations they see their own decline too visible.

What in fact was needed was propor investigation of the tragedy, as to who provoked, why it happened, and its logical next step to punish the guilty. Surely state is well equipped to do this elementary business. But if that is done, the whole 'benefits' of Godhra are lost! So within a single day even when all those who matter amongst Muslim community, secularists and the human rights activists are protesting their heart's anguish out in the streets, or condemning this Godhra tragedy. The lathis (the original RSS weapon, now being a bit extinct to keep pace with times), the *Trishuls* (the symbol of most aggressive RSS wing VHP and Bajrang Dal, currently in use) and more innovative gas cylinders (any semblance with Hitlers gas chambers is purely incidental) come in to action. The hurt of Hindus is coordinated through mobiles and the foot soldiers brave it out while these foot soldiers and the mobile wielders share the loot of business establishments owned by the 'enemies' of Hindu Rashtra, the Muslims.

Many an inquiry commission reports have shown that it is generally some outfit of Hindu communal organisation, which threw the first stone or started the fire (Who Castes the first stone, Teesta Setalvad, Communalism Combat March 1998). These inquiry commissions (Jagmohan; Ahmedabad 1969, Madan; Bhiwandi 1970, Vithayathil; Tellicherry 1971, Venugopal; Kanyakumari 1982), the reports of Bhagalpur, Jamshedpur riots and lastly Mumbai riots have demonstrated beyond any shadow of doubt that the truth is fairly shrouded in mystery and the propaganda that Muslims have started the riot is the triggering point for unleashing the 'much needed' riots to strengthen the base for communal politics. Mostly some pretext is generally made available or situation is such created that minorities are either cornered or threatened in such a way that they are forced to throw the first stone.

When Mr. Vajpayee says that Muslims started the fire, he is following the mould and mindset, which has built the

BJP. Be it the ghastly riots or the Ram Temple movement, the role of Majoritarain communal force is absolutely clear, and made more clear after the cool headed study of the riot reports. But by the time reports are cited, dug up from the archives the 'job' is already done, and the foundation for the new electoral success already laid down.

Now, one hopes the Election Commission will wake up and see the dangers of holding elections in a state, which has suffered such an intense trauma, a state where the whole minority community today is petrified and a state where lakhs are staying in the refugee camps. What one wonders is about the many faces of a man called Atal Bihari Vajpayee. At one time he wrote somewhere, (*Frontline*, August, 1997) we don't fish for votes in the rivers of blood. This was probably before his masks were ripped off by his politics for Hindu Rashtra. Now while eagerly preparing his boats and fishing nets to catch the electoral fish in Gujarat he must be formulating another poem, which can act as a brand new mask for the new occasion.

# 24

# Fake Apology

Mr. Advani, our Deputy Prime Minister was recently (Mid-August 2002) touring UK for rejuvenation of the contact with the UK based NRIs, who like other NRIs are not only a big source of *moolah* for Sangh Parivar but are also promoters of the fundamentalism here by a remote mechanism of sorts. Our Hindutva leaders get a sort of transformation when they travel abroad. And in different forums they play different tunes to win over new friends, to retain the bonds of old friendships and to spruce up the image, which gets sullied due to the acts undertaken to promote their agenda of Hindu Rashtra. Multiple goals; so multiple pronouncements and so multi-speak. One recalls that during a visit to Staten Island our PM, Mr. Vajpayee's carefully painted mask of liberalism fell and he thundered like a swayamsevak. This was obviously to win over the support base of BJP in lands far and wide. One also recalls Mr. Advani in one of his previous visits to London made the famous pronouncement that we want a Hindu Rashtra but it will not be a theocratic state! Incidentally, a bit later Babri demolition was organised under his leadership as a stepping-stone to the blessed Rashtra for the Hindus of Advanis' ilk.

This time around when Mr. Advani was visiting U.K. he has an added burden on his shoulder, the responsibility of Home Ministry and Deputy Prime Ministership. In the face lift exercise he went on to express his sorrow and apology over the Gujarat violence! Did he think London is a better place to apologize for his sins? Is it that a new *fatwa* is in the offing from the Sangh stable that from now on Thames River is a better place for washing one's sins than our own Mother Ganga (river). Whatever be his strategic calculations, the apology could not appeal to those who have gone through the hell orchestrated by Mr. Advani's Parivar. And they humbly rejected the 'apology'. We say that, generous accept the apologies. Could the battered Muslim minority come up to the magnanimity to accept the apology? Is it that they have been too numbed by the stunning blow on their very existence that they are not able to accept the apology of the man of the stature of Mr. Advani? Though they may like to bury the past memory and forgive and forget, is it that they feel that apology is not a sincere one?

Does one doubt the sincerity of our Home Minister? Has there been a change of heart of Mr. Advani so that after seeing all the violence taking place right under his nose he feels a wrong has been perpetrated by him and his Parivar? It is not easy to forget the horrific happenings of Gujarat since they have shown the dumps to which the doctored minds can take the society. Never before has the nation seen the total and gross violation of all the norms of human behaviour. Never before have we seen such a total collusion of the state machinery and the pogrom organizers. Never before have we witnessed such a humiliation of the women. Never before have the children undergone such massive suffering. Even today the refugee camps have the residents who have nowhere to go. Even today their ex-neighbours are telling them that they can return back only if they give an undertaking that they will not file any FIR against them. The net result of this carnage has been that Muslim minority can no more live in Gujarat in a dignified way. They have either to subjugate themselves to the dictates of the Hindu nation or to migrate elsewhere. If this elsewhere happens to be in India then they have to wait in perennial fear as to when another Gujarat type genocide will befall upon them.

Where was Mr. Advani when all this was happening? Barring his Parivar most of those who were witnessing the process were aghast with the complicity of state. Or rather most of the human rights investigation teams could see that it is not a intercommunity clash, it is not a communal violence, it was plain and simple state sponsored genocide, being led by Advani's junior, (Advani being the reincarnation of Sardar Patel as they claim, so in the Sangh terminology, Advani is Sardar; Modi Chote Sardar), Chote Sardar Narendra Modi. And what was Mr. Advani's role, complicity in the genocide. As the central minister of Home, the state law and order is his area of responsibility. And he parroted Modi's words that all is well in the state. And further, to encourage the doings of his junior, he patted the chief of genocide squad, as being the best Chief Minister India has ever seen. He, as home minister could have surely exercised his power to reduce the death dance, if not totally stop it, in Gujarat, but he did not lift even his little finger to stop it. In Goa when his party was supposed to take stock of the situation in Gujarat, he ensured that Chote Sardar is raised in the stature, that Modi is conferred Hero Dom for his labours in Gujarat.

So what is this apology of Mr. Advani? Is it to say that the state has faltered and now the things will be set right? Generally what an apology should mean is that, so far so good (bad) and now as a remorse we will ensure that the injustices done are rectified. That even now whatever is possible to restore normalcy will be done. Whatever is possible will be done to restore the faith of the victims. The ghettoisation of Muslims in Gujarat is complete by now and his junior's Gaurav yatra will be creating a further terrifying atmosphere for them. Is Mr. Advani going to stop all that?

No, plain and simple no. Mr. Advani is more interested in baking the electoral bread in the oven of carnage. He wants to fish in the rivers of blood to consolidate his Hindutva project. He wants to snub the upright Election Commission, to change its decision so that Elections can be held early in Gujarat. The need for early elections in Gujarat is the need of Sangh Parivar, which wants to capitalize on the 'gains' of carnage. Since the polarisation due to the violence is always built up on the basis of the rumours and propaganda that the 'enemies' are going to attack us so lets preempt the attack by destroying them. And so the majority community sees that those perpetrating the barbarism are saviours of theirs'. So the feeling that 'every single days delay in election, is votes lost for Hindutva' and so this hurry by Advani and company to take the Election Commission to Supreme Court via the President.

Clearly Mr. Advani is not just hands in glove with the Gujarat violence, he is currently also adding salt to the wounds of Gujarat victims. That this is a fake apology is as clear to the Gujarat victims as it is to Mr. Advani himself. But if a lie can brighten up your image what is the harm in resorting to such a tactic? But Mr. Advani should know that he cannot fool all the people all the time. The cat, which came out from the bag of Gujarat violence, is growling loud enough to let victims believe what Mr. Advani is saying. And so this rejection of apology. One only hopes there was an element of genuineness in the apology but to expect such a change of heart from a die hard swayamsevak is to expect that Hitler will be leading the Jews to the garden path of bliss and not to the Gas Chamber.

# 25

# Manufacturing Faith

RSS resolution at the end of Bangalore convention (Mid 2002) asked the Muslim community to buy the goodwill of majority community for its own safety and good. Similarly many a spokespersons from this Sangh Parivar have been asserting that since the Hindus are the majority, since Ayodhya is the holy place for them, a la Mecca, the Muslims should strike an out of court settlement with VHP and hand over the 'site' to Hindus for building the temple of Lord Ram. Many 'advisers' have gone on to say that it is the Muslim arrogance, which is responsible for the Ayodhya imbroglio and the accompanying violence in the society.

The assertions made on this wavelength are manifold. To begin with it states that Ram is a symbol of Indian nationalism that Ayodhya is to Hindus what Mecca is to Muslims and finally since Ram was born precisely at the spot where Babri mosque was standing so the site must be handed over to Hindus, i.e., to VHP, to Ram Janmbhumi Nyas, controlled by RSS. In this scheme of things RSS is synonymous with Hindus. Most of these are constructs which have very little to do with truth.

Ram is a mythological figure, Valmiki wrote the epic with Ram as a Hero. Interpretations and worship for Ram is not uniform in different sections of Hindu community. There is no archaeological evidence to show that at the time when Ram is supposed have been born there was any human habitation around Ayodhya. Archaeology does not substantiate the Ram legend in any way. The popularisation of Ram cult began with Tulsidas who wrote Ramayana in Avadhi dialect of Hindi and people at large could access this book.

Before that, story of Ram was available only in Devbhasha Sanskrit so its prevalence was restricted to the upper caste only. As such, Ram is not the only holy figure in Hindu pantheon. Lord Krishna, Brahma, Vishnu, Mahesh and a large number of holy figures are prevalent in Hindu mythology and in Hindu psyche. The choice of Ram as the holy deity may be a bit deliberates one. The other side of this praise for Ram is seen in the interpretation of Ram legend by Phule, Ambedkar and Periyar. Phule saw Ram as the representative of the conquering Aryans, one who was the upholder of gender and caste hierarchy. The story of Shambuk as upholder of upper caste ethos is more than obvious. Just to recall Shambuk was killed by Lord Ram as he was doing penance, an act, which was not permitted to the low caste. Similarly Ram had no hesitation in oppressing Tadaka to insulting Shurpanakha or banishing his pregnant wife Sita on the suspicion of her fidelity.

Ram was never accepted as a symbol of Indian nationalism in the struggle for Indian independence. This struggle based on the secular values kept the holy deities in their sacred precincts while concentrating on the issues of this world, freedom from the clutches of British colonial powers etc. To say that Ram is the prophet of Hindu religion as Mohammad is the prophet of Islam is not true. All the prophetic religions have one prophet, while Hindu pantheon has innumerable holy figures competing for the number one slot. So whatever the birth place of Ram it can not be compared with the holy places like Mecca, Bodh Gaya or Jerusalem as those places are the one's belonging to the 'sole' holy place for the believers of those religions. This can be done only by undermining the status of other holy deities like Lord Krishna, Vishnu or Shiva, which may not be acceptable to many a Hindus who follow them.

Coming to Ayodhya if one spares some thought to the issue, the manipulation of the Hindu Right in raising this as an 'issue of faith' etc. will make it clear that history has not much to do with the issue and what is of paramount importance for the Kar Seva politicians is the political benefits rather than the religious sentiments. Mir Baqui who got the mosque built could not have gone against the sentiments of his chief, Babur. In Babur's reign there was a strong growth of syncretic traditions, while he got the Jain temples of Gwalior demolished on the grounds of nude idols being there. Baburs' will to Humayun advises him to respect other religions especially, Hinduism, as his subjects are Hindus. Babur himself was no bigot and he gives a good account of his respect for other religions in his *Baburnama*. During his reign, in the Guru-Khattri shrine in Peshawar Hindus offered their hair as an offering, and in Kachwa Muslim lived among Hindu Yogis and there was a lofty idol house standing next to a Mosque in Gwalior.

Even Tulsidas, one of the greatest Ram Bhakta's of all the time could not has missed the Ram Temple demolition, had there been one. He lived just a quarter of century after Babur and it is totally unlike for him not to have mentioned this had this taken place as recently as 25-50 years. Also many a Hindus may claim that since Ram was first son of Ayodhya, Kaushalya, Ram's mother, must have gone to her mother's place for delivering Lord Ram.

The claims, which have been made for demolition, also do not mention the reference source of that time. Ram Gopal Pande's *Ramjanmbhumi ka Rakta Ranjit Itihas* mentions that during Babur's reign Hindus attacked the Babri mosque four times, during Humayun's reign ten times; during Akbar's reign 20 times, to recover the site of temple. In this popular book no mention is made of the source of this. As a matter of fact the first confrontation took place at the instance of the British who succeeded in driving a wedge between Hindus and Muslims.

The minor tit bits apart British did want to propagate that Muslim Kings had destroyed Hindu temples and at every point they went on adding this as a matter of practice. The British chroniclers sowed the seeds of controversy. P. Carnegy's 'Historical Sketch of Tehsil Faizabad, Zila Faizabad', Lucknow-1870, and H.R. Neville's Faizabad District Gazetteer, Allahabad 1905 are a good example of this. Without citing any concrete evidence the Gazetteers just put the probability of a hypothesis that the temple might have been destroyed to build the mosque. The underlying current of British officials is best manifest in translation of Babur's memoirs by Mrs. A.F. Beveridge. She suggests in a footnote that Babur being a Muslim and 'impressed by the dignity and sanctity of the ancient Hindu shrine would have displaced at least in part' the temple to erect the mosque.

The events after the night of 22-23 January 1949 are too well known. Some miscreants placed the Ram Lalla idols and the district magistrate K.K. Nayyar sealed the place. Till that time Namaz was being offered regularly.

After this the matter again was in the deep freeze till the Margdarshak Mandal of VHP decided to revive it. Till this time RSS was trying to use the cow protection as the emotive issue to build up hysteria. It failed. After the social changes which had taken place, now a big constituency was there which supported this campaign and BJP itself came forward to reap the fruits of seeds of Ram Lalla idols installed by force. And rest is (or should be hopefully) history. Court injunctions—making the Masjid in to disputed site, its demolition under the leadership of Advani, Joshi and Uma Bharati and declaration of this day as Hindu Shaurya Divas need not be recounted. During the whole process a large section of population came to believe the lies spread by Sangh Parivar. A new 'faith' came into being. This new faith dictated the politics and continues to dictate the politics to quite some extent.

With the recent failures of Chetavani Yatras and other campaigns launched by Sangh Parivar, it is clear that this issue will not succeed in mobilising the gullible any longer. Now to build a Mandir is not like demolishing a mosque. Sangh could demolish it in five and a half hours, but construction will take much longer, so the brute force, which is the hallmark of Parivar may not work now. Also if people don't vote around this issue, if they do not come forward to support the illusions created by Sants and company any longer, (barring of course the lunatic fringe) what is to be the face saving formula? How to convince the core supporters without loosing face? Advice the Muslims to give up their claim and the line that law of the land should prevail. So tell them subtly that there has been anti-Muslim pogroms and that they are insecure in this land, tell them they need security (from its goons) and 'advice' them to give up the claim from the 'disputed site'! One has come around full circle.

Manufacture a faith, agitate around it, destroy the secular fabric around manufactured faith and seeing that there is no exit from this dastardly path, threaten the minorities to behave, to surrender else! And that's where we stand today while reading the resolution of RSS at the end of its Bangalore meeting. Hope the sanity of the society will prevail over these machinations to break the unity of Indian Nation. Hope India will prevail over Hindu Rashtra and we can witness the decline of the fascist manoeuvers of the Sangh Parivar.

# 26

# Commissar Sadhvi's Cow Agenda

It is generally believed that BJP victory in the three assembly elections (MP, Rajasthan, Chhattisgarh, 2004), was on the plank of *Bijali, Sadak, Pani* (BSP). Whatever be the truth of that, the so-called Hindutva agenda is starkly visible in these states with the BJP Governments firmly in power. MP has a unique distinction of having a 'World Renouncer', Sadhvi as the chief commissar of the state. And true to the Sadhvi spirit, she has been bringing in the clerical presence in the matters of state. Right from the word go, i.e., her swearing in ceremony, she has brought in Hindutva into her style of functioning and polices. Not only that her Sadhu brethren were the guests of honour at the swearing ceremony, she also lost no time in banning liquor and non-vegetarian food in the three "holy" cities and to back it up she is now giving a 'cow tilt' to MPs economy by giving primacy to establishing Goshala (cow sheds) (Feb. 2004). Many a previous RSS-VHP campaigns around giving the status of mother to cow went unresponded so far. With Sadhvi Uma finally the 'cow mother' is getting a new place in Indian society. In a society where the young mothers are facing increasing deprivations 'cow mother' will be given the place of honour in the second Laboratory of Hindu Rashtra, Madhya Pradesh.

Why is cow a holy animal, why has she to be given a place above other animals which are equally if not more useful is a long story. Overall cow is the major emotional symbol of the upper caste Hindutva politics, next only to Lord Ram. Lord Ram has been milked heavily for electoral purposes, Ram Janmbhumi campaign was acknowledged even by Advani as having given a fillip in the politics, and now its cow's turn to swell the quantum of the electoral milk for this politics.

One recalls, just a couple of years ago Prof. D.N. Jha a historian from Delhi University had been experiencing the nightmares of 'threats to life' from anonymous callers who were trying to prevail upon him not to go ahead with the publication of his well researched work, 'Holy Cow: Beef in Indian Dietary traditions'. It is a work of serious scholarship based on authentic sources in tune with methods of scientific research in History. The book demonstrates that contrary to the popular beliefs even today large number of Indians, the indigenous people in particular and many other communities in general consume beef unmindful of the dictates of the Hindutva forces who confer the status of mother to her. Currently 72 communities in Kerala—not all of them untouchable perhaps—prefer beef to the expensive mutton and the Hindutva forces are trying to prevail upon them also to stop eating the same.

Jha breaks the myth that Muslim rulers introduced beef eating in India. Much before the advent of Islam in India beef had been associated with Indian dietary practices. Also that it is not tenable to hold that dietary habits are a mark of community identity.

A survey of ancient Indian scriptures, especially Vedas shows that amongst the nomadic, pastoral Aryans, who settled here, animal sacrifice was a dominant feature of theirs' till the emergence of settled agriculture. Cattle were the major property during this phase and they offered the same to propitiate the gods. Wealth was equated with ownership of the cattle. Many a gods like Indra and Agni are described to be having special preferences for different types of flesh—Indra had weakness for bull's meat and Agni for bulls' and cows'. It is recorded that the Maruts and the Asvins were also offered cows. In Vedas there is a mention of around 250 animals out of which at least 50 were supposed to be fit for sacrifice. In Mahabharata there is a mention of a king named Rantideva who achieved great fame by distributing foodgrains and beef to Brahmins. Taittiriya Brahman categorically tells us: 'Verily the cow is food' (*atho annam via gauh*) and Yajnavalkya's insistence on eating the tender (*amsala*) flesh of the cow is well known. Even later Brahminical texts provide the evidence for eating beef.

In therapeutic section of Charak Samhita (pp. 86-87) flesh of cow is prescribed as a medicine for various diseases. It is also prescribed for making soup. It is emphatically advised as a cure for irregular fever, consumption, and emanciation. The fat of the cow is recommended for debility and rheumatism.

With the rise of agricultural economy, the massive changes occurring in the society changed the perceptions of people at large. At the time there were ritualistic practices, with which Brahmins were identified. Even *Manusmriti* did not prohibit the consumption of beef. Buddha attacked these practices, which involved the sacrifices. There were sacrifices, which involved 500 oxen, 500 male calves, 500 female calves and 500 sheep to be tied to the sacrificial pole for slaughter. Buddha pointed out that *aswamedh, purusmedha, vajapeya* sacrifices did not produce good results. According to a story in Digha Nikaya, when Buddha was touring Magadha, a Brahmin called Kutadanta was preparing for a sacrifice with 700 bulls and 700 goats. Buddha intervened and stopped him. His rejection of animal sacrifice and emphasis on non-injury to animals assumed a new significance in the context of new agriculture, which required cattle.

The emphasis on non-violence by Buddha was not blind or rigid. He did taste beef and it is well known that he died due to eating pork. Emperor Ashok after converting to Buddhism did not turn to vegetarianism. He restricted the number of animals to be killed for the royal kitchen.

So where do matters change and how did cow become a symbol of faith, reverence and assumed the status of 'motherhood'. Over a period of time mainly after the emergence of Buddhism or rather as an accompaniment of the Brahminical attack on the Buddhism, the practices started changing. The threat posed by Buddhism to Brahminical value system was too severe. In response to low caste slipping away from the grip of Brahminism, the battle was taken at all the levels. At philosophical level Shankar reasserted the supremacy of Brahminical values, at political level King Pushyamitra Shung ensured the physical attack on Buddhist monks, at the level of symbols King Shashank got the Bodhi tree destroyed. One of the arsenals of rise of Buddhism was the protection of cattle wealth, which was ideally, needed for the agricultural economy. In a way while Brahminism 'succeeded' in banishing Buddhism from India but it had to also to transform itself from the 'animal sacrifice' state to the one which could be in tune with the times while preserving their own interests. It is here that this ideology took up cow as a symbol of their ideological march. But unlike Buddha whose pronouncements were based on reason, the counteraction of Brahminical ideology took the form of a blind faith based assertion. So while Buddha's non-violence was for the preservation of animal wealth for the social and compassionate reasons the counter was based purely on symbolism. The followers of Brahminical ideology accuse Buddha for 'weakening' India due to his doctrine of non-violence. But he was not a cow worshipper or vegetarian in the current Brahminical sense.

Despite the gradual rigidification of Brahminical 'cow as mother' stance, large sections of low castes continued the practice of beef eating. The followers of Buddhism continued to eat flesh including beef. Since Brahmanism is the dominant religious tradition, Babur the first Mughal emperor in his will to his son Humayun, in deference to these notions, advised his son Humayun to respect the cow and avoid cow slaughter. The issue came back with the construction of Hindutva ideology and politics in response to the rising Indian national movement, and asserted the demand for ban on cow slaughter. In post-independence India RSS repeatedly raised this issue as a mass campaign but without any response to its call till 1980s.

While one must respect the sentiments of those who worship cow and regard her as their mother, but to initiate the state sponsored step to promote these emotional symbolisms is travesty of democracy. Madhya Pradesh correctly needs *Bijali, Sadak, Pani*. Cow, bullocks and buffalos do need a tender caring; the ecology has to be respected. But can it take precedence over human problems? As such there is no tussle between communities as for as dietary habits and respect for other's tradition and faiths are concerned. While adhering to one's own faith, one should be tolerant to others faiths and beliefs. The measures as being initiated by the Sadhvi do smack of imposition of her own belief systems on the state as a whole and that too at the expense of state exchequer.

# 27

# Coding the Dress

The recent *fatwa* by Taliban (2001) dictating the dress code to the minorities comes as yet another fanatic move in the name of religion, in this case Islam. Just a few months ago the whole international community helplessly witnessed the insane destruction of Buddha statues in Bamiyan. The reaction to these insanities by Taliban has been mostly condemnatory but shades of the politics of those condemning, are too obvious to be ignored. Most of the liberals unconditionally denounced both these events on the grounds that in civil societies the individual freedom of dress and religion is non-negotiable. The Muslim community at large dissociated from the Taliban version of Islam to state that the Islam does permit the freedom of religion to believers of other faiths (for you your religion for me mine, Koran:109.6). Most of the shades of Muslim opinion was not only upset by the Taliban action, it also feared that vested interests will use this to further demonize Islam and Muslims, which is the order of the day. The Hindu Communal outfits RSS, VHP and Bajarang Dal are sure that it is because of the teachings of Islam that Taliban is behaving in this inhuman manner. They linked the medieval destruction of Hindu temples by Muslim Kings to the Bamiyan and now in the wake of the dress code the threat has been issued that if this code is implemented in Afghanistan then as a punitive measure the

Muslim women in India will not be allowed to wear the *burkha*. On purpose they overlook the fact these Buddha statues have been in Afghanistan before the reign of Muslim rulers and they very much existed during the 14 centuries of rule of Muslim Kings in Afghanistan. The logic for the present threat seems to be that the Indian Muslims are responsible for the acts of Taliban in Afghanistan as much as they are responsible for the supposed destruction of Hindu temple by Babur and his tribe!

Before understanding the acts of Taliban, acts done in the name of Islam here it will be pertinent to recapitulate some of the oppressive and inhuman acts committed by different set of people, belonging to different religions and races, destroying human norms in the name of their race or religion. Moorish Libraries were burnt, inquisitions were conducted, world heritage has been looted from civilised colonies to fill the museums of first world countries by sheer use of force and in the name of Christianity at times. Hitler in his phase of political ascendancy destroyed valuable works of arts and museums and unleashed holocaust for the 'honour' of Great German Race. LTTE has recklessly destroyed the places of worship of Buddhists, Muslims and Christians. In 1981 a library with rare manuscripts was bombed in Colombo. Jews despite having been at the receiving end of the tyranny of racial superiority so very recently, have been doing similar things in Palestine? For many years, while salvaging Jewish archaeology to establish Israeli claim to the land, Arab archaeology has been destroyed.

In our own country we have seen anti-Muslim pogroms for last five decades or so. In the post-independence riots the 12 and odd per cent of Muslim population has been the major victim in the communal violence as 80 per cent of the victims have been Muslims. Not to be left behind from last four years the Christians priests and nuns have been on the firing line along with the burning of churches and bibles and even of the Pastor who primarily was a leprosy worker, was done to death by burning in the most gruesome manner. The nadir of these acts in the name of religion of course remains the Babri demolition and the post-demolition anti-Muslim pogroms. And all this in the name of Hinduism.

Taliban has been propped up by the international powers funneling their resources through Pakistan for the control of oil wealth of the region. And Afghanistan has been facing sanctions for the violation of different human rights due to excesses of Taliban committed against the Muslim and other population. It is only from last six years that they have come to control large part of Afghanistan and while the large populace is suffering and dying due to lack of food, warm clothes, medicines and other essential commodities the Taliban fire is directed to the Buddha statue. While the external manifestation of this rule are seen in Bamiyan and dress code, majority of Afghan people are suffering severe repression at the hands of Taliban, what to say of women who are special target for the 'religion based' policy: they had to discontinue their jobs and the girl children cannot have access to education. The complex story of sanctions, Osama bin Laden and opium trade further worsens the plight of the Afghan people. It is clear from different examples that it is not only in the name of Islam that destruction of human heritage and values have taken place. It is not only in the name of Islam that suppression of human rights and other suppressions of minorities in their respective countries have taken place. The same Gazani who destroyed Somnath Temple passed through the route where Bamiyan is located. The medieval temples destructions were done not only by Muslim kings, Hindu Kings had their own favourite targets in the temples (Raja Harshdev of Kashmir looting temple in Kashmir, Maratha armies destroying temple in Shrirangpatanam, King Shashank cutting off Bodhi tree where Lord Gautama Buddha got Nirvana etc.), Muslim Kings also destroyed Mosques for the sake of power and wealth. If Islam is the only religion, which 'permits' such insanities than what was the religion of Hitler, which religion does LTTE follows and which religion do the 'sons of Ram' who undertook to demolish Babri mosque with the slogan *'Baccha Baccha Ram ka Janm Bhumi ke Kaam ka'* (We the children of Lord Ram are determined to build Ram Temple) follow? What is the religion of Sushama Swaraj who off and has been passing the dictates about the dress code? What is the religion of those who intimidated college girls not to wear jeans?

Taliban is no elected Government of Afghanistan; neither does it represent the aspirations of the Muslims of Afghanistan or any other country. It is an outfit, which is ruling in the name of religion. All the groups who rule or play politics in the name of religion or race indulge in Taliban like actions (Demolitions and dictates) not only in the years past but even today, though with different degree of intensity. We are witness to the similar actions from Jews in Israel, LTTE in Sri Lanka and to 'our' own Sangh Parivar in India. These political organisations, which do their politics in the name of religion or race are thoroughly anti-democratic and capable of going to any length of cruelty to impose their agenda to gain or to retain political power. Democratic and pluralist norms are the first victim in these movements. And while condemning Taliban in no uncertain and uncompromising terms one needs to give a thought to the assault on the democratic values and condemn this malady in whatever superficially appealing terms it is made.

# Section–VII

# Hindutva and Dalits

Is it a mere coincidence that the Hindutva offensive gathered its strength more so after the declaration of Mandal Commission implementation? One recalls in the early eighties Gujarat witnessed massive anti-Dalit riots and in the mid-80s it saw the anti-OBC riots. The first of these was against the reservation of Dalits in the professional colleges and the second was against the job reservation and promotions on the basis of OBC.

Right in the late nineteenth century when the efforts for education and industrial jobs began to pick up there was an opposition to this from the elite sections of Hindus, the one's who formed the base of Hindu Mahasabha and later of RSS. This ideology had to overcome a dilemma, to keep the Dalits down in their social hierarchy and also to use them as their electoral base and to use them as cannon fodder for clashes against the 'others'. This duel strategy expressed itself in various ways. Glorification of *Manusmriti* by the ideologues of Hindutva politics was one mechanism, the putting forward of Integral Humanism (IH) was another major attempt. While *Manusmriti* is blatant in its opposition to the rights of Dalits, IH is more sophisticated. It argues that society like a living being is an integrated, dynamically adjusted being and any change in its inner dynamics will lead to the clashes and disturbances, so status quo is the real way to ward off the inner disturbances.

The strategy of Sangh combine has been very complex and it adapts quickly to the changing situation, to perpetuate its agenda. When it realised that anti-Dalit riots might result in their electoral alienation, it was decided to target the 'external' enemy, i.e., Muslims and to use Dalits-Adivasis as the foot soldiers.

Also there is an attempt to partially quote Ambedkar in its anti-Muslim agenda. This can be quashed with great amount of ease only if one goes through the writings of Ambedkar in a patient manner. Sangh combine has no hesitation at all in using Ambedkar to browbeat the Muslims, even if it involves the distortion of the ideas of Ambedkar. As such also RSS family has handled Ambedkar in various ways. At one level its diehard ideologues like Shourie hit him upfront, while other in the family try to project him as the "Great Hindu Son"! At another level the attempt is taken further by floating organisations like Samrasta Manch (harmony forum). While Ambedkar called for struggle to get justice for Dalits this forum keeping him as one of the icons talks about the harmony amongst various castes.

At another level the assertion of Dalits has been expressed in various ways. One of the impacts of their movement has been their being noticed and some political parties trying to address their grievances. Bhopal declaration is one such attempt by the MP Government under the Congress leadership.

# 28

# Hindutva's Foot Soldiers—Dalits, Adivasis?

The recent Gujarat genocide of Muslims brought to fore a tragic realisation of our polity. Apart from the 'success' of Sangh Parivar in 'efficiently' coordinating this carnage and ensuring that the possibilities of rehabilitation are stifled, the factor most worrisome has been the participation of poor Dalits and Adivasis as the foot soldiers of Hindutva, doing the dirty job for the project of Hindu Rashtra. While the core leadership was with the mobile wielding supporters of Sangh Parivar, a major share of violence and looting was perpetrated through the recruitment of the subaltern sections. It is these sections that did the major part of actual implementation of the street violence. How could the major victims of Hindutva politics be mobilised for the service of RSS project of 'Hindu Rashtra in one state', in the laboratory of Hindutva politics? How could the scum of the earth, the broken people, the poor and pauperised be indoctrinated to undertake the ghastly acts unleashed against the minority community?

**Recent Happenings**

The mobilisation of Dalits for Kar Seva and the subsequent campaigns for Ram Mandir have been very intense. Many of them were sponsored to visit Ayodhya as

Ram Sevaks also. In the anti-Muslim pogrom they could be co-opted because of various reasons. To begin with, Gujarat textile industry, which was the flagship of the industrial status of Gujarat and was foremost amongst the textile trade, has been on decline resulting in job losses for huge section of population. Recruiting these sections in the violence was the major part of the strategy of the organisation of the genocide by Sangh Parivar. The closure of the textile mills in the 1980s and 1990s resulted in loss of more than 100,000 jobs, and collapse of a whole social infrastructure and culture. It also resulted in pauperisation and destitution among Ahmedabad's working class. For sociologist Jan Breman (Breman, 2002); it comes as no surprise that the front organisations of the Sangh Parivar were able to mobilize the lumpenised subaltern castes to assist in the genocide unleashed by them. More so as they were given the signals that there will be no reprisals due to taking part in the pogrom and the assurance that the loot will belong to them.

Similarly Adivasis have been involved in large number to indulge in the violence and looting against the Muslims. Interestingly the victims of the violence do not hold Adivasis as responsible for the attacks on them. They are saying that Adivasis were mobilised by allurement, threat and payment to do what they did against the minorities. Also Adivasis in particular were more involved in looting than any other type of crime during these riots. As a run up to the genocide the Adivasi psyche was carefully cultivated in the direction of anti-Muslim sentiments. The Hindu Bania moneylenders were made to reduce the rates of interest from 120 per cent to 80 per cent or so, in order to project that Bohra moneylenders at 120 per cent are exploiting them.

### The Backdrop-Gujarat in 70s and 80s

Gujarat's socio-economic development explains number of factors, which led to the present genocide, and involvement of subalterns as the foot soldiers. It is interesting that Gujarat has not seen any major reform movement in the past many decades. The neighbouring Maharashtra saw non-Brahmin movement right since twenties and this movement assisted the process of social transformation towards the democratic civil society. Gujarat overall was the house of Right wing politics and conservative social forces dominated the scene. It is here that Swatantra party (the one supporting big capital and opposed to public sector) had a major base; it is here that there were no major leaders from Dalit movement and from communist movement. The hold of Right wing politics was threatened by the KHAM (Kshtriya, Harijan, Adivasi, Muslim) combination in late seventies. The upper caste struck back in the form of anti-reservation riots. Achyut Yagnik (Yagnik, 2002) points out that the educated middle classes, mainly the Brahmins, Banias and Patidars sharply reacted to this by starting agitation against the reservation system. The clashes between savarnas and the Dalits in the industrial periphery of Ahmedabad gradually degenerated into caste war that spread to the towns in 18 out of the then 19 districts. In many villages dominated by land owning Patidars in North and central Gujarat Dalit *bastis* were burnt.

Caste tension resurfaced in 1985 in the second anti-reservation agitation. The BJP leadership drawn mainly from upper caste realised the need to expand their social base to achieve electoral success. They co-opted the Dalit OBC's in to their gambit by different Yatras etc. Advani's Rath Yatra saw pitched battles between Dalits and Muslims. Yagnik further states that RSS 'successfully' created rift between the 'Hindu Adivasis' and 'Christian Adivasis'. In absence of deeper social reforms the modern institutions and values of liberty, equality and fraternity remained weak and Hindutva, by default, provided the much-needed identity to the Dalit OBCs. This process saw its heightened expression in the wake of Mandal Commission implementation. Mr. Vajpayee formulated this response of Sangh Parivar to Mandal

Commission succinctly. He stated that we have brought Kamandal (religion based issues) in response to Mandal (symbolising the aspirations of Dalit-OBCs).

As a matter of fact Gujarat is the 'model' base of Sangh Parivar. It is not for nothing that it was chosen as the laboratory of Hindu Rashtra. The regrouping of social layers in Gujarat has been taking place since last three decades in an intense fashion. Along with urbanisation there has been a parallel process in which the rich peasants of Gujarat have achieved an enhanced social status. These *Patidar* caste (cash crop farmers) has been upgraded by a process of religious maneuvering. The polarisation of middle class (Brahmin, Bania) and Patidar occurred around 1980, around the issue of reservations for the lower castes. In 1980, Gujarat witnessed an extreme form of caste violence directed against the lower castes. The first major move of Hindutva base was to oppose the affirmative action for the Dalits. It got manifested in anti-reservation riots during early 80s. It was argued that due to these pampered 'son-in-laws' of the government who are good for nothing, the children with real merit are suffering in jobs and in admissions in professional colleges. This anti-Dalit riot was the alarm bell of the times to come.

These anti-reservation agitations played a key role in consolidating the base of upper castes and upwardly mobile middle classes. Sangh Parivar stood by to support these upper caste onslaughts. By using clever strategies Sangh Parivar was also able to give an upwardly mobile channel to a section of Dalits, who were aspiring for a better place within Hindu society. In Gujarat one can clearly see the social functionality of creating the 'other' (Muslim). Here, earlier the ultimate object of hate was the Dalit, by a clever maneuver, the Muslim was substituted for that, the Dalit has been unleashed upon the 'other', an atmosphere of terror was created, which helped to maintain a 'status quo' of social hierarchy.

The long-term goal of this politics is to push back the process of social transformation towards the pre-modern hierarchies. Various Yatras and campaigns of VHP gave cohesion to this social base. Sangh Parivar's ideological manipulation of the situation played a major role. It operated on two levels. At ideological level it regarded all those who are not Muslims and Christians as Hindus. This negative definition was given further twist by asserting that Hindus worship Cow, Ram, Vedas, Gita and Acharyas. So in turn all Adivasis and Dalits have to adopt these symbols and ideologies. This move gave a new identity to large section of subalterns. The large proliferation of different Vanvasi Kalyan Ashrams, Shishu Mandirs and other institutions occupied the cultural space lying vacant due to absence of major reform movements. The major challenge, as Shah (Shah, 2002) rightly points out, for the proponents of Hindutva is to build unity among all Hindus without disturbing dominance of the upper castes and class. Hindu Mahasabha had launched the Bharat Hindu Milan Mandir in 1920s and they have been more active in Gujarat since 1970s. Besides undertaking activities to unite various sects and organising religious festivals, they take up welfare and relief measures for the poor. The main thrust of these organisations is to build unity and harmony among the upper and lower castes.

Similarly RSS has also floated the organisation called Samajik Samrasata Manch (Social Assimilation Platform) to attract Ambedkarists and other Dalits for the purpose of developing Hindu unity. Here we again observe two separate strategies, one for Dalits and the other for Adivasis. In both, the common factor is that their material problems are not addressed and an assertive cultural identity is brought to the fore. Amongst Dalits the new middle class aspired for higher status within the Hindu social fold. Sanskritisation process made them to ape for the imitating the upper caste, to ignore and forget the material plight of their deprived brethren. The deprived one's amongst them got swept in the cultural whirlpool of Swadhyay, Asaram Bapus, Swaminarayan type sects and Pandurang Shashtris who proliferated in Gujarat duly supported by the section of affluent middle class. They did bring the traditional Brahminical values in modern garb, laced in sugary syrup. These outfits have spread the idea of Hindutva and the pride in being Hindu, based on Hindutva ideology, cutting across different communities. Joseph Mcwan (Mcwan 2002) points out, "enamored by their wealth and power the Ambedkerite Dalits turned towards BJP. Those who aligned themselves with RSS also managed to acquire power". The core of RSS project through all these mechanisms has been to turn all the castes against Muslims and Christians. Dagger in the velvet cloak was pierced through the material aspirations of Dalits, the ideology of status quo at the level of pre-industrial norms; Hindutva, was imposed in a most respectable form.

It is in this context that the anti-Christian missionary campaign was brought in. The argument that all those living in this country are Hindus was taken to the practical logic. The one's converting to 'other', 'foreign' religions were supposed to be doing so under the allurement of the money or other favours. Hinduism was projected as superior to other faiths as it neither does, nor believes in conversions. Here two birds are killed in one stone. Hinduism, i.e., Brahmanism, cannot undertake conversions in the real sense, as it is an exclusive club. The lower castes do like to convert to escape the social injustice imposed by the upper caste, practicing Brahminical ideology. The argument is cleverly twisted and the 'elite exclusivism' is presented as the virtue. So all those who convert are supposed to have succumbed to the guile or intimidation of the 'foreign religion' so they need to be 'reconverted back' to Hinduism by newly developed rituals. Also they have to be taught to throw away their old gods and taught the virtues of Ram, Gita and Acharyas. And in this direction the Christian missionaries need to be taught a lesson, few Bibles to be burnt, Nuns and Fathers beaten up, etc.

Gujarat has seen all this more than the other places of India where the religious fascism of Sangh Parivar is stalking the streets.

**Cultural Onslaught of Hindutva**

While Gujarat has been the major field of operation, other parts of India have been witnessing similar process. In different states the local cultural metaphors are being substituted by the newly manufactured one's. In his exhaustive appraisal of Surat riots of 1992, Irfan Engineer points out that the propaganda of the BJP has communalised the young in Surat especially those belonging to Machhi, Kharva, Rana, Ghanchi, and traditional OBC communities. According to Engineer earlier they used to be strong supporters of the Congress but have now moved away from it. These communities have prospered in the recent years and are looking for new power equations and broader identities. They are shedding their old customs and *kuldevis* and have begun adopting the customs of upper castes. The BJP has 'successfully' responded to their aspirations by giving them a broader identity through its Hindutva campaign. Also its propaganda has given this identity a nationalistic and patriotic colour. A reform movement to give up certain rituals preceded the desire for a broader identity and subsequent communalisation in these communities. Education is also on the rise among them. Simultaneously their economic base has widened as they have moved into new areas, instead of confining themselves to their original professions. They are also looking for a wider political role for themselves. While the old political equations and arrangements in the Congress provided them with only limited opportunities, BJP as a rising force is providing them new opportunities and greater participation.

The propagation of Hindutva through *Vinayaka* idols is one of the common features. In most of the southern states the VHP and other affiliates of Sangh Parivar have been promoting the Brahminical rituals and are Brahminising the existing rituals and practices. Many sociological studies have shown the tactics adopted by Sangh Parivar in culturally co-opting the subalterns in to the gambit of Brahminical culture. The Sangh Parivar has also used different social facilities like night schools and youth camps to subsume the Dalit identity into a Pan Hindu identity. Many a Dalits have subordinated their caste identity and claimed themselves as Hindus. (S. Anandhi, 1995). The degeneration of Dravida Munetra movement into the AIDMK and the capitulation of present DMK to the Brahminising influence need no recounting. The upwardly mobile aspirations of sections of Dalits have given Sanskritisation process a boost.

This onslaught has operated at three levels. At the level of ideology it has been saying that it does not believe in caste system. Further the origin of caste system itself has been shifted from the original codes of Manu to the influence of 'Foreign' religions!. As per this the invading Muslim kings wanted to convert all and sundry by force. And those who defied this had to face lots of ignominies and had to take resort into jungles and thereby became untouchables. Also it has been propounded that ideas of Ambedkar and RSS on caste system are similar. Here in a clever move the polar opposite nature of both these is hidden from the people. Dr. Ambedkar burns *Manusmriti* and presides over the drafting of Indian Constitution. RSS upholds *Manusmriti* and asks for rejection of Indian Constitution.

At social level long ago, Hindu Mahasabha founded Bharat Sevashram and Hindu Milan Mandir. Lately RSS has founded many an organisations for Dalits. The core philosophy around which these operate state that the caste struggle is not desirable and what we need is caste-harmony, Samajik Samrasata (Social Assimilation). This has trapped many a middle sections of Dalits who have derived benefits of the reservation and other social avenues. These organisations floated by RSS have given a broad Hindu identity to the section of Dalits, who have accepted it as an avenue for upward mobility. The plethora of these organisations apart from organising Hinduised versions of popular festivals also arrange the programmes of interdining (Ram Khichadi) to make their social presence felt amongst the Dalit sections of society. The tendency to blindly worship Phule and Ambedkar has been taken full advantage of by Brahminising them. Sangh Parivar has no problems in worshipping these major contributors to Dalit movement so far as their teachings are kept under wraps.

**Dalit Movement**

Parts of the reason due to which, these strategies have succeeded are the fragmentation of the Dalit movement. Phule identified both the aspects of needs of Dalits, the material and the one's related to Dalit self-respect. His depiction of peasant as a 'Shudra and peasant both' contains the deep understanding of the social situation of the exploited sections. His contribution Shetkaryache Asaud (Cultivators Whipcord) is a good example of his grasp on the situation of Dalits. Similarly Dr. Ambedkar also recognised the need to base the Dalit movement on the material and identity issues. That's why he could found the Independent Labour Party even when talking of Mahad movement for access to public water and Kalaram Temple agitation to get social equality. Later Dadsaheb Gaikawad's agitation for land rights had the germ of this integrated need in it. In early 70s, while Dalit Panthers did come out with brilliant manifesto, even before it could be translated into some agitations most of the leaders of the movement found themselves in the lap of established leadership of upper caste-class parties. The emergence of Kanshi Ram on the horizon of Dalit politics was full of great promise but his lack of assessment of the fascist nature of Sangh Parivar and its difference from other parties is resulted in its opportunist alliance with the party of Hindutva. The intense fragmentation of Dalit leadership in a way is a reflection of the lopsided approach to the problems of Dalits. Last few decades have seen an exclusive focus on issues related to Dalit identity at the cost of their material issues. The Phule-Ambedkar approach of synthesising both these has been forgotten. This may be one of the main reasons for not being able to give a unified direction to the Dalit masses. In the resulting vacuum, the Hindutva ideology has occupied the space and the consequent subordination to Hindutva politics and readiness to act as foot soldiers of the Sangh Parivar's agenda of Hindu Rashtra is there for all to see.

**Aims of Hindutva**

Hindutva is the politics of Hindu elite, propagator of Brahminical values in the modern garb, preserving the birth based hierarchies of caste and gender. In present parlance it is a counter-reaction to the process of social-transformation, which occurred during last century, more particularly after the Independence. The process, by which, the pre-modern hierarchies have been shaken to some extent. It is politically comparable to fascism and fundamentalism. Fascists did this in the name of race while Hindutva does it in the name of Hindu religion, trying to hide the Brahminical content of its current versions. It got boost and power mainly due to the upper caste reaction to the assertion of the Dalits for their rights. It is a counter-reaction of the upper caste-class to thwart the process of social transformation towards liberty. equality, fraternity. It's clever use of cultural mechanisms has given it 'success' in parts to make 'use' of the subalterns for their dirty jobs.

**Future Projections**

Gujarat is the most heightened expression of the state of affairs prevalent in the country. While the balance of forces may be different in different places the broad contours are similar. At many a places the Dalit-Bahujan-Adivasis have better organisations and perspectives but the overall lack of direction leads to its subjugation to Sangh combine in critical times. The decline of left politics and progressive culture has stifled the space and left a vacuum, which has been occupied by the new Brahminical symbolisms. Even existing progressive institutions have been Brahminised to some extent. Global support to the retrograde culture and imposition of the lopsided globalisation has also some role to play in today's pathetic situation. The fragmentation of Dalit leadership and its underestimation of the threats to Indian democracy from Sangh combine by other section of Dalit leadership has contributed immensely to the 'success' of Hindutva politics.

## References

S. Anandhi, *Contending Identities*, ISI, Delhi, 1995.

Jan Breman, *Economic and Political Weekly*, 20-26 April, 2002.

Irfan Enginer, *Surat riots, Investigation and analysis*, pp. 2-3, Centre for Study of Society and Secularism, 1993.

Joseph Mcwan, Society Under Siege, *Seminar*, May 2002.

Ghanshyam Shah, 'Caste, Hindutva and Hideousness', *Economic and Political Weekly*, 15 April 2002, p. 1391.

Achyut Yagnik, The Pathology of Gujarat, *Seminar*, May 2002.

# 29

# Riddles of Hindutva

In the aftermath of Gujarat violence (Feb. 2002), where it is presumed that Hindutva has 'succeeded' and brought dividends for the BJP, aggressive Hindutva of Modi variety is being recommended as the prescription for success of BJP and as a route for the Hindu Rashtra. Pursuing this aggressive Hindutva, Mr. Katiyar, BJP President of UP, has been going hammer and tongs spreading anti-Muslim sentiments. And to buttress his venom he has been using the selective quotations from Ambedkar's writing showing him as anti-Muslim.

What are being misused are the selective quotes from his books on Partition. A complete reading of the book reveals that he studied the problem in its multiple dimensions and in his summary he went on to say two major things. "Strange as it may appear Mr. Savarkar and Mr. Jinnah instead of being opposed to each other on the one nation versus two nations issue are in complete agreement about it. Both agree, not only agree but insist, that there are two nations in India—one the Muslim nation and the other the Hindu nation." he continues, "They differ only as regards the terms and conditions on which the two nations should be. Jinnah says India should be cut up into two, Pakistan and Hindustan, the Muslim nation to occupy Pakistan and the Hindu nation to occupy Hindustan. Mr. Savarkar on the other hand insists that, although there are two nations in India, India shall not be divided into two parts, one for the Muslims and the other for Hindus; that the two nations shall dwell in one country and shall live under the mantle of one single constitution: that the constitution shall be such that the Hindu nation will be enabled to occupy a predominant position that is due to it and the Muslim nation made to live in the position of subordinate co-operation with the Hindu nation." (Third section, Chapter VII)

He was for composite Indian nationalism, "Is it not a fact that under the Montague Chelmsford reforms in most provinces, if not in all, the Muslims, the non-Brahmins and Depressed Classes united together and worked for the reforms as members of one team from 1920 to 1937? Herein lay the most fruitful method of achieving communal harmony among Hindus and Muslims and of destroying the danger of Hindu Raj. Mr. Jinnah could have easily pursued this line. Nor was it difficult for Mr. Jinnah to succeed in it." (*Thoughts on Pakistan*, p. 359)

Rather than being anti-Muslim, he tried to project that both these Hindu and Muslim nationalism are not the democratic nationalism. While chairing the drafting committee of Indian Constitution he picked up the principles, which were totally opposed to the ideologies of communal nationalism. In addition he was concerned about safeguards for minorities and Dalits both. What was the life and mission of Dr. Ambedkar. Is it that Katiyar and company has suddenly been inspired by the ideology of Ambedkar? Today it has become extremely important to understand this again as in Ambedkar's name a politics totally opposed to his values is being brought in. He was the one to suffer and realize the vagaries of caste system, the inalienable part of Brahminical Hinduism. His attempts for social justice in the form of Chavdar talab (right to access public drinking water),

Kalaram Mandir (right to be treated as equals in places of worship) and *Manusmriti* (symbol of caste and gender hierarchy) burning are major landmarks in the history of Dalit liberation. While he went on to burn the *Manusmriti*, the founders of Hindutva ideology have deep reverence for *Manusmriti*. Dr. Ambedkar campaigned for social reforms all through his life. He could also see that in Hinduism the prevalent notions are those of Brahminical stream only. In his book *Riddles of Hinduism* published by Education Department, Govt. of Maharashtra in 1987 he elaborates his understanding about Hinduism, i.e., its Brahminical version, "The book is an exposition of the beliefs propounded by what might be called Brahminic theology... I want to make people aware that Hindu religion is not Sanatan (eternal)...the second purpose of the book is to draw the attention of Hindu masses to the devices of Brahmins and make them think for themselves how they have been deceived and misguided by Brahmins"(Introduction).

He goes on to affirm, "Now the Brahmins have left no room for doubt for they have propounded a most mischievous dogma which the Brahmins have spread amongst the masses, is the dogma of infallibility of Vedas. If Hindu intellect has ceased to grow and if the Hindu civilisation and culture has become stagnant and stinking pool, this dogma must be destroyed root and branch if India is to progress. The Vedas are a worthless set of books. There is no reason either to call them sacred or infallible. The Brahmins have invested it with sanctity and infallibility only because by a later interpolation of what is called Purusha-Sukta, the Vedas have made them the Lords of the earth."

Today the Hindutva is claiming to be a form of cultural nationalism. In its construction of Culture Vedas, Acharyas and Ram have a central place. Vedas' importance is unquestionable for Hindutva as it upholds inequality of caste and gender at deeper level. And Brahminical values do form the base of Hindutva. Though it is said that "we" do not believe in caste system, the caste hierarchy is ingrained in all the ideological projections and symbolisms of Hindutva politics. It is the same Brahminism dominated Hinduism about which Dr. Ambedkar went on to say that I was born a Hindu that was not in my hands but I will not die a Hindu. And that's how his quest began for search of another religion, which can give social justice to Dalits, and that's how he converted to Buddhism with his followers in 1956. And that's what many a Dalits realize at the cost of their lives. In Jajjhar again many a Dalits converted to Buddhism after five of them were killed for skinning the dead cow, another symbol of assertive Brahminism and Hindutva today.

It is not for nothing that the journey to the Hindu Rashtra has been signalled with the agitation for Ram Temple. This movement revolved around primacy of Ram as symbol of Indian (Hindu is synonymous for Indian, in Hindutva ideology) identity. Ram is also the major symbol of cultural nationalism. Lets see what Ambedkar has to say about Lord Ram, "The life of Sita simply did not count. What counted was his own personal name and fame. He of course does not take the manly course of stopping this gossip, which as a king could do and which as husband who was convinced of his wife's innocence he was bound to it." And further, "For 12 years the boys lived in forest in Ashram of Valmiki not far from Ayodhya where Ram continued to rule. Never once in those 12 years this model Husband and living father cared to inquire what has happened to Sita whether she was alive or dead", "...Sita preferred to die rather than return to Ram who had behaved no better than a brute." The signals to the Dalits in Hindutva' cultural nationalism are more than glaringly obvious as the Lord demonstrates in his own life, "...he was a Shudra named Shambuk who was practicing Tapasya with a view to going to heaven in his own earthly person and without so much as a warning, expostulation or the like addressed to him, cut off his head..."(From Riddles of Rama and Krishna). Incidentally the clones of Katiyar in Maharashtra (Shiv Sena) raised hell when this book of Dr. Ambedkar was due to be published by the Government of Maharashtra.

Currently the reigning RSS supremo, Mr. K.S. Sudarshan clarified the relationship between Hindutva and Dr. Ambedkar's ideology. On assuming this highest position in the hierarchy of Hindutva politics, Sudarshan went on to say that Indian Constitution is anti-Hindu, is based on western values and should be done away with and the one based on Hindu holy books be brought in. It does not require too much guessing to find out as to which is that holy book in which the laws of society are given. So Ambedkar stands for burning *Manusmriti* and contributing to making of Indian Constitution while the Hindutva stands for the inverse of this. It is tragic that the person whose all life and struggles were for throwing away Hindutva politics is being misquoted to achieve the goals contrary to his own. It is also tragic that the likes of Katiyar are abusing one the greatest sons of freedom struggle, while those doing politics in his name are either quiet on this or are compromising with the same for the short-term goals of power.

# 30

# Children of Lesser God

From last more than a decade social space and the major newspaper space is full of the news to build the Temple for Lord Ram. The 'Noble People', the saffron robed saints, their associates, the 'Hindu Nationalists' of RSS and their followers have been wielding Trishuls and *lathis* to wipe away the 'symbol of shame'. They assert that as per their 'faith' their Lord was born exactly at the spot where 'symbol of shame' was situated. Thanks to their hard work, at least one symbol of shame, Babri Masjid has been done away with! For the Hindu Rashtra this is the core issue. It is not a coincidence that at the same time the problems of the 'tribe of Shambuk' the Dalits, have been shunted to the margins of social psyche and the media. It is in this backdrop that the Bhopal Declarations of Dalit Rights (Jan. 12-13, 2002) went unnoticed. The Honourable President of India, K.R. Narayanan in his Republic Day speech tried to bring it to our attention but again in vain. Dr. Narayanan in his anguish said, "The discrimination being suffered by women, the scheduled castes and scheduled tribes is a crying denial of the democracy that is enshrined in our Constitution. Recently a conference was held in Bhopal of Dalit and tribal intellectuals and activists. They issued a Declaration called the Bhopal Declaration charting out a new course for Dalits and the tribal people for the 21st century."

What is this Declaration, which the President thought worth mentioning in his Republic Day address? While the popular opinion is being doctored by those in power and those who control the media, for war against the neighbour, against terrorism etc. What business President has got to talk about the plight of Dalits, women and other weaker sections of society? Today Dalits occupy lowest rung of the ladder in social development, access to facilities like water, education, health care and jobs. They do share their plight with the 'dreaded' minority, the Muslims. One can very well ask that when so many provisions, 'reservations' etc. have been made for them, so why this complaint? Is there not a quota for them in jobs, in admissions in professional colleges etc.? Is it not that to pamper these our 'meritorious' children are suffering? So why this advocacy by the President to improve their lot, why this Bhopal Charter, which calls for restoring their land to them with compensation, giving them living agricultural wages, right and opportunity to use the common social property, gender parity in wages, quota in the capital share, access to compulsory quality education and reservation in private sector. It calls for democratisation of capital, proper application of Prevention of Atrocities Act amongst others. Were the earlier provisions not enough? And if the country is to bother about all this for this 'pampered' lot who will take care of the temple of Lord Ram for which even our 'worthy sons of the soil', settled in Dollarland are sending money as a gesture of their 'patriotism' for this Rashtra of theirs'?

In a way the Bhopal declaration and the Ram Janmbhumi campaign are two contrasting poles of our society. With the freedom and bringing in of democratic constitution the politics in the name of religion was quiescent for some time. It is not that the seeds of this politics were not laid. Ram was already given the place of 'Symbol of Nationalism' as the glorious monarch of this land. But the followers of this Hindu Rashtra politics were on the margins. First three decades of the republic saw a painfully slow but sure journey towards the social transformation, towards liberty, equality and fraternity. Even during this period the reservations, which were meant for the downtrodden, were sabotaged by the entrenched upper caste/class hegemony. Some benefits did accrue to the Dalit sections. The rise of these sections, though small, threatened the status quo to which this society had been used to for centuries and the counter-reaction to this minimal gain began with the rise of VHP and other children of RSS, who by word of mouth spread the poison against Dalits, their being non-meritorious, their being the son-in-laws of the government, etc. This poison seeped in to the elite sections of society and it burst out first in the anti-reservation riots in Gujarat in 1981. The think tank of the Hindutva politics soon realised that it may be better to co-opt the elite sections of Dalits in its own gambit and instead target an 'enemy', who is outside the Hindu fold, the Muslim (Christians were to be the next) and keep the social attention sidetracked to the issues which have no real relevance to society.

The idea as one can see in the hindsight was to intimidate the society through communal violence. And in the terrifying atmosphere created through the anti-Muslim violence the social transformation and quest for human rights as such can be undermined in the name of 'patriotism.' And that is how, Lord Ram and the Sants came to the rescue of Hindutva politics. And through the emotive (religious sounding) appeals, Rath Yatras, etc. the elite upper caste/class sections were brought together into the political fold, which supported the demolition and in a way indirectly promoted the communalisation of society. And thus the Ram politics, which was on margins, came to the centre stage and problems of tribe of Shambuk were pushed to the margins. With this, every affirmative action came to be being looked as pampering or appeasement, at the same time shedding the crocodile tears for the plight of 'our Vanvasi brethren', or our 'poor Hindu' brothers.

The 'brilliance' of this strategy has paid heavy dividends to the social elite. It is not only at electoral level. At social level while the guns are targeted against the 'internal threats to Hindu Nation' (Muslims, Christians and Communists, a la M.S. Golwalkar, the RSS ideologue) the real intent of the exercise is to ensure the preservation of status quo or better still push it backwards in the space of time and reverse whatever little could be achieved by these children of the lesser Gods. It is in this direction that the attacks on Christian missionaries have been engineered. These attacks achieve two simple purposes. On one hand the literacy and health facilities being offered by the missionaries need to be stopped, as nothing can be worse than an educated Adivasi, aware of his rights etc. So instead fill the 'vacuum' by Ekal schools, a Hindutva training centre where all 'glorious' aspects of Hindu Rashtra are dished out to make the compliant followers. Where there is no need for the modern education, as it is a 'symbol of mental slavery' to the West. In cities the regular outbursts of communal violence and communal hatred manufactured by different 'innovative' mechanisms will ensure the halting of any semblance of progress, which threatens the social equilibrium.

So we have two alternative paths lying in front of us. Indian Constitution, secularism, democracy, affirmative action, and struggle for social transformation, and in this direction the declarations like Bhopal, on one hand. On the other is the currently assertive politics of Hindu Rashtra, scrapping the 'Western-values based constitution' and return to Hindu Holy scriptures, politics of Ram Janmbhumi, then Krishna Janmbhumi then... till all the vestiges of 'foreign rule' are wiped out and 'self-respect' is infused courtesy the Sants, Mahants and *Khaki Knickerwallahs*, i.e., all those who had nothing to do with our freedom struggle and process of formation of India in to a nation. According to this path Hindu society has already achieved the 'best' set of social and universal values, meaning thereby that pre-independence status quo has to be restored and the deviant path adopted by Nehru (Modernisation) and Ambedkar's constitution has to be buried for good. So today, like no time before in the past, the choice in front of us is starkly clear, towards Ram Temple and all that or Bhopal declaration and improvement in the lot of oppressed and exploited sections of society. Can we dare the dangling Trishuls on our heads and give a thought to the plight of oppressed and exploited, to Bhopal Declaration?

# Section–VIII

# Women and Hindu Right

The ascendance of imperialism, unipolar U.S. dominance and the rise of fundamentalism have another fallout and that is on the gender equations. With secularisation the process of gender justice began. Democracy gives a space to women to struggle for their equality, to struggle for converting the formal equality into substantive equality, i.e., to march in that direction. The organisations, which have come up in the name of religion, have bluntly or subtly tried to reverse this journey. It is interesting to note that Hitler, who smothered democracy in the name of race based nationalism also did the same when he floated, 'Kitchen, Church and Children' as the core value around, which women's lives should revolve. It is no coincidence that the recent rise of fundamentalism, religion-based politics also operates on the similar understanding about the role of women. Taliban through their Fatwa banned the women's working outside family. RSS is exclusively a male organisation and its subordinate body for women, Rashtra Sevikasamiti, does not have the word, swayam or 'self' as accordingly to the patriarchal ideology of Hindutva or Talibans, women's lives are to be controlled by men.

The similarity of basic ideology is no surprise as at one level the political streams basing themselves on religion, revert back to feudal gender equations when clergy were associates of the kings.

Many a debates in the current times revolve around these, be it the issue of supporting the sati tradition by a section of Hindu right or the issue of uniform civil code at another level. The crux of the matter in these has to be gender justice but it is deflected to 'inter religious' issue and thereby sidetracking of the basic issue. Controlling the lives of women by various ideological manipulations and also physically is the cultural accompaniment of the rise of fundamentalist politics. Interestingly many a times a section of women adopts these values in a rabid fashion and they themselves become the vehicle of this ideology. At places the role of women in policy matters shows this. Lately, in communal violence also a section of women themselves participated and assisted 'their' males in intimidating and harassing the minority community.

# 31

# Fundamentalism and Women's Rights

Last few decades have seen a rise in culture of intolerance. This intolerance is being imposed in the name of religion. In different countries of Middle East, Saudi Arabia, Iran, Afghanistan and Pakistan, this phenomenon has been brought in the name of Islam. India has witnessed the similar process in the name of Hinduism, Hindutva to be more precise. These phenomena on one hand stifle the democratic rights of weaker sections of society as a whole and on the other hand suppress the women at social and political level. This suppression comes in the form of *Fatwas* to wear a particular type of dress and particular legislations supposedly based on Sharia. It also comes as dictates in the name of Hindu traditions, ban on wearing particular clothes or warning not to celebrate particular festivals, etc. The currently raging Islamism, politics in the name of Islam and Hindutva, politics in the name of Hinduism are a grave threat to the pluralism and emerging gender sensitive values of our society. These streams have been called fundamentalism or religious fascism. We will use the term fundamentalism for the same.

## Fundamentalism

The word fundamentalism is many times used for the idea of going back to the fundamentals of religions. As a social phenomenon it does not convey the full meaning of the term. In broad sense the term denotes those religious movements, which claim doctrines to be immutable and demand from believers a literal acceptance of the tenets of religion contained in the sacred books as interpreted by them. Fundamentalism rejects attempts at rational interpretation and prefers blind faith to the arguments based on reason. It demands a blind, strict observance of all traditional religious prescriptions. There are three basic trends in this phenomenon, "First, fundamentalisms are inevitably political. Secondly, fundamentalist movements are also genuinely religious: 'We will fail to understand these movements if we neglect their irreducible religious dimension'. Thirdly, religious fundamentalisms are hegemonic, anti-pluralist movements that are constrained in their impact by the conflicting demands made upon them by their dual identity as inherently religious and inherently political entities." (Kanungao, 2002, 15)

This phenomenon increases the intensity of its appeal, it creates hysteria against an internal imaginary or real enemy. In Saudi Arabia it is targeted against women in India against Muslims and Christians, in Iran, the previous ruler Raza Shah was used as a whipping boy. Fundamentalism's projection of past is a ruse while what is being demanded is a pattern of modern practice.

**The Origins**

The term was first used to denote the orthodox trend in modern Protestantism, which emerged in North America just before First World War as a response to the spread of theological modernism and liberalism in Christianity. After 1910 this trend came to be known as fundamentalism. Its proponents demanded stronger faith in traditional Christian dogma and particularly in the unquestioned infallibility of Bible. These beliefs and practices were widely shared in U.S. throughout nineteenth century. The followers of this phenomenon took on the battle through their own institutions and through nation's schools. They organised campaigns against religious liberalism in the churches and the teachings of evolution in the schools. But they did loose out in the battle and modern voices of rationalism prevailed. Irrespective of their defeat they did build up massive institutional infrastructure for spread of their ideas. Even today women in Christian Malawi are forced to abide by state enforced dress code.

**Islamic Countries**

In Islamic countries it came to the forefront since the coming in of Ayatollah Khoemini, who could come to power due to the misrule of American puppet, Raza Shah Pahlavi. Currently some countries are fully in grip of such a movement, while some others are having state sponsored Islamic revivalism and a political and social system through partial implementation of Sharia. In Pakistan it has been coming to fore off and on and Hudood ordinance has been one of the reflections of this trend.

While some Muslim countries are in full grip of Islamic Fundamentalism, there are others where the trends manifest in various degrees. "Ruling classes implement only those parts of Islamic Sharia which suit their political purpose. Islam is sought to be used by them to preserve and strengthen status quo. There was no popular demand in Pakistan nor in Iran and much less in Saudi Arabia to enforce Islamic Sharia" (Engineer, 1994, 86). Even in Iran the upsurge, which was popular and widespread began as a revolt against Raza Shah Pehlvi, whose repressive regime was very unpopular. This popular upsurge against Shah was having dangerous potentials for upper class as the leaders of upsurge, Mujahidin and Fidayin were quite influential, and they wanted to give it the turn towards social change. "As the ruling class of Iran and clergy led by Ayatollah Khoemini were aware of the revolutionary potential of this movement, and they ensured to enforce medieval Islam, a fundamentalist regime, to avoid the loss of their own social status and power. Mujahidin had the motto towards annihilation of exploitation and oppression of every kind and realisation of classless society." (Engineer, *Ibid*)

In Iran interestingly lot of women came forward for the protest against Shah's regime, protesting against the consumerist culture being propagated by his regime. They made veil as the symbol of their resistance. But after the fundamentalists took over the movement and then the regime, they were pushed back to the restricted roles of mothers and wives. For them, "Chador became legally binding requirement, the age of marriage was reduced to thirteen years, divorce became practically impossible, and husbands right to permission for wage work was restored" (Haleh Afsari, 1994)

In Pakistan, the Huddood Ordinance of 1979 sanctioned flogging for adultery and rape, removing the distinction between the two. They brought in a law of evidence whereby weightage of the evidence of women was reduced by half that of a man. The Sharia ordinance was brought in 1988, which advises Muftis to advise the federal governments. In Bangladesh, in 1988 government passed a bill making Islam as the state religion. Women announcers were told to cover their heads and not to wear bindis on their foreheads. Algerian women lost their right to marry in their right and to legal custody of children while men got the right to vote in their wives' name. The Taliban regime of Afghanistan was the cruelest expression of this trend. The Talibans banned women's work outside home, put a clamp on their education and a dictate a day was their norm to suppress and intimidate the women. Today many Islamic countries are in the grip of this phenomenon in a very clear form.

### Hindu Fundamentalism

Hindu fundamentalism is becoming more assertive from 1980s. RSS and its progeny is a mix of fascist and fundamentalist traits. In India the matters are in the different stage. Here the fundamentalist outfit Sangh Parivar has so far not succeeded in capturing the power in toto. Its ideology and some of its actions during last few years are an index of what more is in store for the women as far as suppression of their rights is concerned. RSS, the patriarch of Sangh Parivar (SP), does not permit women to be its members. Like Taliban, it is an exclusively male body. The women are permitted to be the members of the subordinate organisation, Rashtra Sevika Samiti. The prefix Swayam (Self) in the name of this women's body is missing, that does indicates the patriarchal nature of this ideology. Its ideologue M.S. Golwalkar in his book *Bunch of thoughts* clearly states that the rules of *Manusmriti* are eternal and should be applicable for all the times. The current chief K.S. Sudarshan also stated that the present Indian Constitution (based on liberty, equality and fraternity) is based on western values, so should be replaced by the one based on Indian holy books (e.g., *Manusmriti*, etc.).

In the same spirit BJP looks upon women as *matrishakhti* (mother power). Similarly BJP Mahila Morcha (women's wing) proclaims that they differ from what is termed as women's liberation movement in the west. Rashtra Sevika Samiti affirms that we require a sort of readjustment in the social and family set up. "No fundamental change in values is needed. Women in India ever had a pride of place within the household and society. That has only to be re-established and reaffirmed. Even as per Mridula Sinha, ex-President of BJP's Mahila Morcha, women's role in family is primary. In their life and activities family and its unity must be given priority. Too much of freedom to women would break the family to which SP is strongly opposed. This is in stark contrast to the premises of women's movement, which challenges the domination of women within family and society. Ideology of Hindutva aims to subjugate the women with an honourable looking place in society and family" (Puniyani, 2000). Lately one witnessed various assertions from the members of Sangh Parivar, advising the TV newsreaders to dress in a particular way (Sushma Swaraj, I&B minister), the Bajrang Dal volunteers opposing the girls wearing of Jeans, and also opposing the celebration of valentine day.

Despite some differences there are 'core' level similarities between fundamentalists' attitude to women and the Nazi attitude to women. Nazis looked down upon female emancipation and motherhood for women was projected to be the most sacred virtue (Hitler—Motherhood is the greatest honour for women). It was projected that German women have more liking for kitchen, home and rearing children and church, 'German women want to be wives and mothers'. She was projected to be vehicle of German culture and guardian of its racial purity, also being told to be virtuous by accepting sacrifices. Most of women had enthusiasm in Hitler's project due to its social importance accorded to the activities, which they carried out anyway (kitchen, child rearing). Adolf Hitler was quoted in modified form by Golwalkar who said 'wonderful thing about nature, e.g., providence is that there is no conflict between the sexes as long as each of them performs the function prescribed by nature'. Official Nazi doctrine proclaimed the ideology of sex differences between men and women and went on to prescribe sex specific work.

**Fundamentalism and Women**

This phenomenon imposes the role of women as wives and mothers, while other roles of women are relegated to the background. Their concern is to ensure that women are chained in ideological constraints and to increase men's control over women. It aims to restore the birth based hierarchy of gender in which woman is to be the property of man. These controls operate through the emotive appeal of religions. Most of the women tend to internalize it and collude with fundamentalist groups and in the process find their comfort. This is possible as religious beliefs are not imposed but generated and developed in the process of appropriation and reconstruction of social and personal existence.

The countries where the rise of imposition of *fatwas* and dictates on women is being seen are the one's where the secularisation process (removal of the hold of clergy on the social affairs) is not complete. Some of these countries see the coming up of women in the social space due to the industrialisation process. This changes the social dynamics of genders. Women becoming equal citizen's comes to the fore and the vested interests are opposed to this new equation of genders. The women's going out for work creates a new situation and a threat to the loss of control over their lives. It is the strongest form of patriarchal control, and is brought through the language of religion.

In a way fundamentalism is a strategy of vested interests of society who stand to oppose social transformation. They do this in the form of revival of set of doctrines from scriptures or religious traditions, which they project to be opposed to the changes society is witnessing. They oppose the changes in the name of defending the faith of religious community, whose identity is threatened as per them. In order to preserve this identity the social norms of the era gone-by are reasserted. The retrieval of doctrines is very selective. These 'fundamentals' are redefined as per their social contingency. Essentially this exercise aims to fend off the new set of social values, which threaten status quo. And all this is done in a religious language for better effect. It does not intend at artificial imposition of old practices and life styles nor does it aim a simple return to a sacred past, a golden era, "Instead religious identity thus renewed becomes exclusive and absolute basis for recreated political and social order that is oriented to future rather than the past. By selecting elements of tradition and modernity, fundamentalists seek to remake the world in the service of dual commitment to the unfolding eschatological drama (by returning all things in submission to the divine) and to self-preservation (by neutralising the threatening other) (Marty M.E. and Appleby R.S., 1994). Fundamentalists are involved with political life even when they attempt to preserve their separateness from secular society. They do participate in the matters related to modernisation, development political structure, etc.

Thus it can be inferred that it is a social movement targeting against liberal values of society against society's potential march towards non-hierarchical relationships. It is an imposition of retrograde conservative values, selectively culled out from religious books or practices. It suppresses the fact that there is no homogeneity within religions, and constructs the version of religion suitable for vested interest. Despite the superficial opposition between different fundamentalisms they share these basic creeds, each claims that theirs' is the only true creed based on divine law. All fundamentalisms feel threatened by pluralism.

## References

Afsari Haleh, Quoted in Amrita Chachi, Women and Religious Fundamentalism in South Asia, in Andreas Nehring Fundamentalism and Secularism, Gurukul Summer Institute, 1994.

Engineer Asghar Ali, *Islamic Fundamentalism, In Religious Fundamentalism in South Asia,* (Ed. V.D. Chopra), Gyan Publishing House, 1994, p. 86.

Kanungao P., *RSS's Tryst with Politics,* Manohar, Delhi, 2002, p. 15.

Marty M.E. and Appleby R.S., *Accounting for Fundamentalisms,* Chicago Press, 1994.

Puniyani Ram, *Fascism of Sangh Parivar,* Media House, New Delhi, 2000, p. 86.

# 32

# Hindu Right and Women

I would like to begin my talk by drawing your attention to the fact as to why an organisation like Mahila Jagruthi feels the need to be concerned about communal problem. As per my understanding of Hindutva phenomenon, it primarily aims at suppressing the rights and aspirations of the most exploited and weak sections of the society. It is not only the Christians and Muslims who are victims of this oppression, but also the women, who I feel, are the worst targets.

While pondering over this topic, there are contradictory points, which come to our mind. First point is regarding Hindutva against women. How do we understand the same party, BJP, which is calling for 33 per cent reservation for women is also the party whose women and men functionaries have passed opinions against the women's rights? Second, in the Education Minister's (organised by Murli Manohar Joshi, a top leader of BJP) conference, a proposal was mooted for special provisions for educating the girl child. And what were these special provisions? Girls in middle and high school should be taught cooking and home management as part of their curriculum. I would not treat this as a minor issue. It is certainly very significant and we shall now see how we can understand this issue.

The Hindutva phenomenon is opposed to women's liberation movement on the grounds that "Well in India, why are you talking about women's liberation? India is a land where women are always worshipped. And we do not need any particular ideology about women's liberation as we have already given them a high place in the society as goddesses."

I'll come to the other statements by Sangh Parivar a while later. Let us travel back to the ancient days, when the so-called Hindu religion prevailed and women were worshipped. It is true that a few women did contribute to the Vedas and the Upanishads but that was again a very marginal participation. However, the major statement about the status of women at that particular point of time was from *Manusmriti*.

*Manusmriti* was not a fictional or imaginary piece by Manu. It was representative of the type of society at that time. And what does Manu say about the position of women? A woman is always a dependent being. She is dependent on her father at a young age, later on husband and son. Woman was always regarded as property of man. She was equated to a field where men plough and so the production of the field belonged to the men. This was in 2nd Century AD now travelling straight to 15th Century AD; a period when Tulsidas, the famous poet saint lived. He said "*Dhol, pishach, shudra, pashu, nari/sakal tadana ke adhikari*" which means, the drum, untouchable, animal and woman deserve to be beaten. That was their status in society. The point I'm trying to make here is that the position of women in the second and 15th century was little different from the second century. The first conscious fabrication by Hindutva ideologues is that we in India always had a place of pride for women. This was said so that the women would not be able to struggle for equal rights in the society. Also it is being said that it is due to Islam and the 'barbaric' Muslim invaders that women's position in society degenerated. Let's remember here that Islam itself came into existence from 7th century. The position of women in the society started changing with newer ideas that underlined liberty, equality and fraternity as basic hallmark of the society. This marked the particular point of transition from where the terminology—man and wife—changed to 'husband and wife'.

The first efforts to change the situation in India began with Raja Ram Mohan Roy. He was a strong opponent of the Sati tradition where a woman was burnt on the pyre of her husband. After this we come to two parallel streams, parallel in the sense that they could never meet and they were equally opposed to each other. On one hand we have Mahatma Phule, Pandita Rama Bai and on the other we have Savarkar, Golwalkar and other Hindutva ideologues. Among the first stream of thinkers, Phule said that women should come out in the social field and for this they should be educated. It is in this period that some women broke the shackles imposed by the society.

I'll straight go into Ambedkar and Hindu Code Bill. Ambedkar was given the responsibility to draft the Hindu Code Bill and in the Bill Ambedkar tried to give as much equality and fairness to women. The Bill was strongly opposed by Hindu right wing and reactionary elements within Nehru's cabinet. The opposition was so severe that Ambedkar was forced to resign from his cabinet post. In India, after 1960 when Mathura rape case came to be known, the women's movement started picking up and articulating the aspirations of women in the society.

Now we shall see what the other stream was saying. I shall begin with Savarkar. In one of his writings he criticizes Shivaji, who is respected by people of all religions and women in general. He is commenting on the episode when Bassein Nawab's daughter-in-law was brought as a part the loot. You all know that earlier it was a prerogative of kings and feudal lords to pick up a beautiful woman and to make them part of their Harem (Concubines). The daughter-in-law was brought to Shivaji and Shivaji respectfully commented, "Alas if my mother was as beautiful as you, even I would have been a good looking person." Shivaji was not like other kings who would misuse women. Now we shall look at our great ideologue's comment on the episode. He says, here there are Muslims who have raped our women and Shivaji had an opportunity to teach a lesson to these Muslims by giving them tit-for-tat. Savarkar sees this episode as a battle between two communities and he is of the opinion that as a retaliatory measure, the need to rape the Muslim woman is justified. This is what Savarkar is trying to imply in his criticism. So what is the great ideology of our Hindutva activists? If you want to take revenge against a community, you can do so by defiling the women of that community. Women are the symbol of honour of a community. So if you want to humiliate a community, the women of that community should be subjected to ill treatment. Savarkar's advice was 'well taken' by the people of Surat in the massive riots of 1992-93!

Now we go to the next major Hindutva ideologue Golwalkar. Golwalkar in his writings says that nature has created different types of place for man and woman and they have different roles to play in the society. What is important is to maintain or see that there is harmony between the two and not equality. What is important is the harmony, which is prevalent in the society. Golwalkar goes on to say that the primary duty of a woman is to take care of her children and rear them in the Hindu way of life; to make them good children with proper Hindu *Samskar* (traditional norms).

In 1936, one woman relative of a RSS worker, Laxmibai Kelkar made a request–Why are the men alone doing hard work to 'build the nation'? Let us also contribute. And she was told that RSS was purely a male body and there is no place for women in this male body. What we Hindu men are capable of doing, you women are not. RSS is not open to you. If you also join this who will look after our children? Who will cook?

Now I want to make a point here. While the women were refuse entry into RSS, they were advised to form

Rashtrasevika Samiti or organisation of servants of the nation. The issue I'm trying to make is that the male can be self-driven according to Hindutva ideologues (RSS means National Volunteer's Organisation). The male can be a volunteer. The female can only be a servant. The job of Rashtrasevika Samiti members was to see that their male members in the community, working for RSS, were taken care of. Before I come to BJP Mahila Morcha, which tells us more about the way they look at women, we should make another interesting point. The VHP and other organisations of Sangh Parivar generally propagate that women should not go out and work in the society unless there is a dire need in the family. And one of the best examples I remember is VHP in America. Among the many NRIs, who are top supporters of RSS, one of them was a top woman executive in a bank. Prompted by the RSS's advice, she quit her job to bring up her children in the Hindutva way of life. After a few years she got so frustrated that she went into a mental depression.

Now I shall straight come to the organisation called BJP Mahila Morcha. This is a subordinate body of the BJP and I shall draw your attention to one of the interviews given by Mridula Sinha, president of BJP Mahila Morcha. This interview appeared in the *Telegraph* in 1993. I shall put forth a few points from the interview Ms Sinha says:

1. "Well dowry is bad but what can we do? I gave dowry for my daughter and received dowry for my son.

2. Wife beating is bad. But if it has to be done to bring the woman on proper track, it's all right because it is the woman who is wrong in her new home, new situation in life.

3. Women in their own life should not take independent decisions about marriage and other things. The family should take these decisions.

From here I go on to Ms Vijaya Raje Scindia, vice-president of BJP. For many years now she has been a very prominent leader of BJP. Now all of you may remember the Roop Kanwar incident. She was forced to become a Sati (burnt on the funeral pyre of her husband). In response to this incident in Rajasthan, there was a good deal of protest from many women's organisations. Ms Scindia went on to say, "Who are these Western-oriented groups who are protesting against the incident, is this Indian tradition?" Not satisfied with that, she led a *morcha* of women to Parliament in Delhi. The slogan of the *morcha* was "to commit Sati is a glorious tradition of our Hindu society and those who are opposing this tradition are western-oriented anti-nationals."

I shall quote two more incidents before I say how I understand this game of Hindutva. Take the case of Bhanwari Devi. She was a social worker in Rajasthan. She went from village to village to do reform work like preventing child marriages. Disliking her work, some upper class men raped her. The court acquitted the rapists in due course and they were publicly honoured by one of the branches of Sangh Parivar. Lastly I come to the most deceitful face of Sangh Parivar in the form of our Prime Minister Atal Behari Vajpayee. In 1990, in one of the interviews to *Dharmayug*, a Hindi magazine, he says that all those women who want to become equal to men are worth the ridicule. It is a wrong demand on the part of women to be equal to men.

Friends, until now, I put forth before you so many anecdotes simply to show that the way Hindutva wants to deal with women is very, very complex. The gender hierarchy, the superiority of men, which is prevalent in society, is breaking down under different strains. One important factor is women's movement.

Now I will try to draw two analogies in the geographical sense. First from German fascism. Hindutva has lot of similarities with German fascism. During the Nazi regime, what was the stand of Hitler about women? Hitler went on to say that German women primarily like to be at home. They love to be mothers and love to take care of their husbands. Here he sounds as if he is talking on behalf of the women but he is basically articulating the demands of a fascist movement to straitjacket, to limit the role of women in a particular society. Therefore he goes on to say that women should primarily be attached to kitchen, church and children.

Secondly, in the case of our neighbouring state, Afghanistan', things are happening right in front of our eyes. Taliban is trying to impose different kinds of restrictions on women to control their lives in a very direct and crude way. My basic surmise is that Hindutva is more dangerous than Taliban at one level. Why? In Taliban's case, one can easily make out that they are trying to restrict the space for women. In the case of Hindutva, it is a very, very subtle manoevre, a very subtle way of controlling women. On the one hand they are saying that "We demand reservation for women in the Lok Sabha, " and on the other the primary identity they want to impose on women is that of a mother. And when you impose this identity as the primary identity, then you are already imposing on her certain restrictions.

From here, if we try to understand whatever we have tried to outline so far, it is clear that different aspects of the life of women are aimed at for being controlled but the language used is modern and the presentation is very refined. I began with some incidents from *Manusmriti*. Today it is clear that *Manusmriti* cannot be implemented and imposed in the same manner as before. Now the clever Brahminical ploy or the clever Hindutva ploy is to ensure that similar values are brought into the society in a more refined and modernised language.

The last point I want to make is this: Initially if you see, women had been the major victims of communal politics, which comes forth in the form of communal violence. Now the picture becomes more complex in today's time. We see some of the middle sections of women being drawn into the politics of Hindutva not only at a political level but there are also instances where these women have assisted in communal violence and have helped the communal people in various ways.

As such also if we see, total gender equality does not prevail in the society. There are pulls from both the sides to the type of situation that is prevailing today. On the one hand we have progressive women's, and liberal movements which strive to see that more rights are brought to women so that they can determine their own lives. On the other, there are factors, which are trying to pull back these efforts striving for gender equality. And I see Hindutva as the most sophisticated way of trying to control the lives of women and to oppose gender equality.

I shall end my talk with an incident in Dadar, Mumbai recently. There was a seminar and the name of that seminar was '*Purush Hakh Protection Samithi,*' meaning 'Seminar for the protection of rights of men'. In that seminar, it was said that women are unnecessarily fighting cases against domestic violence and this should be stopped. This is contrary to the trend where the major cases of violence are against the women. But such attempts are picking up at this point of time to bring pressure on women from different angles and are an ideal foil to the Hindutva.

# 33

# Hinduism and Gender Justice: Transitions in Nineteenth Century Bengal

***(Book Review)***

(Book Reviewed: *Hindu Wife Hindu Nation-Community, Religion and Cultural Nationalism* by Tanika Sarkar, New Delhi, Permanent Black, 2001, Pages-290, Rs. 575)

During last few years many a valuable contributions, which are giving great insights in to the process of transition from the pre-modern structural hierarchies to the values of liberty, equality and fraternity, have been added to the sociology. The one under review will find an important place amongst these significant contributions. This one is study of transition towards the modern social relationships and also gives an insight into the seeds, which were to give rise to the genesis of Hindu communal politics later. These seeds explain the quiet acceptance of some conservative, orthodox values: values of birth based inequality in the name of tradition and cultural nationalism even today. Tanika Sarkar's contribution does not just remain an academic exercise but also gives a valuable framework for understanding the ideology and dynamics of Hindu Right.

Sarkar's focus is on the deeper social processes in the mid and late nineteenth century Bengal. While the major concern is on the issues related to the travails of middle class Hindu families, one gets precious understanding of the social roots of the rise of Hindu nationalism also. These give insight into the ideology, which gave rise to Hindutva politics in early twentieth century. Interestingly most of the themes dealt in this collection of essays relate to the lives of middle class people who act in response to or in reaction against people who are Muslims, low castes, peasants and labourers. And nothing can define the agenda of present Hindutva onslaught, which is based on the affluent and medium sections of middle classes, who, threatened by the movements of workers, Dalits and women are resorting to this religion based nationalism. The 'need' for constructing the edifice of Hindutva on 'threatening other' (Muslim, Christian and Communist) is well explained by Sarkar, "Its cultural politics has been based on tensions between Arya Samaj reformist chauvinism and Sanatani conservatism, each trying to grapple with the development of low-caste separatist sects and cults, their defection from Hindu control, their cultural and political self-assertiveness. The Samaj and Santanists eventually converged on a shared anti-Muslim politics and sought to short circuit internal fault lines within Hindu community via a threatening Muslim."(p. 2)

With the introduction of modern education a new 'culture of debate' got roots in social norms and a broad awareness of social issues emerged. The process of Secularisation was in slow motion due to the slow industrialisation process. Release of workers (Dalits) from land slavery was the phenomenon of the day. This period also saw the beginnings of the aspirations of women to be part of the social space. While the nationalists of the mould of Indian National Congress saw these as an essential accompaniment of the process of freedom from the clutches of British Empire the Hindu nationalists began to register their reservations against this transition process. These subtle and overt resistance to the change started being articulated through different forms of literary expressions. Sarkar in brilliant interpretations of the literature of that period brings to our attention the ideology of the Hindu revivalists who were later to become the base of Hindu nationalism.

The theme essay, 'Hindu Wife: Hindu Nation' delineates the linkages between the domesticity, control over women and the concepts of Hindu nationalism. The pan-Indian aspirations began from 60s and different native associations of newly thrown up classes started looking forward to national association, which could articulate their demands vis-à-vis British authorities. At social level the modern values were introduced through modern education and newer socio-economic conditions. These led to the questioning the deeply entrenched domestic-social customs like *sati, kulin* marriage and widow re-marriage. Print medium enhanced the new expression of urban popular culture and revolutionised the reading habits. The emergence of newer equations and possibilities was perceived by sections of society. Up to this time the association of modern relationships and their introduction through Western (British) influence gave a distorted picture of the deeper social processes. Both liberal and revivalists saw these as imposition of the West. Liberals, in addition, also saw conservative practices as distortion from the earlier purity and a symptom of decay. Hindu revivalists glorified these customs and according to them any deviation from these would signify the surrender of native glorious traditions.

Different conservative tracts glorify the joint family as the core and all encompassing institution. Many of these books advised the *karta,* head of the family, to marshal all his resources to control the rebellious women. Revivalist forces trained their guns against any endeavour on the part of reformist-cum-colonial-cum-missionary effort to bring reform in the marriage acts, proposals to introduce divorce and the like. The battle of revivalists was as much on this front as on opposing the politics of Indian National Congress aiming at bits and pieces of provisions for independence. The glorification of child bride and in-dissolvability of Hindu marriage finds its repeated mention in the conservative literature. The child bride is described with adorable awe: little, lovely, ravishing, pleasure, infant, doll etc. Soon enough from 1860s women themselves started describing the travails of women and child brides. The trauma of child bride, the deprivations of widows and the absence of love in the lives of wives were well articulated. In 1884 the matters were precipitated when a low caste Maharashtrian girl Rukhmabai, sought to repudiate an unconsummated marriage contracted at her infancy with an illiterate, dissolute, sick husband. The reformers came up with the demands to raise the age of marriage and to provide for divorce while the Hindu nationalists opposed this on the ground that raising the age of consent will jeopardize the Hindu tenet of *garbhadhan*, i.e. obligatory ritual cohabitation as soon as the wife attains puberty, else their womb is tainted and her offspring's loose the right to serve up ancestral offering. This showed in clear light the two streaks of attitudes towards the social transformation process and two strands of political attitudes, the secular nationalism and the Hindu nationalism. The attitude of Hindu nationalists towards women is portrayed in most clear terms in a quote from Hindu patriot. As per this Hindu wife is "an article of gift...she is given away as a cow or any other chattel'. (p. 51)

It is argued that in Hinduism there is no hold of clergy and that Hindu religion itself is secular. Sarkar's essay on 'Talking about Scandals' elaborates in precise sociological details the hold of Mahants and others (like temple in charges etc) on the social matters. In one such episode one powerful Mahant, a manager-cum-guru of the rich and popular Saivaite temple and pilgrimage centre in Hoogly seduced and than raped the young wife of one person who had to be away from his town for the job in the printing press in another city. And this is a sample of many such scandals spread over in the newspapers, literature and other forms of artistic expression. British authorities were in a bind. English owned newspapers debated the morals of native society, British justice and the desirability or otherwise of the intrusive course of action vis-à-vis Hindu institutions. Time and over again British authorities had to do the tight rope walking between the demands of reformers for measures towards gender justice and the demands of Hindu nationalists to preserve the Hindu values.

It is not a mere coincidence that the British attempts for affirmative action for Shudras coincided with the simmering of self-respect movement among the low-caste Namsudra peasants. These developments were deeply threatening the hegemony of largely upper caste Hindu gentry, the majority of whom were later to support the religion based nationalism of Hindu Mahasabha and RSS. Sarkar sums up the new status of holy men in a very apt manner, " While the sexual and financial corruption of holy men in control of sacred places had long been common knowledge. The new challenge made their continued acceptance in such embarrassing locations". (p. 77)

The essay on the autobiography of Rashsundari Devi's *Amar Jiban* makes very absorbing reading. In the secularising social circumstances how a woman learns to read and write in a secret manner and than goes in to pen a portrait of her life, reflecting the pains of women come out excellently in the essay, 'A Book of Her own life'. A few quotes from the autobiography speak more than many a commentaries on the book can, "(On getting married) 'I went straight into my mother's arms, crying, Mother, why did you give me away to a stranger?' (After marriage) 'My day would begin at dawn and I worked till two at night…I was fourteen years old…I longed to read books…But I was unlucky, those days women were not allowed to read.'"

To oppose the education amongst women orthodox Hindus believed and spread the word that literate woman was destined to be a widow. And also that educated women had loose morals. It was difficult to question the firmly held belief that the observance of prescribed ritual, caste and gender norms that had been spelt out by the Vedas and subsequent sacred law codes (*Manusmriti* being the best known amongst them) would constitute the pious life or Dharma. Sarkar delves at length about the notion of *Sansar* (family life) and its place in the ideological framework of orthodox Hindu life. One does know how much the things have changed but Rashsundari, the girl bride's sentence reveals a lot about the mother-in-law daughter-in-law relationship even today, "Every time my mother-in-law looked at me a pint of blood would dry up in the body". Sarkar describes the debate of age of consent and its opposition by orthodox Hindus on religious ground at length. According to the beliefs held by orthodox Hindus the girls should be in their Husbands homes when puberty set in. In another essay while delving on similar theme she points out that number of girl brides had to suffer the torture of sexual life as they were biologically not ready for it. In contrast to the 'in our glorious Hindu tradition women had a very high social status', Sarkar demonstrates the reality of glorious status. Sarkar quotes Rashsundari Devi to buttress her point, "I was caged for life, in this life there will be no escape for me...I was snatched away from my people ...and given a life sentence...I would shed tears in secret but since I had to spend my life with these people, I eventually became a tamed bird...", comments Sarkar "The love she gave her in-laws was not a spontaneous affection but the result of training and necessity, the habit of a caged bird". (p. 121)

Bankimchandra has a place in Indian history, which spans more terrain than just being writer of the song Vande Mataram, which is used time and again by Hindu communalists for their political agenda. He wrote in a prolific manner and Sarkar does demonstrate his reflections of the contemporary society, his concerns about social reforms and also his transition from a concerned reformer to Hindu nationalist. Interestingly as he made this transition his attitude towards the problems of low caste and women also changed. Sarkar points out that with this transition, "...he tried to reorient the location of patriotism from his earlier vision of freedom for the woman, the low caste and the peasant, and now he sought it within the disciplined regime of Hindu sacred order, which needed to prove it had earlier glorious history than the Muslims." (p.139) It is in this phase that he could glorify the 'purity of Sati', and reject liberal reformist schemes on the grounds that they would fatally disrupt the very existence of Hinduism. Here lies the genesis of anti-Muslim stance developed by him and later practiced by Hindu nationalists. In this scheme of things since internal reform was ruled out the Hindu could redeem and prove himself through acts of militant heroism against the 'external enemy' constructed through the particular interpretation of the past. This part of the book is very brilliant and cogent interpretation of Bankim's writings. This part of the book also demonstrates the link between the Hindu nationalism and glorification of the hierarchical suppression of women and Dalits.

In 'Imagining Hindu Rashtra' the potential controversy around Vande Mataram is elaborated very well. To RSS and Hindutvavadis this song in its homogeneity and completeness represents their concept of undivided Hindu nation and that's why in their *shakha bauddhiks* it is sung in full unlike the abbreviated version sung by others. While some shades of nationalists used the abbreviated version of the song as a projection of history of colonial exploitation and patriotic struggle, the RSS, which had strayed away from the anti-colonial movement right from the beginning and was exclusively devoted to communal agenda, took this song as a vehicle of its ideology which spelt the need for historical struggle against Muslims. The novel Anandmath, whose part this song is, is set in the backdrop of famine of 1770 and Bankim under the spell of nascent Hindu nationalism pictures the combat between the ascetic warriors of Naga Dasnami sect, against the puppet Muslim Nawab, representing the British crown. Here he ignores the role of Muslim *faquirs* who led the starving crowds, which went on to plunder. The Nawab is ousted and direct rule of British is restored. Nationalists took this as a call for struggle against foreign power while RSS takes it as an achievement of the goal of getting rid of Muslim rule.

Vande Mataram projects the homogenous uniformity of the motherland suiting the politics of Hindutva brigade, the same communal forces are not comfortable with *Jan Gan Man*, which is the national anthem, as it gives the picture of diversity of the country. Most of the communalists give the status of Holy to the wars they wage against their enemies and Bankim is no exception in describing the war against Muslim Nawab as a *Dharmayuddha*. That may be an added reason for the Hindu right to iconize him. He served as a bridge between nineteenth century Hindu revivalism and later anti-Muslim, violent politics by providing powerful image of communal violence and by giving it the status of Holy war. Essay 'Conjugality and Hindu Nationalism' takes up the debate on age of consent in all its depth and breadth. The last essay, 'Aspects of Contemporary Hindutva Theology' analyses the phenomenon of Hindutva through the voice of Sadhvi Ritambhara, one of the three ascetic women in the top rungs of Hindutva political hierarchy. Her hate-filled cassette and her role in exhorting the Kar Sevaks played no mean role in demolishing the Babri Mosque. Sarkar argues that communalism is not just plain politics masquerading as religion. It draws life from two modern forms of Bhakti *Deshbhakti* and *Rambhakti*, the aspects forcefully brought forward by the combination of Sadhvis, VHP and the political components of Sangh Parivar.

Surely this is a major contribution in expounding the details of secularisation process. It does deserve a serious attention from those struggling for secular society, those bringing forward the goal of gender justice and those trying to understand the process of social transformation in colonial societies.

# 34

# Farzana, Nisha and Uniform Civil Code

Two cases of dowry tyranny came to light recently though in contrasting backdrops. Nisha Sharma, a Hindu girl refused to get married because of increasing demands of in-laws for dowry grew. Farzana, a Muslim girl, refused to accompany her husband because he demanded dowry. So far so bad. The dilemma begins now. RSS mouth piece *Organiser* (June 1, 2003) compares these two victims of dowry and brings in its usual vitriol of anti-Muslim anti-Islam projection to these events. While commending Nisha who according to this paper has become a role model and has received other marriage offers, according to *Panchjanya* Farzana, has still to find a way through stifling tentacles of Islamic practices perpetuated by medieval minded clergy. And so it revives the demand for uniform Civil Code as the panacea for this ailment of 'Islamic society'!

Are these comparable situations? Is it that so far all was quiet on dowry front and these two cases have come as a reminder of this abominable practice. Anti-dowry campaign has not been on the agenda of the RSS, which has more 'serious' issues like temple and 'Hindu Pride' as the major issues to address. Is RSS family serious about the issues of gender justice as such or this is a convenient stick to beat the minority community with?

The dominance of patriarchal values has been the foundation on which the social bias against women perpetuates itself. Also most of the civil codes are gender unjust and so mere parroting the uniformity has no meaning. The proper campaign has to be for gender just civil codes, which will necessarily be uniform and this has to be implemented through social reforms. Also it needs to be introspected as to what are the social conditions under which the communities can accept the reforms for gender justice. Though the demand for uniform civil code emerged from women's liberation movement it was soon realised that gender justice rather than uniformity is the core around which the laws should be formulated. Also social conditions have to be geared in a direction where the justice can be given to the women who have occupied the lower rungs in the social hierarchy from centuries. As far as suppression of women's rights are concerned it transcends the religious boundaries and clergy of all religions is more or less unanimous as far as subjugating women's rights is concerned. Though some holy books have given better status to women, by and large religions have been primarily a male bastion, a reflection of the gender hierarchy as a whole. This is best reflected in the concept of God. The question can generally be raised as to why generally God is a male? That apart none of the women's right organisations will resort to the umbrella of religion to seek and enhance their rights and status in the society.

Where do matters differ in different religious communities? One need not go to the fate of Hindu Code Bill drafted by Dr. Ambedkar but one does concede that in first three decades of the Indian republic a good deal of progress was made by the Hindu community as far as struggle for gender justice is concerned. It is nobody's case to show that all is well amongst Hindus as far as treatment of girl child and equality of women is concerned. But last two decades have overall seen an intimidation of rights movement due to the rise of fundamentalism of different hues at home. Rise of Hindu fundamentalism has also been accompanied by ghettoisation of the minorities. One recalls that the pitch and intensity of communal riots has gone up tremendously during last two decades and during these riots the Muslim community is the bigger sufferer. Rough estimates prior to Gujarat riots show that this community has population of 12.6 per cent and amongst the unfortunate riot victims its percentage is around 80 per cent. The minority psychology is greatly shaped by this insecurity and this works on the social norms even of those who are not directly affected by the violence. Added to this is the international phenomenon where American imperialism is out to demonize Islam and Muslims by all means possible so that it can gobble up the world oil resources.

Muslim women have been struggling for reforms in their civil code from last many decades. Every cycle of violence is a big setback to their movement. The communal violence has been blatantly intimidating minorities and the communalised state apparatus has been aiding the Sangh Parivar outfits in conducting these pogroms. Can such an intimidated community go in for reforms? There are contradictory tendencies in every community and society. Same Muslim community, which is recognised by the Burqua clad woman, has Kinetic riding Muslim girls trying to make their own living as teachers or journalists. One of the *India Today* issues of 91, which showed one Muslim girl riding a horse, another one driving a Kinetic, reflected the trends of time of reforms in the community. The issue is what does the communal violence do the social psychology? By now the likes of Thackeray (Mumbai 92-93) and Modi (2002-03) have perfected the art where the victim community is shown to be starting the riots and these saviors, the soldiers of Hindutva, the Hindu Hriday Samrats (Emperor of Hindu Hearts) merely rush to the 'defense' of the majority community and become the victors in the elections which follow. In addition to grabbing power through the rivers of blood they also walk away with the trophy titled 'Hindu Hriday Samrat'.

It is a difficult time for Islamic community world over. At the global level Samuel Huntington is providing the arguments for imperialistic ambitions of U.S. administration and at home RSS has been developing expertise in Muslim demonisation from last many decades. It is an interesting fact that the RSS progeny is honing its skills in demonising the Islam and Muslims on one hand and is subservient to the U.S. imperialists on the other.

As it is difficult to 'defeat' a Modi who 'successfully' polarizes the communities through orchestrated communal violence, so it is equally difficult to stall the rise of Mullahs and obscurantist in a threatened Muslim community. While it is unfair to compare the Farzana and Nisha it does teach many a lessons. Nisha boldly stands to defy the patriarchy and its manifestation in the form of dowry. Farzana is no less when she refuses to join her husband on the same ground. These acts of individual valour do reflect the stirrings amongst young of the community to break the shackles of male domination. But there the comparison ends. Both these girls have to live in the different milieu. While Nisha's milieu is not adorable in the least, Farzana is a double victim, that of patriarchy and that of minority bashing and resulting ghettoisation. While condemning the forces of Mullahs one recognizes the challenges faced by the Muslim liberals. On one hand there is a tremendous pressure to withstand the onslaught of crippling anti-Muslim propaganda, which by now has become part of social common sense, on the other they are stretching all their strength to battle the obscurantism promoted by the Mullahs and their ilk. No doubt Islam is the much-maligned religion today. The teachings of Koran are in the book. The practices of Muslim community have been shaped by the bad cruel world dominated by lust of colonialists of the past and imperialists of present. Both these have suppressed the democratic aspirations of Islamic societies. Starting from formation of Israel, overthrow of Mossadeq regime in Iran and training of Jehadi youth through the conduit of Pakistan the world's superpowers have created a situation where the popular dissent gets expressed though the worst form of Islamic obscurantism.

Where does the Muslim community go from here? Can it bear the double burden of Hindutva attack from outside and the grip of Mullahs from inside? Farzana has to be nurtured and supported in her decision to boycott the marriage cemented on dowry. It is difficult to think of reforms in a ghetto, amongst the community threatened by regular onslaught of violence. It is difficult to bring in reforms in a community whose religion is demoniosed not only nationally but internationally as well. Come what may against all the odds Farzana has to be nurtured. The goal of bogus defenders of women's rights, the RSS and its progeny has to be understood in its proper perspective. An ideology, which is deeply seeped in the patriarchy, Hindutva, has no place for women's rights for equality. Time and over again its ideologues have defended the violation of the 'being' of the women of 'other' community. It has no interest in protecting the rights of minority women, but we have to do that irrespective of who raises the issue. One of the major needs in the direction is to ensure that ghettoisation which is the aftermath of violence is checked. The Muslim community has to rise to the occasion and against all external and internal odds to chose the direction of progress and justice. It has to join the progressive elements of other communities and close the ranks with them to ensure that the Hindutva onslaught from outside and Mullahs from inside are not able to intimidate its dynamics of progress and reform.

# 35

# Caging the Women

## Age of Consent Debate

A proper legislation to curb the child marriage is one of the markers of the democratic modern societies where the equal status and rights of woman are accepted as a norm. But it is not with ease that the conservative elements permit such bills to go through. On various grounds, in the name of religion, sacred traditions etc. the conservative elements have opposed the raising of age of marriage for the girls. The earlier girls fall into the domesticity, easier it is to cage them and have a slave and companion for the men, with religious sanctions.

It is in this light that one looks at the Muslim Personal Law Board's decision (2003) to oppose the Child Marriage restraint Act 1929, which puts 18 years as the lowest age on which girls can be married. One recalls that it was opposition to the Shah Bano judgment and creation of hysteria 'Islam in Danger' that made Rajiv Gandhi to concede to the demands of Mullahs to get the judgment overruled by a new act of Parliament. Needless to say, most of the Muslim majority countries have brought in legislations which give a due justice to the woman in matters of marriage, divorce and the like. In India this is something, which is the sore point for the civic society. While on one side it affects the Muslim women, on the other it gives the much-needed pretext to the Hindu communalists to launch one more offensive on secular fabric and the Muslim minorities themselves. The story is quiet complex. We have been witnessing the rise in communal violence over a period of years. In these communal riots the number of Muslim victims has been over 80 per cent. We have to note that after partition the elite, salaried and section of educated Muslims left for Pakistan in the longing for 'greener pastures' (pun intended). The sections left behind were more from the lower and illiterate sections, who due to the discrimination policies of the Hindutva infected state apparatus, could not come up and easily be the part of mainstream. Despite odds a large section of Muslims was still able to struggle for modern education and try for decent employment, business etc. Till Nehru was alive his impeccable secular credentials and policies gave confidence to the minorities. After his demise the Hindutva elements in Congress did become strong and in future first Indira Gandhi and later Rajiv were to use Hindu communal card for electoral purpose.

Communal violence went up in intensity by and by. The violence not only paralyses the minorities for a long time, it also creates the Ghettoisation, the fertile ground for the rise of conservative elements in the community. This also increases the power of Mullahs within the community and this retrograde thinking imposes practices, which are detrimental to the status and rights of woman in particular. It is remarkable at one level that despite such odds the Muslim women covered lot of ground towards a honourable place in family and community. After Babri demolition in particular the retrograde march has picked upsteam and chances of Mullahs ruling the roost have become stronger and stronger. This is precisely what Sangh Parivar wants; this is precisely what adds fuel to the communal fire being ignited by the Hindu Communal onslaught from 1980s. The two, imposition of conservative norms on Muslim minorities and the strength of Hindutva offensive, have a circuitous relationship. Each feeding in to the other to create a vicious cycle, the result of which is the social atmosphere where what gets sacrificed on the altar of religious nationalism is the Human Rights of weaker sections of society.

At another level it rings a different bell also. In Hindu community also the age of consent was a major debate amongst the progressive and conservative sections of society. With education and secularisation process beginning in the middle of 19th century, many a women had started articulating their problems. Despite the glorious picture that women have a very respectable place in Hindu society, the literature of late 19th century gives an accurate picture of the condition of women at different levels. Early marriage resulted in enslaving of the women to the household of the husband where the patriarchal powers operated through different complex mechanisms. A book written in late 19th century by Rashsundari Devi, Amaar Jeevan (My Life) gives an elaborate description of the travails of women in those times. Early marriage and lack of education was the major bane of women's life. The efforts of reformers worked on the twin levels, age of consent and education. Starting from Savitribai Phule number of initiatives were undertaken to spread education amongst women. The education process was opposed by spreading the rumours that educated women become widows earlier and that they have loose morals. When the state wanted to bring in the legislation to raise the age of marriage, it was opposed staunchly by the conservatives on the ground that as per Garbhadhan, the obligatory ritual cohabitation as soon as the wife attains puberty, (else their womb is tainted and her offspring's loose the right to serve up ancestral offering), early marriage is a must as per our religion. It was a serious battle, with Hindu nationalists on one side opposing the raising the age of marriage and the reformers seeking it staunchly.

The post-independence efforts of Nehru-Ambedkar also met the stiff opposition for reforming the Hindu codes. The bill drafted by Ambedkar, on request from Nehru came under serious attack, to the extent that a frustrated Ambedkar resigned from the cabinet and the bill was diluted greatly making it ineffective. By and by, many improvements had to be introduced under the pressure of the rising women's movement from mid-nineteen seventies onwards. And lot of strides could be made under the influence of women's movement for equality, gender justice. From mid-eighties the counteraction has followed. This pertains to the rise in the assertion of Hindu conservative elements, consolidated under the umbrella of Sangh Parivar and its paraphernalia. And this time around, the retrograde move has taken the form of a cultural and propaganda offensive. At cultural level the likes of Pandurang Shastri Athwale are propagating an early marriage, within three years of puberty, the declining age of puberty to 10-11 years notwithstanding. Effectively this tantamount to advising that a girl should be married off by the age of 14-15 years. It is not a coincidence that Mr. Athwale is greatly appreciated by Sangh Parivar and his reach has increased during the period when the communal poison spread by RSS started going up. This 'saintly' advise is being backed up by the visual media where the tele-serials like *Sas Bhi Kabhi Bahu Thee* are reinforcing the patriarchal norms in the modern and sophisticated guise.

Essentially, starting from the opposition of Hindu nationalists in late 19th century to the efforts of RSS, affiliated and adjunct pracharaks (propagators) like Athawale the demand for early marriage of girls is being reinforced. The efforts of Muslim Personal Law Board fall in the same category. They mean to stifle the transformation of society towards the democratic norms of gender equality. In case of Hindu community the gains of last century and quarter mean to be reversed by the current Sangh Parivar affiliates who pass the Fatwa about women's conduct off and on. Be it Dharam Sansad of VHP advising women to play the role of 'loyal wife' to the *trishul* wielding Bajrang Dalis ordering the girls not to wear jeans to the Muslim Personal Law Board's opposition to the Child Marriage Restraint Act, they operate on the same wave length. And of course they boost each other. Here one must concede that that *trishul* wielders are calling bigger shots and are the prime movers of communal politics, while the Mullahs and Law Boards of this variety give the ammunition to the offensive communal politics. The Indian nation needs neither of these.

One also concedes that in current times the communal violence, in which Muslims turn out to be the bigger victims of the violence, aggravates the conservatism in both communities, more so amongst the Muslims. Every bout of riot leaves Mullahs in a stronger position. In the aftermath of Mumbai riots the Muslim women's struggle for abolition of triple *talaq*, polygamy and *burqa* got a big setback. It did take a long time before the local groups working in this direction could regain the rhythm of their work for reforms amongst the community. Also one will like to add that the struggle for preservation of democratic norms, minority rights has no meaning if the rights of women are not taken up with utmost sincerity. It is the joint struggle of men and women from minority community along with other democratic-secular forces, which has the potential of being a strong pillar in the struggle against religious fascism, which is the major threat in India today. The moves like the one proposed by Muslim Law Board will put the struggle back by miles and so needs to be opposed by all those striving to curtail the march of Hindu religious fascism in the form of the increasing social and civic domination of the institutions of Sangh combine.

# 36

# Uniformity or Gender Justice

Chief Justice Khare's observation (July 23rd, 2003) about the need to work for uniform civil code has rekindled the debate, which has been raging from last decade or so. Different groups have responded to it in a different fashion, with Muslim League opposing it right away and BJP jubilantly welcoming it. These are the two opposite poles of the reaction to the observation of the Chief Justice. It is likely to bring forth the debate about this vexed issue. Different social groups have seen the demand for uniform code in different perspectives. One of the arguments is that such a code will strengthen the national unity.

As such the issue of uniform civil code was raised in the beginning by the women's movement in its quest for gender justice. During Shah Bano case the immaturity and mistakes of Rajiv Gandhi regime sowed the seeds of dissatisfaction to this judgment reversal by the act of Parliament. As the orthodox section of Muslim leadership banked on the preservation of male domination in the name of Islam, the RSS and its progeny intensified the campaign for uniform code. It came in as a convenient handle to beat the Muslim community with. It was asserted by BJP leadership that a uniform code will draw from different prevalent codes and that's what will bring in a 'model' code. Realising that a mere uniformity cannot bring in justice the women's movement began to call for gender just code and that's where it stands today. There is a crucial difference in these two simple concepts. A uniform code need not be gender just while a gender just code can be uniform for the whole nation. As such the civil code relates more to the laws of inheritance of property, divorce and custody of children. And in these matters most of the prevalent codes are biased in favour of men without any shadow of doubt.

Going back early to the days of Nehru-Ambedkar, one recalls that Nehru had requested Dr. Ambedkar to begin the process of drafting civil codes, beginning with Hindu code. Hindu being the majority it was more pertinent to begin with that. In due course Ambedkar-Nehru duo realised that the serious opposition to this within the ruling party itself will not permit the passage of the bill and the justice cannot be delivered to women so easily. Meanwhile the women's movement started picking up and it in due course started articulating for equality before law and need for legal provisions in that direction. While even the process for Hindus is not complete the women from minority community started suffering from other disadvantages. The regular recurrence of anti-minority violence intimidated the minorities, minority women in particular. Till 91-92 the contradictory trends of progress and regression of minority reforms was fairly in balance. Post-Babri the regressive trends became stronger and the ghettoisation of Muslim community started setting in. The Muslim community as a whole and Muslim women in particular became subject to a physical-psychological intimidation. Every round of violence left a scar on the minority psyche. The Mumbai riots were a severe blow to internal reforms within the community. The Gujarat carnage has exceeded all the imaginable barbarities against women and the same battered women had to take shelters in the mosques. What will be the result of this phenomenon, 'mosque as the only saviour for Muslim women'? To say that it will further strengthen the hold of

Mullahs is to state the obvious. The movement of Muslim women for justice has been on in a small but significant way. This gets a severe jolt every time a bout of anti-Muslim violence breaks out. The Muslim women are double victims. On one hand they have to face the violence of Hindutva from outside and on the other they are victims of the intimidation of Mullahs from inside.

To begin with no civil code can be imposed from outside. We require a feeling of security to ensure that reform process begins. In the current scenario the Hindutva movement is repressive not only to the Muslim minorities but it also targets at the gender equality. It asserts that notion of women's liberation is licentious, synonym with loose morals. It moans about the glorious position of Indian women in the past where women were worshipped. And so we do not need any notions of "Western" ideas of gender equality as Hindus worshipped 'their' women. The Hindutva women's organisations, which are subordinate to male RSS, propagate an opposition to the ideas of struggling for equality and justice. The parallel cultural expression is being percolated through the current Hindi serials like *Saas Bhi Khabhi Bahu Thi* and its clones on different channels, which merely propagate the patriarchal notions in different guises. Also with the ascendance of Hindu right movement all the other Human rights movements are facing a setback.

Today it is an impossibility to take up the issue of gender just code right away. The doctored minds are talking of the great traditions, unmindful of the fact that what is being paraded as the great tradition is nothing but the values enshrined in the *Manusmriti* in more refined form.

We do need uniformity, but of course it has to be based on justice. This justice is the biggest victim at the hands of the religion based nationalism. We need to restore the democratic culture and spirit in all aspects of social life as the prerequisite for justice. No threatened and insecure community can go in for reforms. It is commendable that even in the shadow of terror of this atmosphere, created by Togadia's and Modi's, a large section of Muslim community and leadership are talking of progress and reforms. The Shahi Imams are being marginalised. This is a positive trend in the nation. While BJP will try its best to use this handle of uniform code, it is imperative that democratic movement works for a riot free India, a harmonious atmosphere where communities feel secure and thereby strive for progress and justice. More than Muslims, the major opposition to tie gender just code will come from the same Hindutva forces that today are demanding for uniform code. Once the terrain is shifted to justice as the first principle and uniformity as an accompaniment Hindutva will oppose it tooth and nail as its very foundation is on the concept of patriarchy and male domination. It's a clone of Talibanism or Islamism as being practiced by the Pakistani ruling junta where Mullahs hold the sway.

There is an urgent need to shift the debate to issues of security and justice which are the core issues, the basic foundation on which uniformity can be built and brought in for all the communities.

# 37

# Whither Gender Parity?

## Women and the Patriarchal Values Today

The Muslim Personal Law Board's meeting gave the hope that it will abolish triple *talaq*, will take a step towards justice for Muslim women. But that was not to be. While there are multiple factors coming in the way of reform in Muslim personal laws, things are not too bright for Hindu women as well. The rise of politics in the name of religion has created an atmosphere where the social relations, the one between men and women, between upper caste and Dalits are going in a reverse gear.

There are multiple glaring instances, which have happened during last few months, which force one to think as to where are we heading for as far as gender parity is concerned. We did hear about many cases of honour killing in Pakistan during last few years. Cases where the male relatives of the women killed them as they decided to choose their own life partners against the wishes of their men folk, father, brother etc are on the rise. This abominable practice was heard of and one understands has been prevalent in Pakistani society. One heard of two cases of women being burnt alive as Sati, and then glorified by the respective families. Sati was a custom against which reformers like Ram Mohun Roy struggled in the late nineteenth century. Cases of its occurrence in late twentieth century did shake the conscience of most of us. While a large number of people condemned it, there were people who came up with the concept of Rani Sati temples to 'honour' this custom. Of all the condemnable reactions, which took place in the wake of Roop Kanwar being burnt, the worst of course was the protest march taken out by the then Vice President of Bhartiya Janata Party, Mrs. Vijaya Raje Scindia, a widow herself. This march which was taken to the Parliament, the highest law making body in the country, had the slogan that to commit sati is not only the glorious tradition of Hindu women, its their right also. This march was meant to stall the legal measures, which were being contemplated to prevent such incidents in future.

One and a half decades down the line, things are no better. If at all new forms of women's oppression are coming up. The worst amongst them being the replication of honour killing, the practice which one was hearing of in Mullah dominated Pakistan. Somewhere in March 2004, a young man killed his sister and brother-in-law in Thane. After being arrested for the crime he gloriously proclaimed that his sister had married against the wishes of the family so he undertook this crime and that he is proud of what he did. Somewhere in June 2004, a boy killed his sister in Nagpur. The girl apparently was talking to her boyfriend on phone. She had made up her mind to marry him. Her decision to marry the boy of her liking was not approved of by the family, i.e., father and brother, and so in the rage of anger the boy killed his own sister.

The latest issue (July 2004) of a national newsmagazine reports a speech by none other than the Chief Minister of Madhya Pradesh, the firebrand Uma Bahrati. As per the report, RSS ideologue Govindacharya had proposed to her through Mr. Advani. She apparently was favourable to the proposal. She sought permission from her brother for this. Her brother, Swami Lodi, did not approve of the alliance so she rejected the proposal and took *Sanyas*. Why the all-powerful person of the stature of Uma Bahrati has to get the nod of her brother for marrying the person of her choice.

The rising occurrence of incidents of girl being either denied permission to marry the person of her choice or being killed because she exercises the option and goes ahead, is reflective of the deeper cultural rot which is setting in the society due to the rise of politics in the name of religion. The ideology of this politics is based on the pre-modern feudal values. Feudal society, where the nexus of landlord and priest ruled the roost in the society, was founded on the hierarchical notions of caste and gender. In this scheme of things the supremacy of landlord is unquestionable as he had the divine power. And it was the priesthood, cutting across different religions, which propagated and upheld these values. According to this in European society the serf was bonded to the land and the feudal lord was the controller of his life.

In India, the things were parallel but different. Here there was no centralised Church, but the local alliance between the landlord and the priest served the same purpose. In Maharashtra this alliance goes by the popular name of Shetji-Bhatji (Landlord-Brahmin). In this scheme of things the peasant the Shudra was tied to the land, was himself a semi-property of the landlord, so could not own his property. As far the woman is concerned, the pattern in most of the geographical locations and in the prevalent norms in most religious communities was the same. Its that woman is the property of man. So obviously a property in turn cannot own a property herself. She needed protection and in turn control. In her childhood this control is the prerogative of father, during adult life that of husband and in old age in case of husbands death its son or another male relative who is the controlling authority. In one of the colloquial languages a word is used for women, *Trimmat*, the one guided by opinions of three persons, depending on the stage of her life.

Secularisation process breaks the authority of landlord not only on land but also of his control over, serf, shudra, who now is an independent landowner, land to the tiller, if that takes place. At times guillotine, at times revolutions brought to end this divine power of landlords and Kings. *Bhudan* (donation of land) or half-hearted land reforms could not end this hegemony totally. As far as women are concerned, the introduction of education, and their entry into social space should have abolished the concept that woman is the property of man. One hears of the word *Kanyadan*, donating of daughter, at the time of marriage. There is nothing like *Putradan* (donating of son) as an equivalent. As son is the recipient of the property. Husbands in many traditions are addressed as Master, *Dhani*, and *Swami*, etc.

The process of transition of women from property, controlled subjects to the people in their own rights began and Savitribai Phule is the major initiator in this direction. The coming times saw the emergence of the likes of Pandita Ramabai, Anandi Gopal, etc., who took extreme pains to come out of the shackles of patriarchal control. India's freedom movement also saw a great participation of women in the struggle for freedom. As India's secularisation process was not complete the remnants of it kept hierarchical values alive even after independence. The Indian Constitution did accept the total equality of caste and gender. But can any deprived section get its rights just for asking. No way. A struggle to get one's social and political goals is the only way to get it. The laws and constitution provide the ground on which such struggles can stand and march ahead.

It is likely that these tendencies became stronger in Pakistan after the Mullah influenced changes brought in by Zia Ul Haq in early eighties. In India the rise of the social power of Hindutva around the same time has given a fillip to the retrograde values as far as gender is concerned. At this point, Hindutva defends the subjugation of women as a political agenda. For that matter any politics, which goes on in the name of religion, does the same. Hindutva ideology is joined in this arena by post-modernists, the ilk of Ashish Nandy's, who will come forward to defend these traditions, closing their eyes to the social relations, to the notions of hierarchy. The question is not just whether Uma Bharati can marry the person of her choice or not, the question is a broader one. And it pertains to the surge of politics, which aims to suppress the human rights of weaker sections of society. The question pertains to the abuse of the emotions associated with religion for the sake of power. One hopes that the cases of honour killings reported around are the last one's. One hopes that rather than asserting that women were worshipped in ancient India (! before they were consigned to the 'holy' flames of her husbands funeral pyre) one comes to recognize that women are equal citizens, equal in social rights, and both genders have to have parity in all matters of our social and political existence.

# Section–IX

## Faith and Reason

Faith in the dictates of clergy is the norm of the feudal societies. The journey of rational thought is very painful and many a scientists and thinkers have to sacrifice a lot, including their lives. Right from early times there have been thinkers who have refused to submit to faith, to the authority of clergy, Charvak being one of the best example in India. During the period of reformation this process picked up with great speed in the West and the authority of clergy and faith-based knowledge met their nemesis.

In India the process saw its mild ascendence with the introduction of industries and modern education in the mid and late eighteenth century. This process ran parallel to the rise of the national movement. Since in India the process of secularisation has remained incomplete, this rational thought and the knowledge based on that did come up but could not occupy the substantial social space. With BJP led coalition coming to power at the centre (1998), the major throw back in times was the introduction of astrology and art of religious rituals in the University education. While it may sound innocuous at one level it does hide the deeper agenda of bringing in a culture and power equations where the pre-modern power relations come to the fore in newer garbs.

# 38

# Rational Thought in Indian Tradition

Last two decades have seen the rise of faith-based traditions and religiosity is on the rise. Overall only some of the traditional systems of thought are being glorified to the exclusion of other and more prevalent one's. Also their 'scientific nature' is being asserted by intellectual jugglery. It is during last two decades in particular that impact of the very rational traditions as represented by Ambedkar, Periyar and Nehru face severe challenges from the Hindu right. In the case of Ambedkar the man is being glorified and worshipped but his system of thought is being deliberately sidelined. The traditional faith based systems like Jyotishi, Karmakand and similar so-called disciplines are being brought to the mainstream university education, courtesy the BJP led coalition, and RSS swayamsevak Murli Manohar Joshi's impositions in the field of education. The trend to rationalize our education and thought is getting a severe jolt in the current times. It is being asserted that rational thought based disciplines are Western, unsuitable for our great 'glorious' traditions. Further the faith and blind faith are being brought back through official and unofficial channels. When the journey back to traditions is affirmed as the goal, it not towards the materialist, rational Lokayat but towards the Brahminical system, which is being brought back. Those working for religion-based nationalism are concerned only with those ideas, which have rooting in the concepts and philosophies, which can uphold the hierarchies of caste and gender in the modern garb. It is because of this that the traditions and values of Lokayat-Charvak find no place in the newly found love for traditions.

**Religion in Social Space**

This trend is an accompaniment of the religion-based nationalism, which is again on ascendance due to various complex reasons. This religiosity is again of the particular variety, the one revolving around the clergy, the dharmgurus. Ram Temple movement, Babri demolition, and 'Islamic terrorism' present a picture of India, which is much different than the one seen in the earlier decades of the republic. This scene is duly backed up by the rise of religiosity in different walks of life. The religious cults, Asaram Bapu, Aniruddha Bapu, Pandurang Shastri Athwale and their ilk are drawing large followings. The temple visits and temple functions have become the major events of communities. The media is devoting more and more space on the discourses of swamis and saints; columns on religious values and religious functions are aplenty in the media. Television serials depict the 'guiding role' of clergy and there are special channels like *Astha, Sadhana* and *Sanskar* to propagate particular versions of religiosity. The struggling middle class hero of the previous decades is replaced by the stinking rich patriarch constantly in touch with the priest for guidance in his regular affairs. "Current events in India reveal the continuing importance of religious nationalism...the religious aspects of Indian nationalism have yet to receive adequate attention." (Peter van der Veer, 1998, ix)

The Non Resident Indians are importing priests, building grand temples, dime a dozen, in the countries of their adoption and helping the religious campaigns and its associated political hate propaganda here, thereby helping the deepening of religiosity and religion based politics in India. The returnees from Gulf countries, with bagfuls of currency prefer to promote Madrassas and mosques or the temples as per their religions.

It is not only the religion based nationalism, which rules the roost, a type of religiosity, has come to be the prominent phenomenon of the society today. The understanding of religion fluctuates between religious identities and religious community on one hand to the moral values of the religions on the other. Somewhere the role of clergy, with different prefixes like Acharya, Mahant, Guru, has gone up in dominance. Their social power has also risen along with rise of religious cults and their following amongst diverse sections of society. The existence of rational thought in Indian's past is deliberately undermined and sidetracked for the political agenda, which is trying to work for the reinstatement of the feudal hierarchies of caste and gender.

**Indian Traditions**

Most of the religions have two streams of practices and philosophies. The one and the more dominant one is an accompaniment of powers that be, i.e., the feudal lords and the kings. These forces rule in alliance with the clergy, which manufactures the ideology, whose basis is the needs of the ruling elite. In Indian history this got crystallised in Brahmanism and the books, which this tradition brought up. These in a way were the ruling ideas of the society at that time, and faith in the holy books and the clergy was central to this. The rebellion or the opposition of the weaker sections of society got manifested in the form of alternate systems, which were more popular amongst the average people of society. In the power struggle between the elite, affluent, those living on the land revenue on one hand and the labouring people on the other, these two streams were standing in total opposition to each other. These popular traditions were hounded and their left over description is available mainly from their criticism found in the 'mainstream' Brahminical texts.

**Faith or Reason**

With the emergence of caste society in India the hold of Brahminical ideology and clergy became strong and the sanctity of caste system was derived from the Vedas and Smritis, the most well known amongst them being *Manu-smriti.* The rebellion against Brahminical ideology kept coming up in different forms in Indian society be it the materialist Charvak tradition or the one brought forward by Buddhism, they all resorted to the use of critical reason to oppose the propagation of 'faith based ideologies', which were used to numb the social rebellions against the system. Brahminical system discouraged the use of logic in various ways. Indra had to be born as a jackal for the 'sin' of using logical thinking; he explains, "(In the previous life) I was attracted to logic, the technique of fruitless argumentation. I was a scholar in a degraded sense, because, in the capacity of a free thinker (*haituka*), I was vilifier of scriptures (*veda-nindaka*)... I used to refute Brahmins and was hostile to what Brahmins said. I was disbeliever (*nastika*) and I entertained doubt about everything. Hence, I was just a fool with pretentious learning"(Gangopadhayay, 1990, 11). In Ramayana too we have the similar type of denunciation of free thinking. While advising Bharat as to how to rule, Ram advises Bharat to be careful about *Laukayatika-s,* who are free thinkers. Manu in his tome repeatedly warns against too much involvement with logic, which may go against the holy scriptures questioning their authority. According to him "in fact, preoccupation with logic is almost as good (! bad) as committing a crime"(Gangopadhyay, 1990, 12). "Even Brahmagupta, who, as Al-Beruni, the 11th century traveller to India notes in his writings, was craven in his submission to religious orthodoxy, attacks the writings on the eclipse of the earlier astronomers Varahamihira and Aryabhata not on the grounds of any scientific error but only because they openly reject the version of the orthodoxy. Brahmagupta's concern is that if generally accepted by the people at large, such attitudes would lead to defiance of religious authority. Despite this criticism, Brahmagupta goes on to a detailed calculation of the eclipses based on the method of Varahamihira and Aryabhata, leading Al-Beruni to suggest that what underlay Brahmagupta's criticisms was more a lack of courage than any conviction in mythology" (Jayaraman, 2001).

The case of development of medical science in India is very interesting. The Charak school, which was based on empirical observations, was able to make a good headway in understanding the dynamics of human body to the extent of the reasons of diseases, and it rejected the supernatural explanation of human ailments. But in due course the remedies based on observations had to give way to the pressures from Brahmins, "Even such physicians as believed and stood by rational scientific medicine had to insert various compromising passages under pressure from the Brahmin priesthood...where as Samhita rejects all supernatural intervention in Ayurveda, it also narrates tale of Bhardwaj, considered the first human source of Ayurveda, having received his knowledge ultimately from Brahma. The priesthood always insisted that no human knowledge could ever originate from anyone except Brahma"(Sardesai, 1986:174).

**Brahmanism and Others**

All the Indian traditions criticising the authority of Brahmins and Vedas are termed as atheists, *Veda bahya*, outside the pale of Vedic orthodoxy. These in turn are Lokayata, Charvak, Buddhism, and Jainism.

This dominant tendency, which condemned the traditions like Buddhism, derived its legitimacy from faith in Vedas. It is surprising that various ideologues of Hindutva politics trace the lineage of secularism, liberalism and scientific temper in Vedas. Here we see two attitudes towards the traditional dominant Brahminical ethos. While upper caste nationalists did not go deep into critiquing Braminical values, the oppressed castes have an "inherent interest not simply in rising in the system but in overthrowing it" (Omvedt, 1994:31). In different forms the 'reason' has been the engine of the movements whose ideologies were opposed to the rule of the landlord-clergy nexus. In our own country, "The intellectual resources and political motives for critical reason or "scientific temper", have been with us since the Lokayats, which surfaced again, after centuries of suppression and ridicule by Vedantists, in the naturalism, skepticism and pragmatism of Phule, Periyar and Ambedkar. These ideas took a bourgeoisie form in the Nehruvian ideal of 'scientific temper' (Nanda, 2001:2555). Charvak called for the use of rational materialism against the prevalent system, Ambedkar called for the use of reason in the 'annihilation of caste'.

## Lokayat-Charvak Tradition of Rational Thought

It is in this overall backdrop of the struggle between reason and faith, the struggle between the exploiting elite and the toiling masses, that understanding the Lokayat tradition becomes important even today. Lokayat was the popular thought system amongst the masses. Their concepts and ideas were attacked and looked down upon in a contemptuous manner by the dominant Brahmanic stream.

This Lokayat tradition was alternatively called Carvaka or Barhaspatya. It meant the rational philosophy, the materialist philosophy. "It was called Lokayat because it was (lokesu) prevalent amongst people" (Chattopadhayay, 1981, 3). It meant philosophy of the people. It was looked down as the crass, immoral, consumptionist philosophy. It was materialist not in the sense of crass immoral consumption but in the sense that the world is material, primary and the source of consciousness. It regarded this world as concrete material world and denied everything beyond. Manibhadra explicitly defined it as, *lok* meant *padarth-sartha* or *padarthsamuha* that is the totality of material existence. "Thus Lokayat meant not only the philosophy of the people but also the philosophy of this worldliness or materialism" (Chattopadhayay, 1981, 3).

Brahaspati (c. 7th-6th century B.C.) is believed to be the founder of the Charvaka-Lokaytika school, author of its Sutras. Like many other progressive Indian traditions it was a materialist philosophy. Its salient features can be outlined as follows (V. Brodov, 1984, 86).

(a) Recognition of the fact that external world, of which man is a part, exists objectively and is therefore not a product of his brain but exists independent of any consciousness.

(b) Recognition of the fact that the external world manifests itself in the law governed fashion, the laws being capable of change only through physical action rather than through ideas, magic or prayer.

(c) Negation of the existence of supernatural forces; the view that the world develops spontaneously without outside interference.

(d) Recognition of the man's perception of the objects or phenomenon of the outside world (sense perception) as the only source of knowledge.

(e) Recognition of the fact that the nature of man's life and activity is determined by conditions of life and not by a deity.

There are many philosophers who contributed to this system of thought, focusing on different aspects of this worldview. Bhishan, one of the outstanding contributors of this school, came under severe criticism from Lord Manu and other Brahminical philosophers. "Expressing the hope and moods of poorest strata of Indian society, Bhishan was sharply critical of Brahmanism, the Vedic religion, and the ideology of priests. The compilers of Vedas, he says were hypocrites and swindlers. "Invoking the Vedas, the priests dupe the simple people with meaningless jumbles of words, living in luxury at the expense of poor people bringing them offerings. Who the offerings were for? Gods were non-existent and had never existed. Should there be offerings for deceased relatives? Even if the dead relatives need the food why should we pass it on to priests?" (Borodov, 88). Charvaks held that the combination of four elements earth, fire, water and air produce all the objects and phenomenon of nature, material and spiritual.

Charvaks decried religious superstition, which according to them kept the people in chains of bondage to the priests and blind faith. Jawaharlal Nehru wrote, "The materialists attacked the authority and all vested interests in thought, religion and theology. They denounced Vedas and priest-craft and traditional beliefs, and proclaimed that belief must be free and must not depend on pre-supposition or merely on the authority of the past. They inveighed against all forms of magic and superstition. Their general spirit was comparable in many ways to the modern materialist approach, it wanted to rid itself of the chains and burden of the past, of speculation about matters which could be perceived or worship of imaginary Gods..." (Nehru, 100)

Brahmins, priests, persecuted the Charvaks and their works were destroyed, Nehru further points out, "Among the books that have been lost is the entire literature on materialism, which followed the period of the early Upanishads. The only reference to this, now is found, are criticisms of it and an elaborate attempts to disprove the materialist theories." (Nehru, *op. cit.*)

Brahmanism held that Lord Brahma is the source of all the holy books, so they are unchallengeable, to be reversed and followed uncritically. In contrast, Lokayat denied the authority of sruti and smriti, ridiculed Brahmanical rituals and mocked the ideas of the other world or heaven. It is to be noted that Lokayat philosophy was not preached just by few skeptics or philosophers, "In all probability, it was a body of beliefs and practices, deeply rooted in the lives of masses and at the same time hostile to Brahminical doctrines" (Chattopadhayay, 36). Their rituals were in direct contrast to the Brahminical one's, their rituals were rooted in the concept of this world as they denied the existence of the other world. They were referred to as *Nastiks* or *haitukas* by Lord Manu. The followers of Lokayat tradition were under severe condemnation from Brahmins, and these Charvaks were called *asuras, demons, rakshashas, daitayas*, etc.

The Charvaks main purpose seems to be to denounce the Brahminical ideology. This philosophy can be summed up as follows:

1. The basis of all the life is the four elements, fire; water, earth, air. It is their nature (*swabhav*) which determines the character of the things.

2. There is no After world. This world is the only reality.

   "While Life is yours, live joyously;

   None can escape Deaths searching eyes;

   When once this frame of ours they burn

   How shall they e'er return?"

(S. Radhakrishnan, p. 281)

They were critical of the idealist proposition that "consciousness is the property of immortal soul".

3. They held that God is the invention of the rich to dupe the poor. They saw the clergy (Brahmins) as having motives to keep the poor in the ideological bondage for the benefit of powers that be.

4. They also denied the existence of soul. For them thought cannot exist independent of matter.

5. Law of Karma (requital for both good and bad) is an invention employed by vested ideologies. They held that source of evil should be looked for in the injustices which are prevalent here.

6. Sense perception is the source of knowledge. The theory that knowledge comes from divine sources is a construct of the clergy. (After Brodov)

## Conclusions

Charvaka-Lokayat tradition is a very profound Indian tradition reflecting the travails of the poor and struggling sections of society. It shows in a clear manner as to how the downtrodden developed their resistance to the hierarchical exploitative system sustained by the caste system and its upholder, the Brahmanism. This tradition shares not of commonalities with various other Shramanic traditions in India. The materialism and reason of this tradition was picked up in the current times first by Jotiba Phule and later by Bhimrao Ambedkar. The class affiliation and the correlation with system of thought becomes all the more clear when one sees the re-imposition of the faith based Brahminical values by the BJP led Government. BJP, the affiliate of RSS, the one to have the agenda of Hindu Rashtra is again a ploy to bring back the caste and gender hierarchies in the modern garb. And it is no wonder that in the name of traditions it is bringing back only the Brahminical one's while totally ignoring the values of Shramanism embodied in Lokayat and Buddhism.

## References

Brodov V., *Indian Philosophy in Modern Times*, Progress Publishers, Moscow, 1988.

Chattopadhayay D., *Lokayat*, People's Publishing House, 1981.

Gangopadhayay M.K. (1990), *Philosophy in India*, Navakarnataka, Bangalore.

Jayaraman, T., (2001) Vedic Astrology and all that, *Frontline*, May 12.

Nanda, Meera, Breaking the spell of Dharma, (2001), *Economic and Political Weekly*, July 7.

Nehru Jawaharlal, *Discovery of India*, Asia Publishing House, 1961.

Omvedt, Gail, (1994), *Dalits and the Democratic Revolution : Dr. Ambedkar and the Dalit revolution in Colonial India*, Sage, New Delhi.

S. Radhakrishnan, *Indian Philosphy*, Vol. I, George Allen and Unwin Ltd., London, 1977, p. 281.

Sardesai, S.G. (1986), *Progress and Conservation in Ancient India*, People's Publishing House, Delhi.

Veer, Peter van der, *Religious Nationalism*, OUP, 1998, New Delhi.

# 39

# Science and Society

Science is a human activity concerned with organising perception about the world into a body of knowledge. Human society has come far from the initial phase when the understanding about universe, earth and life were a mystery to human thought and, in due course, it started getting applied to the field of production and planning related to various aspects of life.

Science initially, was limited to material ideas and social processes, which were restricted in scope. It is only in the late medieval period that scientific and rational ideas began to make an impact on the understanding of social organisation and relationships. Gender inequality or class difference (slavery, caste) was explained as destiny. Exploitative relations were projected as the will of god and clergy made them acceptable to the society in the name of religion. Till roughly before the industrial revolution, the role of clergy in modulating social relations was primary. And science-rationalism remained restricted to the arena of explanation of natural phenomenon. Gender, class and caste equations were frozen in time till the advent of the 'industrial era' when the application of technology in the process of production began in right earnest.

It should be noted here that the impact of science started changing 'qualitatively' from the late medieval times on two fronts. On the one hand, the production process started getting a boost due to application of science and technology, which required the earlier subjugated classes to be released from their bondage, and on the other hand, rational thought started making an impact on social relations, also as now the cover of 'divine-powers' in hiding the exploitative relations started weakening in a broad sense. The feudal class and the clergy treated the advent of new ideas with extreme hostility, be it the germ theory of disease, or the earth revolving around the sun or the theories of evolution. Most of the ideas related to modern science came in for severe opposition from vested interests. The vested interests and the priestly class saw the threat to their social hegemony in the areas of property relations and to impact of constructs, which pointed to the divine forces being the authors of the uneven social relations. Along with this the authority of priestly class also changed its nature qualitatively. The feudal classes and clergy perceived the dangers to preserving the status quo in the society. This was manifest in a very clear form in Europe where the clergy was well-organised in the church and growth of science and the emergence of newer social relations had to take place in opposition to the authority of the church. Many scientists had to face inquisitions, imprisonment and other punishments for their scientific discoveries and ideas which had the potential of increasing the role of human reason in the social affairs. Due to industrial revolution in some countries, the production relations changed and introduced concepts of liberty, equality and fraternity. These ideas brought a liberal space where struggle could take place for the actualisation of these values.

It meant that the oppressed classes could demand the implementation of the norms related to these ideals. It saw a huge release of social forces mainly of the vassals from land and women from domestic slavery. This initial model of introduction of science was restricted to few countries only. In the colonies, this process took very different forms. In some countries the conservative sections, which stood to loose due to this change started opposing the values of science in the name of fundamentals of their religion. This was first seen in late nineteenth and early twentieth century in America where the faith-based values were asserted as the fundamentals of religion.

The Age of Reason opens a vast space for the advancement of science, not only in the sense of technological advancement but also in the sense of rational scientific values forming the base of social thinking, norms and relationships. In the colonies, the polarisation could be seen due to women and shudra and their equivalents (vassals, semi-bonded labourer, Dalits etc.) challenging old values. In the quest for liberation, they did value the offshoots of scientific principles.

Most of the social reformers took up rationalism and encouraged modern education in contrast to the study of holy books etc. Pioneers like Jotiba Phule did advocate the study of science education in preference to the learning of holy books. The setting up of industries and the consequent release of Shudras from the land-slavery was the initial phenomenon, which started breaking the shackles of caste system in India. Similarly, reformers like Raja Ram Mohun Roy, who stood for abolition of Sati, also promoted literacy and modern science amongst these sections.

Initially, most of the feudal elements and religious clergy rejected science outright as opposed to God and sacred traditions. Once the impact of science became visible in different areas of life, this initial phase of outright rejection of science was followed by a period when the precepts of religion themselves are presented as being most scientific. New concepts were brewed to propagate that religious concepts themselves are very scientific. The case of 'creation science' vis-à-vis theory of evolution, 'Islamic science' (Koran being the source of all scientific knowledge) and Vedas (being the fountain-head of most of the knowledge in general and nuclear science, ecological science and aviation science in particular) are just a few examples of this. What these hide is an attempt to reassert the hold of pre-modern values of birth-based hierarchy and the hold of feudal elements and clergy on affairs of society.

Those groups, which have control political power also control the direction of scientific research. A discipline, which has the potential of abolishing the material deprivations of the world and can bring material abundance of unimaginable magnitude, is primarily put to use for strengthening the hold of those in power. A discipline which can boost the production to infinite limits, help in easing out the miseries of day-to-day existence of millions, can give basic amenities, health and education in abundance, is predominantly used for making weapons of mass destruction and increasing the luxuries of few elite.

The case of fundamentalists, those using selectively culled out religious practices and doctrines for political use is very complex. Fundamentalism in Christianity asserted that basic biblical doctrines should be accepted without question, absolute accuracy of Bible, (story of miracles etc.). This went along with imposing restrictions on women in the social sphere and subjugation of poor and marginalised. In Pakistan and many Islamic countries where mullahs rule the roost, something like 'Islamic Science' is supposed to be the ultimate in knowledge, with claims that Koran contains all possible science. This absurdity goes to the extent of positing that Koranic evidence supports the existence of djinns, who are a source of infinite energy and which could be utilised as fuel. Things were much better in India for quite sometime with scientific temper having a respectable place in social and political affairs. With the resurgence of fundamentalism in the name of Hindu religion, similar ideas are gaining credibility with vehemence.

Today, science cannot be rejected outright so what is being done by fundamentalist forces is to project that their obscurantism itself is science. The most galling example of the recent imposition of obscurantism is the (BJP led NDA) government's move to introduce astrology courses through UGC. Hindu fundamentalists claim that astrology is a science. Astrology's foundations are far removed from this. It is basically made up of religious and magical beliefs. One such belief is that Saturn, which now is known to consist of rings of frozen gases, is a demon who can harm us and that the power of demons can be kept in check through practices like *yajnas*.

Science keeps transcending itself with newer facts and is subject to change. While religious beliefs by their very nature are to be revered blindly and are fixed for all times to come, astrology is based on beliefs where there is no scope for change. Today, the discoveries of biology prove irrefutably as to how the sex of the foetus is determined. Yet the most sought after 'putreshti yajna', is believed to lead to the birth of a son. Gautam Buddha and Jain prophets came down heavily on astrology prescribed *yajnas*, particularly those prescribing animal sacrifice, such as the 'ashvamedha' yajna, which involved the burning of a horse. Social sciences, the late entrants in the realm of science are the biggest victims of the kar seva exercised by the warriors of fundamentalist politics. Social science has the potential of showing the truth of human relationships to great extent, but it is unfortunate that currently, the social sciences in general and science of history in particular are being so presented as to prove the clash of communities. Even today, when information technology is trying to lift the remaining veils of secrecy over knowledge, there are sections in society who in pursuance of their political agenda are parading partial, half-baked or blatantly false and concocted observations as science.

# 40

# History, Science and Social Change

There are many a changes being brought in the field of Education. One is the immediate deletion of certain portions from the current History textbooks, written by the historians who are amongst the best in the world. These changes are pending the introduction of new books in which, History will cease to be taught as a separate discipline. History portions of the proposed books will be written in consultation with the holy people of the religions. The second major change is the introduction of faith-based courses like Astrology, Karmamkanda and Paurohitya in our Universities.

In Pakistan where the hold of Mullahs has been strong from last few decades History is not taught as a separate discipline and the period of History from Harappa to invasion of Sindh by Muhammad bin Kasim is totally missing from the books. History is projected as the History of glorious Mughal kings. This is in tune with the History pattern introduced by the British, who presented Indian History according to the religion of the rulers. Though this type of History persists to some extent in India major efforts have been made with the formation of NCERT in 1961 to change the orientation to incorporate the lives and concerns of the average people in the same. The efforts are now on to reverse this and bring back the communal view in consultation with the Dharmagurus (Clergy) of different communities. In a hurried manner some portions have been deleted on the ground that these hurt the feelings of certain communities. Like one portion dealing with Guru Tegh Bahadur, which has been deleted states that Guru's armies plundered in the neighbouring areas. The argument has been put forward that mentioning that, some Kings plundered is an insult to the King and the community to which he belonged. It is interesting to note that while so much is being made of plunder, it is being forgotten that plunder into territories of other kings was 'normal' during those times. One remembers as to how Shivaji's armies used to plunder the areas in Surat, as to how the daughter-in-law of the Subhedar of Kalyan was brought in as a part of the plunder and Shivaji rose beyond the accepted norms of the times in respectfully sending her back to her home with due honour.

It is being alleged that national heroes have been insulted in these textbooks. Let us see one example of this 'insult', "The Guru, while being a religious leader, had also begun to be a rallying point for all those fighting against injustice and oppression... for the Sikhs, the Guru gave up his life in defense of cherished principles." In what way does it tantamount to insult to the heroes of communities one fails to understand.

Interestingly the other deleted portions give the real reasons of this exercise. There are three major themes around with this censorship is applied. First relates to the distinction of mythology and History, mention that there were no human settlements around Ayodhya in the times when Lord Ram is described to be living. This scientific truth breaks the back of the whole Ram Janmbhoomi movement. Second is the mention of cultural and dietary practice of eating beef. There are innumerable passages in different treatises which mention about the beef eating practices, *Taittraiya Brahman* categorically tells us: 'Verily the cow is food' (*atho annam via gauh*). Yajnavalkya's insistence on eating the tender (*amsala*) flesh of the cow is well known. Even later Brahminical texts provide the evidence for eating beef. *Manusmriti* also did not prohibit the consumption of beef. One wonders if there is a move to take back Bharat Ratna from one of the tallest Vedic scholars, Mahamahopadhya P.V. Kane, who in his *History of Dharma Shastra* categorically states about the beef eating practices based on impeccable Vedic and other sources of that time. Cow, projected, as equivalent to Mother, is central to the communal politics. Any mention of beef eating is dangerous to this politics. That is one of the reasons of Prof. D.N. Jha going through the nightmares of suppression and persecution for the crime of writing a scholarly book, *Holy Cow, Beef in Indian Dietary Tradition.*

Also the portions, which mention the rigidification of caste system by the ideology of Brahminism and prevalence of caste has been deleted. We can overcome the evils of the past only if we can understand the situations in which they came up and got perpetuated. So why delete these? There seems to be the overall pattern to emulate the system prevalent in Pakistan so that History is reduced to a mere tool in the hands of communal politician.

Currently the other equally dangerous path being pursued in the field of education is to introduce courses, which promote blind faith, e.g., courses in Karmakand, Paurohitya and Astrology etc. Introduction of astrology in the face of great advances in astronomy give us the insight about the contrasting methods of Faith and Reason. Faith based Astrology has non-existent planets like Rahu and Ketu as the key players, it regards Saturn, which in reality comprises of rings of frozen gases, as a demon. As per Astrology one can get the 'much sought after' male child by doing Putrakameshti Yagna, while even the knowledge of elementary biology will tell us that the sex of child is determined not by pleasing the planets but by X or Y chromosome, which meets the ovum. These moves are aimed at stifling and rooting out the very basic aim of education, to cultivate critical and independent thinking amongst the children. The current move is the prelude to the long-term goal of controlling the mindset of the society in the communal direction and to create a conformist society.

Communal politics is the politics of elite of the society who project the communities as uniform homogeneous mass. Here the interests of communities are understood to be determined solely by the religion one follows. So the interests of people of two religions are supposed to be opposed to each other and here the History becomes the history of different kings fighting against those belonging to other religions. This a bogus theory as we know that kings had alliances cutting across their religions (Akbar+Mansing opposite Rana Pratap+Hakim Khan Sur, Aurangzeb+Mirza Raja Jaising opposite Shivaji+Siddi Sambal etc.). This totally overlooks the social practices of Bhakti and Sufi where people across different religions follow these Holy Saints or Peers. Also the economic and political factors controlling the decisions of the kings are put under the carpet and all their policies and actions are evaluated from the religious motives. So the destruction of Somnath Temple, which was done to plunder its wealth is seen as attack of one religion over the other, while overlooking the parallel fact of destruction of temples Hindu kings (by Raja Harshdeo in Kashmir, by Maratha armies in Shrirangpatnam, Tipu Sultan's territory).

Fundamentalism is a further intense presentation of this political ideology and it aims to push back the social relations of liberty, equality and fraternity. Its aim is either to oppose the social change. What we mean by social change is the elimination of birth based inequality of caste and gender or the birth based inequality between feudal lord and vassal. It is opposed to the human rights of women, Dalits and workers and promotes itself by basing its politics on the emotional hysteria, around the religious symbols as against the ethical aspects of religion. Politics of democracy and liberal norms are the major victim in the fundamentalist regimes. In the countries wherever fundamentalism has come to power it has done away with Democracy and the concept of human rights of weaker sections of society and promoted the interests of only a section of people. It has resorted to faith based knowledge. Also in the times of transitions and social struggles where the weak have tried to articulate their rights they have put forward the values based on reason and logic.

In India this struggle has been between the low caste untouchables and the Brahminical stream. Buddha and Charak both opposed the caste system and prevalent social hierarchy of caste and gender. They also opposed blind faith and the concept that knowledge comes only from Brahma through the holy books alone. In due course their teachings were suppressed and the anti-low caste offensive reaction was brought forward by Shankaracharya at ideological level and by kings like Pushyamitra Shung and Shashank at political level. This counter-reaction banished Buddhism from India. With the secularisation process proceeding in late 19th century, Mahatma Jotiba Phule brought it back the process of social change on Indian scene. This tradition was carried forward by the freedom struggle, which again was based not on any religion but on the values of liberty, equality fraternity. Ambedkar gave it the most precise expression. And these ideas became the vehicle of social change. Now since the social change has proceeded to some extent the values of faith-based knowledge are being brought back through the introduction of astrology etc.

In Europe this process took place from late seventeenth to early 19th century. The discoveries of science, the process of industrialisation and social transformation towards liberty, equality, fraternity were opposed by the feudal elements and the clergy. Many scientists had to face inquisitions, imprisonment and other punishments for their scientific discoveries and ideas which had the potential of increasing the role of human reason in the social affairs. It is because of putting forward rational doctrines that challenged the deeply held beliefs of the Church that Galilio was condemned, Giordano Bruno and Servatus were burnt at the stake. Due to industrial revolution in some countries, the production relations changed and introduced concepts of liberty, equality and fraternity. These ideas brought a liberal space where struggle could take place for the actualisation of these values.

This initial model of introduction of science was restricted to few countries only. In the colonies, this process took very different forms. In some countries the conservative sections, which stood to loose due to this change started opposing the values of science in the name of fundamentals of their religion. This was first seen in late nineteenth and early twentieth century in America where the faith-based values were asserted as the fundamentals of religion.

Initially, most of the feudal elements and religious clergy rejected science outright as opposed to God and sacred traditions. Once the impact of science became visible in different areas of life, this initial phase of outright rejection of science was followed by a period when the precepts of religion themselves are presented as being most scientific. New concepts were brewed to propagate that religious concepts themselves are very scientific. The case of 'creation science' vis-à-vis theory of evolution, 'Islamic science' (Koran being the source of all scientific knowledge) and Vedas (being the fountain-head of most of the knowledge in general and nuclear science, ecological science and aviation science in particular) are just a few examples of this. What these hide is an attempt to reassert the hold of pre-modern values of birth-based hierarchy and the hold of feudal elements and clergy on affairs of society.

The knowledge systems based on faith have been propagated by those who are opposed to social change. While the philosophers of social change have promoted the 'reason' based knowledge systems. We can see that faith-based knowledge has been used by clergy and feudal elements to oppose the process of social change and communal politics and fundamentalist politics resort to faith based knowledge to oppose the process of social change, while philosophers of the movements of oppressed groups can articulate their longing only through reason or logic-based knowledge system.

# Index

## Q



## R



## S